Going Scapegoat

Going Scapegoat

Post–9/11 War Literature, Language and Culture

DAVID A. BUCHANAN

McFarland & Company, Inc., Publishers
Jefferson, North Carolina

The views expressed in this article are those of the author
and do not reflect the official policy or position of the
U.S. Air Force, Department of Defense, or the
U.S. government.

Excerpts from *The Yellow Birds* by Kevin Powers
copyright © by Kevin Powers 2012. Reproduced by permission of
Little, Brown and Company and Hodder and Stoughton Limited.

Numerous quotations from *Billy Lynn's Long Halftime Walk*
by Ben Fountain copyright © 2012 by Ben Fountain.
Reprinted by permission of HarperCollins Publishers.

Excerpts from *FOBBIT* copyright © 2012 by David Abrams.
Used by permission of Grove/Atlantic, Inc. Also published by
Harvill Secker; reprinted by the permission of the
Random House Group Limited.

LIBRARY OF CONGRESS CATALOGUING-IN-PUBLICATION DATA

Names: Buchanan, David A., 1976– author.
Title: Going scapegoat : post/9/11 war literature, language
and culture / David A. Buchanan.
Description: Jefferson, North Carolina : McFarland & Company, Inc.,
Publishers, 2016 | Includes bibliographical references and index.
Identifiers: LCCN 2016036391 | ISBN 9781476666587
(softcover : acid free paper) ∞
Subjects: LCSH: War stories, American—History and criticism. |
American fiction—21st century—History and criticism. | Soldiers as
authors. | Powers, Kevin. Yellow birds. | Fountain, Ben. Billy Lynn's
long halftime walk. | Abrams, David, 1963– Fobbit.
Classification: LCC PS374.W35 B83 2016 | DDC 813/.609358—dc23
LC record available at https://lccn.loc.gov/2016036391

BRITISH LIBRARY CATALOGUING DATA ARE AVAILABLE

**ISBN (print) 978-1-4766-6658-7
ISBN (ebook) 978-1-4766-2673-4**

© 2016 David A. Buchanan. All rights reserved

*No part of this book may be reproduced or transmitted in any form
or by any means, electronic or mechanical, including photocopying
or recording, or by any information storage and retrieval system,
without permission in writing from the publisher.*

Front cover concept of War in the Middle East © 2016 Hal Bergman/iStock

Printed in the United States of America

*McFarland & Company, Inc., Publishers
Box 611, Jefferson, North Carolina 28640
www.mcfarlandpub.com*

To my sister Katie.

Acknowledgments

This book was made possible by the close reading, editing, instruction, inspiration, and guidance of a number of people. Thanks are in order for Dr. Billy J. Stratton, my friend and academic mentor, as well as Dr. Linda Bensel-Meyers. Linda introduced me to Kenneth Burke and taught me about the technique of keeping a commonplace book. Both were crucial to the completion of this project. I also owe a note of gratitude to Dr. Clark Davis, Dr. Dean Saitta, and my peer reviewers. All of them brought clear and helpful suggestions to an early draft of this work. This book is better because of them all. I should also thank my mother Rita Buchanan. She was my junior high school English teacher, and I owe much of my writing ability and none of my mistakes to her. She's retired now, but during this process, she was a worthy copy editor. And finally, I thank my wife, Dr. Cindy Buchanan, who has, for years, been a patient and supportive partner in this endeavor in addition to so many others. She has been the most important influence on my personal and professional lives for fifteen years, and I owe her everything. She is my biggest fan, my strongest motivator, and my best friend. I am lucky to have her on my team.

Table of Contents

Acknowledgments — vi

Introduction: The Resilience of Racist Language, Symbols and Rhetoric — 1

One: Literature, Criticism and the Fetishization of Experience — 15

Two: Kenneth Burke: A Method for War Literature — 47

Three: Confounding Expectations in Kevin Powers's *The Yellow Birds* — 61

Four: The Comic Corrective and Ben Fountain's *Billy Lynn* — 96

Five: The Convenient Scapegoat in David Abrams's *FOBBIT* — 122

Six: Representing *Hajji*: This Generation's Enemy "Other" — 155

Conclusion — 195

Chapter Notes — 203

Bibliography — 209

Index — 221

Introduction
The Resilience of Racist Language, Symbols and Rhetoric

> Men build their cultures by huddling together, nervously loquacious, at the edge of an abyss.—Kenneth Burke, *Permanence* 272

This project began during the summer of 2005, when I was deployed to Saudi Arabia in support of the so-called Global War on Terror. It was my first trip to the region, and though I am a pilot in the U.S. Air Force, I was assigned to a diplomatic position with the Royal Saudi Air Force. It was a great job, one full of ample free time, a small amount of additional responsibility, and very little oversight. Another officer—a major—and I were responsible for overflight clearances for coalition aircraft as they crisscrossed Saudi airspace. This meant that—to obtain the proper approvals and signatures—we had to hand-carry a form to the Royal Saudi Air Force headquarters building in downtown Riyadh two or three times a week. One morning, when the Major and I (I wore the rank of captain) were leaving our extremely secure American compound on the outskirts of the city, the gate guard, a young Marine from Minnesota, checked my identification card and said, "Watch you don't get scalped by no injuns out there."

My career in the Air Force has taken me to some interesting places. I flew a KC-10 refueling tanker around the world, including 120 missions in the skies over Afghanistan and Iraq. I was a speechwriter for a three-star general. I teach literature and composition at the Air Force Academy in Colorado Springs, Colorado (my alma mater). In all that time, however, I have never stopped thinking about that young man's statement. It struck me then, as it does now, as sad and disturbing, and I have never stopped pondering the cultural forces that were at work there.

I initially intended to write this book about the specific nature of the stereotype that worked its way into that nineteen-year-old Marine's psyche only to be chewed up and spat out in Riyadh, Saudi Arabia, to another man about to drive through a modern metropolis in a Toyota Land Cruiser. But then I began to—much to my chagrin—discover that such misplaced and recycled metaphors and historical stereotypes are a linguistic tradition when Americans go to war.[1] That is, the most convenient stereotypes and proverbs that Americans tend to recycle for use in our contemporary metanarratives of war tend to relentlessly revert to the same language of the United States' conquest of the American West and the so-called Indian Wars of the nineteenth century.

This cultural habit has existed for generations, but it was popularized and normalized during Vietnam. An Army general during Vietnam named Maxwell Taylor, in testimony delivered before the Senate Foreign Relations Committee in 1965, once described the situation in Vietnam by saying that "[i]t is very hard to plant the corn outside the stockade when the Indians are still around. We have to get the Indians farther away in many provinces to make good progress" (qtd. in Drinnon 369). Forward firebases near Vietcong territory often colloquially were called Fort Apaches, and territory not controlled by the United States anywhere in Vietnam widely was referred to as "Indian Country" by soldiers, journalists, and elected officials alike. Indeed, *Indian Country* is the title of Philip Caputo's 1987 novel about a veteran who buried his lifelong friend, an Ojibwa man named Bonny George, on a Vietnam battlefield.

I read Caputo's novel during one of my five deployments to the Persian Gulf, a time when it became quite clear to me that little has changed in the way Americans linguistically fashion their experiences of war since the nineteenth century. I once sat through a briefing delivered by a high-ranking officer who, with none of the healthy ambiguity of Caputo's tale, described the entire nation of Iraq and the Arabian Peninsula as "Indian Country." Another supervisor often repeated the tired aphorism that there were too many chiefs and not enough Indians in my squadron. When I took a daytrip to do some shopping in a fancy mall in Abu Dhabi, before my co-workers and I left base, a middle-aged woman sergeant lectured us on proper behavior and decorum while we were "off the reservation," as she put it. When I spent a few days on an American airbase in Kyrgyzstan, I saw a T-shirt for sale in the base's store (or Post Exchange, the PX, as it is called on Army bases) that read "Taliban Hunting Club" above a gun sight centered on a silhouette of a bearded, bin Laden look-alike that was plastered on an Old West "WANTED" sign. In David Abrams's novel about the Iraq war, I read this line: "The PX, run by the U.S. Military, is the equivalent of the Old West general store. Its aisles are stocked with potato chips, beef jerky, cases of soda, sunglasses" (52).[2]

Of course, none of my observations was necessarily new, even though I was noticing such problematic language for the first time. As Winona LaDuke, a well-known activist, actress, and politician of Anishinaabekwe ancestry, writes in *The Militarization of Indian Country* (2013), "the military has named us and claimed us" throughout history (xvi). And, as LaDuke goes on to point out, "Native nomenclature in the US military is widespread. From Kiowa, Apache Longbow and Black Hawk helicopters to Tomahawk missiles, the machinery of war has many Native names" (xvii). I long had noticed this disturbing naming trend as well, but it wasn't until that day in Saudi Arabia in 2005 that it became painfully clear to me that the appropriation of native American stereotypes, proverbs, metaphors, or symbols often goes unchallenged in the discourse of war. Sometimes, it is even celebrated. With every encounter, I became more and more exasperated by the resilience of racist language and symbol abuse in America's war culture.

In *Facing West: The Metaphysics of Indian Hating and Empire Building* (1980), Richard Drinnon writes in this thorough examination of America's habit to fashion images of the enemy according to a long heritage of "Indian Hating" in American culture: "every generation of Anglo-Americans down to the present has followed the pattern set then and has repeated, with minor variations, such justifications for burning natives in their villages and rooting them out of their swamps" (xii). The pattern still holds true today. For an essay published in *The Stranger* shortly before the U.S. invaded Iraq in 2003, Sherman Alexie wrote, "Thus, the United States was founded, in part, on the demonization of Native Americans, and it's damn easy to justify the mass extermination of demons, isn't it?" Al Carroll, in his carefully researched *Medicine Bags and Dog Tags* (2008), notes, "the Second Iraq War marks the fifth war in U.S. history where war supporters have invoked the image of the enemy as 'Indians' and have used Wild West imagery" (200). As Alexie explains, this cycle reflects that, behind America's war culture, there lurks an abiding hypocritical manipulation of language:

> We will only win the metaphorical and clichéd war on terror when George W. Bush proclaims a metaphorical and clichéd victory of terror ... as a Native American, I find it ironic that the United States wants to go to war with Iraq because it keeps breaking treaties.

Many other scholars—such as Drinnon, Carroll, and LaDuke—have examined the ways that native American stereotyping and metaphor recycling tenaciously emerge whenever Americans go to war.³ Similar to Alexie, all of these scholars remind us of the troubling linguistic, cultural, and historic legacy in the United States that, as LaDuke puts it, treads on "dangerous ground," a ground that today extends from battlefield violence in Iraq and Afghanistan to cultural violence in native communities across the United States (xvii).

In the *Chronicle of Higher Education*, shortly after 9/11, Richard Slotkin warned that, in response to the fear and hatred that grew out of the attacks, the U.S. likely might revert to what he called the "savage war," a scenario he predicted would express "the profound sense of rage we feel when we have helplessly suffered a terrible trauma" (B11). He rightly pointed out that this type of war is "so at odds with reality that [its] imperatives can never be fulfilled" (B11). In a *New York Times* column from 2005, Patricia Limerick agreed, adding that "much of what we have taken to calling 'the lessons of Vietnam' ... could just have easily been learned as 'the lessons of the Indian wars'" (A23). She called the metaphorical reframing of Indian War epithets and stereotypes examples of "historical amnesia" and declared that it is "a national misfortune that the Indian wars have faded from the memory of most citizens" (A23). From Slotkin and Limerick to Carroll, LaDuke and Alexie, many other scholars (Billy J. Stratton, Michael Yellow Bird, Don Trent Jacobs, S. Elizabeth Bird, Vine Deloria, and Gerald Vizenor) have written extensively about the persistence of the savage/civilized binary and the myriad manifestations of Indian stereotyping in a hyper-militarized, post–9/11 culture in the United States. Collectively, this body of work encourages a shift away from the language of conquest to that of a more accurate recasting of native people, the Indian Wars, and any group of human beings that might become an enemy of the United States.

This deeply held habit of racial Othering is a difficult feature of American war culture to dislodge though. As Robert Ivie and Oscar Giner write in *Hunt the Devil* (2015), "The incantation of evil casts a spell of militant insecurity on the American people. War is the national sacrament of atonement. It sacrifices a scapegoat in whom the world's evil is invested" (12). Elizabeth Bird writes, "[t]he fact that these stereotypes have been around so long demonstrates the way they have become entrenched in white mythology" (89). Entrenched they most definitely are. A few months after President Bush made his "mission accomplished" speech aboard the USS *Abraham Lincoln* in May of 2003, Secretary of Defense Donald Rumsfeld put the stereotypes and myths to use in a speech at Fort Carson, a large Army base south of Colorado Springs. He made the obligatory expression of gratitude to the troops for their service, and he vowed the eternal support of a grateful nation. He also made an explicit link between soldiers fighting in Afghanistan and nineteenth century Indian fighters: "In the global war on terror, U.S. Forces, including thousands from this base," Rumsfeld said, "have lived up to the legend of Kit Carson, fighting terrorists in the mountains of Afghanistan, hunting the remnants of the deadly regime in Iraq" (qtd. in Miles). Behind Rumsfeld's podium stood a color guard of cavalrymen, astride horses, dressed up in cavalry-style costumes from the nineteenth century (of Custer's 7th Cavalry no less) with the Rampart Range of the Rocky Mountains in the background. Forget facts and history, it is the heroic legend of Kit Carson that Rumsfeld put to use in his rhetoric, a rhetoric that scapegoats both terrorists and Indians and recasts the soldiers behind him as imperialist saviors.

Robert Kaplan, a White House consultant during the invasion of Iraq in 2003, went so far as to encourage such appropriation. In a 2004 op-ed for *Wall Street Journal*, Kaplan wrote:

> The American military is back to the days of fighting the Indians. The red Indian metaphor is one with which a liberal policy nomenklatura may be uncomfortable, but Army and Marine field officers have embraced it because it captures perfectly the combat challenge of the early 21st century.[4]

Kaplan isn't alone in this approach. In an essay titled "The 'Old West' in the Middle East: U.S. Military Metaphors in Real and Imagined Indian Country" (2008), Stephen Silliman cataloged the many instances of Old West metaphor raping in our post–9/11 war culture. Actually, Silliman logs seventy-seven different Indian Country metaphors that appeared in news stories and weblog commentaries across various media outlets. As he concludes,

> Transplanting the "Indian Country" metaphor across regions, through time, and in military contexts mobilizes a complex framework of already understood but national symbols to explain events, people, the nature of battle, and the very reasons for war in 21st-century Iraq [238].[5]

In May of 2011, the exploitation of history and language in the service of American conceptions of modern war culminated during a Navy S.E.A.L. raid in Abbottabad, Pakistan, the operation that resulted in the death of Osama bin Laden. News quickly spread that the phase of the operation that included bin Laden's death had been coded and reported by the S.E.A.L.s (over the radio) with the word "Geronimo." Many defended the coding, then and now, with dubious claims that ignore, as Billy J. Stratton puts it, the "deeply problematic nature of Native representation in American culture" (141). For example, in an afterword to a celebratory graphic novel titled *Code Word: Geronimo* (2011), John Del Vecchio suggests that—based on self-serving concepts of vagaries like bravery and valor—the military's appropriation of "Geronimo" for use in a raid against the most hated man in the world was "a great honor to a great man, a great spirit. His name has come to embody the ideals of bravery and valor we ourselves wish to emulate" (77). This argument not only dictates to the native community what one should consider a great honor, it also, as Carroll explains, ignores the fact that "most Natives attach fundamentally different meanings to words and phrases such as *patriotism, our land, fighting for my country,* and *the flag* or *our flag*" (3; italics original).[6]

Indeed, Harlyn Geronimo, the great-grandson of the Apache chief and a veteran of two tours in Vietnam, describes—in a statement submitted to the U.S. Senate Commission on Indian Affairs—the use of "Geronimo" as a "grievous insult," despite the military's intent or the specific context of its use:

> And to call the operation to kill or capture Osama Bin Laden by the name Geronimo is such a subversion of history that it also defames a great human spirit and Native American leader. For Geronimo himself was the focus of precisely such an operation by the U.S. military, an operation that assured Geronimo a lasting place in American and human history.

In this special hearing titled "Stolen Identities: The Impact of Racist Stereotypes on Indigenous People," Suzan Shown Harjo, a Cheyenne and Hodulgee Muscogee advocate for American Indian rights, also delivered a statement that succinctly summarizes the basic offensiveness of such misappropriation in the context of modern war:

> Geronimo was picked for the same reason that the term "Indian country" is still used to mean enemy territory. The "savage savage" Indian-as-enemy stereotype is so deeply embedded in the American psyche that there are those who fear that Indians, once in control of anything, will treat white people as badly as the historic white man treated us.... When people representing the U.S. reach back a century to take a gratuitous swipe at Geronimo as an enemy and to equate him with a terrorist, they are insulting all Native American nations and people.... That is why we take the matter of stereotypes so seriously and believe that we should not be subjected to denigrating names, imagery and behaviors in polite society.

Stratton, in *Buried in Shades of Night* (2013), explains the issue further:

> [T]he fear and loathing invoked by the horrific images of modern terrorism reaches to the core of America's national psyche and extends renewed meaning to the age-old struggle between the forces of good and evil, civilization and savagery, and Christian and pagan—recalling a time, a place, and a world where the very fate of civilization is put into peril by savages who lurk in the dark and howling wilderness, waiting to descend anew upon unsuspecting settlements [143].

This urge to alter this unfair bias determined the direction I ended up going with this book. Yes, the persistence of appropriated language in the service of modern war and its deleterious effects on native people and their cultures is difficult to dispute. Moreover, it is equally disturbing to note that these racist habits are central tenets of American conceptions of the "enemy" in our post–9/11 wars. It is baffling that Americans—both soldiers and civilians—expect war to be justified and explained according to such myopic stereotypes and metaphors. In everyday life in the military *and* in the growing body of literature that takes the wars in Iraq and Afghanistan as its subject, our military members overlay the terministic screens of the scapegoated "savage Indian" on their own war experiences because such symbols are a subconscious part of their national identity, regardless the ethnocentric version of history it reflects, regardless how poorly applied the metaphor may be. For an all-volunteer military that has been at war for almost fifteen years, this unconscious impulse is, clearly, a risky manipulation of language and history. As Simon Harrison explains in his book about the way American soldiers treat the bodies of dead enemies in modern war, "many transgressive forms of behavior are shaped and motivated by the same cultural metaphors as normal behavior" (14).

In his collection of essays on semiotics and societal symbol use—*The Message in the Bottle: How Queer Man Is, How Queer Language Is, and What One Has to Do with the Other*—Walker Percy writes,

> Man's capacity for symbol-mongering in general and language in particular is so intimately part and parcel of his being human, of his perceiving and knowing, of his very consciousness itself, that it is all but impossible for him to focus on the magic prism through which he sees everything else [29].

The linguistic appropriations outlined above fall right in line with other, deeply embedded representations of any group of human beings that can be considered enemies of the United States. Sadly, as far as the discourse of modern war is concerned, it seems that the American symbol-monger has mastered the use and misuse of Indian War symbolism, be the monger Robert Kaplan, Donald Rumsfeld, or a teenaged Marine from Minnesota.

How, then, should a scholar of literature apprehend the work that is emerging from our post–9/11 wars? Considering the depth and embeddedness of appropriated and misappropriated symbols that observe war and represent it in literature, I suggest that it is most appropriate for the critic to examine war literature according to the symbolic scapegoats it creates (as opposed to realistic reportage of traumatic combat experience). This Kenneth Burkeian approach may not stop the racist use of Indian War stereotypes in American war culture and our desire for witness-based tales of heroic redemption, but as I will show, it does fully expose symbol use (and misuse) as part of a larger pattern of loathing, victimization, and redemption (Kenneth Burke's scapegoat mechanism) when America goes to war. Moreover, when the genre under consideration is as vast as war literature, a method of analysis like Burke's resolves a major salient issue that has long dominated the literature of war: the tendency for the genre to be assembled and governed by an untenable and extremely limiting aesthetic, one that privileges combat experience and the witness account above all other forms and styles of war writing.

Kate McLoughlin, in her richly informative book *Authoring War* (2011), expresses the conventional critical account regarding war and its representation in literature; as she writes, "War, in other words, resists depiction" (6). But is this truly the case? Does war's experience truly resist depiction any more than any other topic that might be represented and depicted in words? Or, is it more precise to say that the readers of war literature often resist accepting depictions of war that don't provide vicarious experience or provide a common tale of tragic redemption or the chance for hero worship? Perhaps this is what McLoughlin is arguing, not that war is necessarily any more difficult to write about than any other subject, but that in this genre, all such literature faces an aesthetic tension, one based on popular demands and expectations. After all, the many cultural functions of literature in general would make it an imperative for literature to represent war and to do so effectively. That imperative is even more pronounced when literature serves to counterbalance or correct the metanarratives enumerated above, narratives that often resort to the use of a scapegoat as symbolic action in war's representation.

McLoughlin's commentary deserves a fuller citation here:

> The reasons that make war's representation imperative are as multitudinous as those which make it impossible: to impose discursive order on the chaos of conflict and so to render it more comprehensible; to keep the record for the self and others (those who were there and can no longer speak for themselves and those who were not there and need to be told); to give some meaning to mass death; to memorialize; to inform civilians of the nature of battle so as to facilitate the reintegration of veterans into peacetime society; to provide cathartic relief; to warn; and even, through the warning, to promote peace [7].

McLoughlin doesn't reference Kenneth Burke once, but it seems to me that Burke's dramatistic approach to literature, one that seeks "to fall on the bias" (*Attitudes* 47), covers every purpose she lists above in addition to the ones she doesn't (to my mind, the glorification of combat and a justification of war designed to placate or satisfy a complacent public through the use of a convenient scapegoat). The various expressions of war experience—depending on medium, style, and authorial biography—have their advocates. So, considering McLoughlin's long list, it would be irresponsible to suggest any "right" way to record the extreme reality of war in art. What this book will show, however, is that it is possible to read any reduction of war's reality into representation and avoid the legitimization of violence, the glorification of heroic sacrifice, and the racist stereotyping of an enemy Other.

As Burke points out in his book *Permanence and Change* (1954), throughout much of history there has existed a "usual way" by which societies seek to create "social cohesion" according to a "fluctuating" cycle of symbolic "mystification" followed by a period of "unmasking" (294). But, as Burke goes on to point out, this symbolic mystification has "been so often misused in history by the defenders of special sinister interests, (that) we clearly see its limitations" (294). This does not mean the literary critic is helpless in the face of such a cycle, for, in literature, we can observe "individual persons enacting roles in the social order" that enact extensive scapegoating mechanisms in service of war and violence (294). However, as Burke suggests, these observations must be accompanied by a method so that we can note the cycle without becoming part of it. He explains: "might it not be possible that, were an educational system designed to that end, this very fluctuancy could be intelligently stabilized, through the interposing of method" (294). As this book will present, Burke's method will not end the American urge to demonize our enemies according to shopworn and inaccurate Puritanical conceptions of native Americans, but it can work to stabilize our social instincts to symbolically mystify and unmask in the literature of war that we read and write.

If the art of war strains to make sense of war, its agents, and its victims, then the close study of that art does so as well. Thus, this book demonstrates how a rhetorical examination of the scapegoating mechanism in the literature from and about our wars in Iraq and Afghanistan can help us refrain from further reductions of indigenous cultures of the United States into caricature and lead us further away from seeing the enemy as Other. I ask: can a rhetorical study of war literature illuminate aspects—undesirable though they may be—about the way Americans expect war to be fought and represented, no matter who does the observing, no matter who does the reporting? I suggest an answer to this question through a rhetorical analysis of three war novels published in 2012 (*The Yellow Birds* by Kevin Powers, *FOBBIT* by David Abrams, and *Billy Lynn's Long Halftime Walk* by Ben Fountain). I show how we can examine the terministic screen each books creates in such a way that the criticism subverts and redirects the dominant scapegoating metanarrative that the United States incorporates into its war fighting culture.[7]

It takes time for honest art to emerge from war. Likewise, my study of literature (not my deployments to the Persian Gulf) has made one thing clear; it is not necessary to loathe a population or an enemy in order to provide "security." In effect, that is what we encourage when the painful history of our Indian Wars is twisted into misused symbols time and again. If we honestly and self-critically look at our post–9/11 wars and the scapegoats their stories create and discard (as this book does), we can avoid the fear and paranoia that is inherent to past and current American militarism and conquest. The three works of fiction considered exhibit a range of approaches to the soldier's tale. All of them are involved in storytelling problematics. This book assesses those problematic tales and the scapegoat mechanisms they complete. In this way, I have constructed a cautionary note regarding the grand narratives of modern war culture.

The questions I ask of these novels are based on similar analyses of combat memoirs and non-fictive reports from the front written by non-professional writers—or, as Keith Brown and Catherine Lutz call this body of literature, "Grunt Lit" (322). Compared with the war novel, I examine how this mass of writing, some of it designed to titillate and vindicate a removed civilian populace through what Kenneth Burke calls "vicarious atonement" actually works (*Permanence* 90). Ultimately, I put forth the idea that all representation is misrepresentation, that absolute authenticity is unattainable, and that conveying war's significance in literature demands a critical eye, one that is best informed by Burke's rhetorical methods.

Chapter One surveys the status of the genre that I have chosen to refer to as "war literature." I propose two reasons why McLoughlin might suggest that war resists depiction. First, considering that this is a genre of memoir, autobiography, history, fiction, journalistic accounts, and poetry, and considering that all of these forms and modes of war writing are linked by subject only, the genre is too vast for easy generic analysis. Second, I examine the ideological underpinnings of the genre of war literature as being made up by the guiding principle of "combat gnosticism," a term coined by James Campbell in 1999 to address the navel-gazing focus on combat experience as a spiritually essential quality in war literature studies. When combat gnosticism and a healthy dose of exceptionalism and what William Spanos calls the "specter of Vietnam" combine in contemporary American war literature, a corresponding literary aesthetic forms in contemporary war literature, one that perpetuates the language of scapegoating from earlier wars and one that allows a steady supply of books that reading war tourists can consume safely in order to find redemption through the vicarious victimage of easy targets.

In *American Exceptionalism in the Age of Globalization* (2008), Spanos' phrase—"the specter of Vietnam"—describes the ways that the memory of Vietnam has come to

> haunt America as a contradiction that menaced the legitimacy of its perennial self-representation as the exceptionalist and "redeemer nation." In the aftermath of the Vietnam War, the dominant culture in America (including the government, the media, Hollywood, and even educational institutions) mounted a massive campaign to "forget Vietnam" [ix].

These words should be read as cautionary ones for our post–9/11 wars and contemporary war literature, especially since the phenomenon he describes ultimately "transform[s] a healthy debate over the idea of America into a national neurosis" (ix). It takes no leap of logic to wonder if we are already collectively forgetting Iraq and Afghanistan. When convenient hierarchical national narratives such as manifest destiny or the enemy Other persist as symbols in the literature of war, the public reader too easily assumes exasperating but responsibility-displacing attitudes that justify war along similar lines. The ideology of combat gnosticism, as I examine it, is one of the main culprits.

Chapter Two establishes Burke's methodology and philosophy regarding rhetoric and scapegoating as the appropriate ones to bring to war literature. Using Kenneth Burke for theoretical refinement, I examine how the seductive nature of combat gnosticism tends to crowd out the vast and varied war experiences and war narratives of other Americans. I suggest that it is dangerous to allow war stories to carry too much of a tragic, yet redemptive mission in our culture even though this is, perhaps, the most common trait of popular American war writing. Since Burke focuses on the psychology of the audience, not of the hero, I argue that his method offers the proper perspective on war literature, one that allows a fruitful negotiation of titillating, unambiguous propaganda alongside other, purely decorative works of war literature. Specifically, I focus Burke's logology through the use of his concepts of hierarchical psychosis, scapegoating, and the cult of the kill; and I establish how we can, when we read war literature, redirect the tragic cycle of vicarious victimage that often dominates the genre.

Chapter Three uses Burke's scapegoat principle to trace the symbolic presence of purgative catharsis and vicarious victimage within Kevin Powers's novel, *The Yellow Birds* (2012). If we accept the scapegoat principle, as Burke would have us accept it, as "not primarily as a survival from earlier eras, but as a device natural to language here and now," then we can, perhaps, witness the spell of the ritual as it occurs in contemporary war literature like Powers's ("Dramatism" 451). When we trace the curative victims in *The Yellow Birds* according to Burke's philosophy of literary form, a goad emerges from the criticism, one that could urge a movement away from a cultural need for such sacrifice.

Chapter Four examines the extent by which Ben Fountain's *Billy Lynn's Long Halftime Walk* (2012) deploys what Burke terms the "comic corrective" in its satirical message to complete an underlying scapegoat mechanism. Burke labels the human being as an "animal exceptionally adept in the ways of symbolic action" ("Dramatism" 353). For Burke, symbols dictate experience, not the other way around. And so, in *Billy Lynn*, Billy Lynn and his buddies become misused symbols to such an extent that their inner humanity is occluded by their roles as redemptive vessels of the national guilt associated with the invasion of Iraq, 9/11, and a nation's rage. I examine the novel's fluctuation between what Burke considers the extremes of literature, from "the extreme of utterance" to "the extreme of pure beauty" (*Counter-Statement* 54). As Burke says, in that

> fluctuating region, between pure emotion (which leads to barbarism or iconoclasm in art) and pure decoration (which leads to hagiography), humanity and craftsmanship, utterance and performance, lies the field of art, the evocation of emotion by mechanism, a norm which, like all norms, is a conflict become fusion [56].

Fountain's novel takes big swings between unambiguous propaganda and real-seeming satire; it is only through analyzing those swings that one can reveal the artistic evocation of emotion that accompanies Billy's heroic scapegoating for the benefit of a culpable public.

Chapter Five assesses the hierarchical psychosis (as Burke terms it in *A Rhetoric of Motives*) that dictates the social order on an American base in Iraq in a novel by David Abrams: *FOBBIT* (2012). Like *Billy Lynn*, *FOBBIT* is a satirical assessment of American war culture, but his satire details the way soldiers live and interact with each other on one small Forward Operating Base (called FOB Triumph) in Iraq in 2005. With Burke's ideas about order and hierarchy, we can assess Abrams's scapegoat mechanism as a dialectic treatment of the status of Fobbits (support troops who never leave base) and combat troops (the real warriors). As Burke writes in *Attitudes Toward History*, any propagandistic strategy like Abrams's "must be employed as an essentially *comic* notion, containing two-way attributes lacking in polemical, one-way approaches to social necessity" (166). My treatment of *FOBBIT* shows how Abrams's comic frame "is neither wholly euphemistic, nor wholly debunking," so we can gain from it a *"charitable attitude toward people that is required for purposes of persuasion and co-operation"* (*Attitudes* 166). I examine the extensive hierarchical psychosis on FOB Triumph, and I show how such an order engenders scapegoats so that the order can survive. This chapter minimizes the typical combat scene in favor of an exploration of the scapegoat mechanism in *FOBBIT*, resulting in a chapter that interrogates the social order of hero worship as it operates in post–9/11 American culture.

Chapter Six is a thorough examination of the epithet *hajji* and the ways it has been popularized in both Iraq and Afghanistan. I outline the ways *hajji* operates as a tool of scapegoating in a militarized American culture. I make the case that *hajji* is an extension of the metaphysics of Indian hating while it is also one that incorporates religious vituperation *and* the demonization of the enemy into one harmful term of denigration via a complex scapegoat mechanism. If the existence and use of the word *hajji* (an Arabic term of respect for those who complete the pilgrimage to Mecca) is not direct Indian hating, Indian hating at the societal level certainly trains soldiers how to use it effectively. Thus, Indian hating excuses, authorizes, and provides the model for the *hajji*-fication of the United States' post–9/11 scapegoated enemy.

A Note on Terminology

This book refers extensively to "wars" that the United States has waged in Iraq and Afghanistan in the years that followed the tragedy of 9/11 with full awareness that "war" is a bit of a misnomer. Technically, the United States has never declared war on Iraq or Afghanistan, and the last time the United States declared war against any country was in June of 1942 when Congress voted to do so against Romania, Bulgaria, and Hungary. A number of critics take issue with the use of "war" to describe the American military operations in Iraq and in Afghanistan. Suman Gupta, for instance, spends considerable time in *Imagining Iraq* (2011) explaining his selection of "invasion" to describe what the United States and the United Kingdom endeavored to do in Iraq with military forces in 2003 (19–23). While I accept his reasoning—and at times adopt "invasion" to describe the initial phases of the United States' military operations in Iraq—I prefer the term "war" when I describe any armed conflict that has been endorsed by the United States government and/or enacted by the United States military since 9/11.[8]

It also is worth noting that, in official terms, the most accurate way to refer to our various post–9/11 military adventures would be with the appropriately labeled "operation." This naming convention is important within the military, at least as far as funding and planning and logistics are concerned. As of the writing of this book, one official American military "operation" is ongoing: Operation Inherent Resolve, which describes all military actions in Syria and Iraq that seek to thwart the Islamic State in Levant/Syria (known as ISIL and ISIS). Operation Enduring Freedom (OEF), which describes the United States' actions in Afghanistan, began on 7 October 2001 with airstrikes by American fighters and bombers, and missile strikes from American and British warships and submarines. OEF officially ended on 28 December 2014 when NATO took over with its mission, known as Resolute Support. Two other "operations" that can be considered part of the so-called Global War on Terror have also officially ended: Operation Iraqi Freedom (OIF) lasted from the invasion of Iraq in March of 2003 until the drawdown of troops was completed, a date officially marked as 1 September 2010. Thereafter (from 1 September 2010 through 18 December 2011, when the last U.S. troops departed Iraq), the conflict in Iraq was known within the military as Operation New Dawn. Again, considering the comprehensive intention of this project, I refer to all of the above operations, conflicts, invasions, and missions as "war."

One

Literature, Criticism and the Fetishization of Experience

> There is no violence in Faulkner, there are no bull-fights in Hemingway.—Kenneth Burke, "Realism" 44

The Cyclical Pattern of War's Representation

Since 9/11, the literary landscape that assesses and represents the wars in Iraq and Afghanistan has been dominated by non-fictive accounts of combat, be those accounts marketed as memoir, autobiography, or as journalistic reports from the battlefield. This phenomenon is perhaps the most consistent trait in American war literature. As David Lawrence puts it, "fiction takes longer to gestate" (168). Roger Luckhurst agrees: "the conventional account is that there is a traumatic time lag between war and its novelistic assessment, as if the immediacy of war experience is irrecoverable" (55). In a speech delivered at the U.S. Air Force Academy, Roxanna Robinson, the author of the Iraq war novel *Sparta* (2013), describes the "strict chronological pattern" of war writing in more detail:

> There are three different kinds of war writing: journalism, memoir, and fiction (poetry, too) and each tells a different kind of truth. They follow a strict chronological pattern: first comes journalism, reported at the time, from the field; next comes memoir, after people have come home and transcribed their notes. Poetry may come next, the last is fiction. Fiction is long, and it requires knowing more than the facts. Journalism is meant to be neutral, memoir is meant to render factual experience, but fiction is meant to tell an emotional truth. This truth must work its way through the heart as well as the mind. Emotion takes the longest to write about, because our understanding of it is slow [7].

And, in an essay published in *The New York Times* in 2014, Michiko Kakutani repeated the same theme, pointing out that before novel-length war fiction can emerge, the actual event of war must "recede in time" (A1). Again, these critics aren't observing anything new about war literature. War fiction just takes longer to appear, and this makes sense for both logical and logistical reasons. As David Langness, a book critic for *Paste* magazine, points out, the youngsters who fight wars simply do not possess the emotional or intellectual maturity to translate experience into art: "You cannot write a great war novel if your fatigues still fit."

I'm sure this truism is at least partially accurate, but Langness is talking to a rather small number of people: those who have, as the saying goes, "been in the shit." Nevermind how difficult it is to actually define combat in the conflicts that the United States has entered in the last fifteen years, a number of questions immediately come to mind. Must the chronological pattern Robinson describes be so strict? What if the author never wore fatigues? Why, during war fiction's gestation period, do we insist on waiting for this very small group of people (combatants, usually men) to develop the writing skills and maturity to turn experience into emotional truth? What is it about war and war writing that forces civilians to wait for an artistic turn? Yes, truthful and meaningful war fiction—written by civilians *and* veterans—takes time, but that may not necessarily be due to the traumatic nature of war itself. Rather, the delay seems to grow out of an abundance of deference to direct combat experience in war literature's authors.

We can track this throughout a century and half of American wars. Ambrose Bierce participated in the Civil War as a soldier in the Union Army, but his short story collection, *Tales of Soldiers and Civilians*, didn't appear until 1891. Melville and Whitman both experienced the Civil War as civilians, and both published war poetry during the Civil War.[1] But Whitman's prose recollections of his own experience of war—*Specimen Days*—didn't appear until 1892. Other creative prose about the Civil War took just as long to appear. Hamlin Garland's short story, "The Return of a Private," wasn't published in the magazine *Arena* until 1890, after Garland visited home and heard his father reminisce about his Civil War experiences. Mark Twain may have been a volunteer member of the Confederate Army for one week before he lit out for the territory (where he stayed for the duration of the war), but his humorous tale of his limited time in the military—"The Private History of a Campaign that Failed"—wasn't published until 1885. Twain's scathing prose piece, "The War Prayer," never appeared at all during his lifetime.

Similar conditions attended the imaginative literature that sought to represent the American wars of the twentieth century as well. John Dos

Passos published *Three Soldiers* in 1921, and Willa Cather's Pulitzer Prize–winning novel, *One of Ours*, didn't appear until 1922. Of course, a number of combat gnosticators of Cather's day, including Ernest Hemingway, castigated Cather for daring to represent combat without having experienced it firsthand. As Steven Trout writes of Cather's novel, "such a candid and sustained portrayal of military violence, a subject then perceived as the exclusive domain of mail *eyewitnesses*, was nothing short of audacious" (105; italics original). Dalton Trumbo, a civilian, didn't publish his World War I novel, *Johnny Got His Gun*, until 1939. Norman Mailer, a veteran, published *The Naked and the Dead* (1948) relatively quickly, but it took Kurt Vonnegut until 1970 to transform his experiences in Dresden during World War II into the novel *Slaughterhouse-Five*. Serious fiction about the Vietnam War saw the same delay. Tim O'Brien's first book appeared in 1973, a work that served as a cerebral, immediate reaction to firsthand combat experience, but it was, of course, a memoir (*If I Die in a Combat Zone Box Me Up and Ship Me Home*). O'Brien's first work of fiction, *Going After Cacciato*, didn't follow until 1978. Yusef Komunyakaa took fourteen years to begin writing war poetry, and Gustav Hasford's autobiographical novel, *The Short-Timers*, wasn't published until 1979. Stanley Kubrick adapted Hasford's prose into the film *Full Metal Jacket* in 1987, the same year Phillip Caputo's first novel about Vietnam, *Indian Country*, appeared, though his memoir—*A Rumor of War*—appeared in 1977.

For better or for worse, this same cycle seems to be holding true today in the genre of contemporary war literature. However, it may have everything to do with the nature of the craft and very little to do with war and time. The delay between war and war's representation in fiction is far from unique to the subject, and the wide range of civilian successes with war writing suggests that contemporaneity may not matter in any war novel, at least as far as the emotional truth contained within a book is concerned. The difference with war literature, then, may be that, unlike other subjects, strong voices (usually veterans) protect the field of war literature from being penetrated by the noncombatant voice when they argue about the distracting details and issues of authenticity and accuracy.

A few war novels did quickly appear in the United Kingdom following 9/11—Pat Barker's journalist-in-Afghanistan novel *Double Vision* (2003) and Ian McEwan's poorly reviewed *Saturday* (2005)—but nothing similar gained traction in the United States until Siobhan Fallon (a military spouse) wrote *You Know When the Men Are Gone* and Helen Benedict (a civilian) crafted *Sand Queen*, both of which were published in 2011.[2] Thus, as Robinson mentions above, 2011 and 2012 likely marked a turning point in the most recent iteration of the cycle of war literature's production.³ Serious American contemporary war fiction finally began appearing during those years, much of it written by civilians, and it continues to do so today in ever increasing numbers.⁴ Throughout, however, these civilian-penned war stories have taken an epistemological backseat to the witness-based account of combat.

Somewhere in the middle of this predictable, but confounding, generic cycle is where the field of war literature studies finds itself today. Drawing from such landmark studies of war literature as Paul Fussell's *The Great War and Modern Memory* (1975) and Samuel Hynes' *The Soldier's Tale: Bearing Witness to a Modern War* (1997), a number of recent books seek to reframe the art of previous wars in a more contemporary context, but very few escape the crippling cycle described above. In *Coming Out of War: Poetry, Grieving, and the Culture of the World Wars* (2005), Janis Stout points out that if the twentieth century was a century full of war, then the art of war since World War I is remarkable primarily for being the art of "opposition" (xi–xx). While she doesn't directly politicize her criticism toward the United States' latest wars, she does explicitly express a driving hope that, by studying war literature and poetry, "we can indeed *come out of* war, in the larger sense, and learn peace" (xx; italics original). Mary Favret's *War at a Distance: Romanticism and the Making of Modern Warfare* (2010) doesn't discuss America's post–9/11 wars either, but it returns to the work of Austen, Coleridge, and Wordsworth to examine the marks left there by these authors' distant relationships with war. In similar manner, *The Cambridge Companion to War Writing* (2009) attempts a more comprehensive approach to the genre. Edited by Kate McLoughlin, the *Cambridge Companion* begins with *Beowulf* and ends with Martin Amis in an attempt to trace centuries of American and British war literature according to a conflict-specific organization.⁵ McLoughlin followed the *Cambridge Companion to War Writing* one year later with a monograph that is a more thorough examination of works of war literature as cross-cultural artifacts, entitled *Authoring War: The Literary Representation of War from the Iliad to Iraq* (2011). This second text examines a wide range of war literature according to a thematic structure, one that "offer[s] a transhistorical and cross-cultural study of war writing" (19). In 2014, Christopher Coker published *Men at War: What Fiction Tells Us about Conflict from the Iliad to Catch-22*. This study focuses on the "existential appeal" of conflict in cultures throughout history, and Coker points out that it is war's tenacious grip on human behavior that makes war fiction "so important" (2).

My project takes a somewhat different approach to three novels that appeared in 2012 as part of the first wave of war novels that specifically deal with American war fighting in a post–9/11 world. While many existing book-length examinations of war literature are concerned (as Paul Fussell was) with the blurred line between fiction and nonfiction in war's art, very few contemporary critics seek to answer Margot Norris' question in *Writing War in the Twentieth Century* (2000): "Can art," she asks, "overcome its internal constitutive difficulty in addressing the violent, the cruel, and the ugly without transforming it into beauty, without endowing it with aesthetic effects, without arousing pleasure, without bringing to redemption what should be irredeemable?" (20). It is difficult, but as I will show, it can be done.

Interestingly enough, all three of the novels I examine in detail appeared within months of each other in 2012, but each one comes from a different source of authorial wartime experience. An Army machine-gunner wrote *The Yellow Birds* (Kevin Powers); a civilian with no military experience crafted *Billy Lynn's Long Halftime Walk* (Ben Fountain); and a noncommissioned officer who worked in Army public affairs wrote *FOB-BIT* (David Abrams). In 2013, David Lawrence described this trio as "'The Big Three' war novels" from our wars in Iraq and Afghanistan (168). To date, no extensive or comparative critical treatment of any one of these three novels exists.

The Ideology of Combat Gnosticism and the Genre of War Literature

Times are good for war literature and writers of war fiction. Phil Klay won the National Book Award for his collection of short war fiction, *Redeployment* (2014), and rarely does a month pass that a major imprint does not issue another war novel that takes the conflicts in Afghanistan or Iraq as its subject. As more war fiction continues to appear, though, one salient concern continues to control the genre: the ideology of what James Campbell calls "combat gnosticism" (203). In a 1999 essay that appeared in *New Literary History*, Campbell writes, "Perhaps the single most important defining element of the genre is this emphasis on personal experience" (205). Requiring or even simply valorizing combat *bona fides* in authors of war literature, Campbell says, has resulted in a critical tradition and epistemological ideology that is unique to war literature, one that has a silencing or controlling impact on the genre as a whole (203). Campbell proposes that when we (readers, critics, and writers) canonize and privilege white, male, combatant voices over all others, the result is not an increased understanding of war, its symbols, its depravity, its victims, or its agents; rather, it produces an elite combat gnosticism, "a construction that gives us war experience as a kind of gnosis, a secret knowledge which only an initiated elite knows" (204). Seventeen years after Campbell made those observations, combat gnosticism continues to be the driving force within the war literature genre.

In one sense America's post–9/11 wars are no different from any other American wars of the last century; that is, large-scale violence leaves very few people—civilians *and* members of the military—untouched by war. Even when we consider the all-volunteer nature of the military and the widespread apathy with which many Americans consider war after fifteen years of continuous conflict in two countries and sporadic conflict in many others, war's experience occurs now—as it always has—at all levels of citizenship, both with intense combat or none at all. Regardless, experiential authenticity and a literary obsession with various concepts of accuracy, still, are major issues for unsophisticated readers, writers, and critics of American war literature, and it has been this way at least since Stephen Crane published *The Red Badge of Courage* in 1895. Crane was born after the Civil War ended, but without ever pulling a trigger or ducking a cannonball, he produced what Ernest Hemingway called "that great boy's dream of war that was to be truer to how war is than any war the boy who wrote it would ever live to see" (Intro xvii). Crane never saw war or combat. Hemingway barely did (as a combatant). Yet, despite both men's literary successes with war writing, today's dominant approach to war literature remains rooted in a preference for the very authorial experience they both defied. As Roger Luckhurst explains, "Ethical criticism on the aesthetic representation of war is often pulled between the demand for witness and documentary record versus the call for indirection, aporia or the foregrounding of the impossibility of representation of such traumatic violence" (52). Thus, it is no overstatement to say that war literature is a suffering, and sufferable, genre. McLoughlin explains:

> The literature of war is writing stretched to its limits, demanding extraordinary resourcefulness from those who seek to produce it. Its readers also have significant responsibilities. Understanding how and why truths and lies about war are conveyed, perceiving the status of those who convey them, and appreciating the surrounding ethical issues are nothing less than necessary acts of global citizenship [Intro xiv].

These issues place heavy demands on any work that might be classified as war literature, and the result is an infinitely capacious genre with critical blind spots and facile appraisals everywhere.

The ideology of combat gnosticism can have disastrous effects on what McLoughlin, in *Authoring War*, considers the "parapolemical" of war literature (3). In an introduction she wrote for a three volume war literature anthology, McLoughlin agrees with Campbell's central argument: "Confining the right to write about war to combatants," she writes, "has the result that those traditionally denied access to the war zone (women, the enemy) are also denied access to the genre" (xiii). In *Coming Out of War*, Stout also criticizes the privilege attending the experience-laden trench poets of World War I, arguing that it was and still is "distorting and invalid" (58). Indeed, Stout encourages a turn from witness poetry to "significant but less often recognized body of poetry of the war that eschews the hard-boiled factual mode altogether in favor of meditation, lament, or moral pronouncement" (163).

The very concept of a genre known simply as "war literature" is at least part of the problem. Margot Norris, in *Writing War* (2000), describes war writing as "postgeneric" (23). What war and its corresponding literature have created at the end of the twentieth century, she says, is "a kind of collage assembly of different discursive and representational styles only loosely united by the common topic of war" (8–9). In war literature, all styles and forms and subgenres are lumped together, and while this has led to a rich and extensive tradition in American letters, the genre's incoherence has never resolved the running battle that has long existed regarding experience, authenticity, and aesthetics in the criticism that follows. In Norris's words, "modern war writing" is "fit only to problematize the very concept of genre, to question the representational and ethical fitness of all genres" (23). She is right, of course, but authors and critics of war literature don't always bother to problematize anything about the way war is represented or discussed.

The fallacious story of battlefield experience is a seductive trait of the war literature genre, and from the collage that Norris describes above, critics often pluck such a tale and its attendant experience-based authenticity for scholarly attention. To be fair, such sharing and telling of war's experience and war's trauma can bring therapeutic service to the victims or agents of war. Yet, merely appreciating the author's or the protagonist's catharsis does very little to address the way these stories operate within a society that created the possibility of the war in the first place. Since the ideology (combat gnosticism) that privileges the experience of combat is also the easiest and most obvious guide for authors and critics alike, it enjoys a curious resilience even though, at its core, this ideology ignores the inherent, generic paradox that drives the field itself. McLoughlin summarizes:

> The argument for realism in war literature is that the facts must be presented as accurately and objectively as possible.... Formal decoration and imaginative license have no place in this strict regard for truth. But the realist project falters as soon as it states its terms. "Fact," "accuracy," "objectivity," "truth," and "realism" are infinitely contestable concepts [Intro xii].

The demand for experienced truth and realism could be contestable elements of any genre, but with war, they somehow never fade into the critical background.

Christopher Coker dates the frustration over what Norris describes as "art's epistemological inability to totalize, to encompass all aspects of a phenomenon" as beginning with the very birth of the novel (20). Most contemporary critics of war literature, however, trace the battle between modern war and its representation to modernism and W.B. Yeats' famous exclusion of Wilfred Owen from *The Oxford Book of Modern Verse* in 1936. "Passive suffering," Yeats writes in the introduction, "is not a theme for poetry" (xxxiv). The exclusion angered critics and civilians alike, though, as Yeats explained in a 1936 letter to Dorothy Wellesley, his editor:

> When I excluded Wilfred Owen, whom I consider unworthy of the poets' corner of a country newspaper, I did not know I was excluding a revered sandwich-board man of the revolution & that some body has put his worst & most famous poem in a glass-case in the British Museum—however if I had known it I would have excluded him just the same. He is all blood, dirt, & sucked sugar stick [Wellesley 124].

Wyndham Lewis and T.S. Eliot also complained about the banal trauma-trumpeting soldier-author and the way his voice tends to crowd out other voices and, in turn, dominate literary criticism. The artist who writes about war without witnessing it, they both objected, is forced to wait and watch while war memoirs and other forms of reportage prepare the literary ground for a more imaginative seed.

In 1915, Lewis wrote in the "War Number" of his short-lived journal *Blast*:

> The quality of uniqueness is absent from the present rambling and universal campaign. There are so many actions every day, necessarily of brilliant daring, that they become impersonal. Like the multitudes of drab and colourless uniforms—these in their turn covered with still more characterless mud—there is no room, in praising the soldiers, for anything but an abstract hymn. These battles are more like ant-fights than anything we have done in this way up to now [25].

Eliot agreed, at least partially, with Lewis' argument, suggesting that art stands above and beyond the universal limits and bloody realities of modern war. In a 1919 issue of *The Egoist*, Eliot argued that the best war poetry eschewed, not necessarily experience, but the reporting *of* that experience. In a review of Herbert Read's recently published collection of poetry, he writes that Read's work is "the best war poetry that I can remember having seen" (39). Eliot goes on:

> It is better than the rest because it is more honest; because it is neither Romance nor Reporting; because it is unpretentious; and it has emotion as well as a version of things seen. For a poet to observe that war is ugly and not on the whole glorious or improving to the soul is not a novelty any more [39].

As Eliot and Lewis argue, the experience of the soldier is too savage to contribute to the creation of art, and we can suggest the same about much contemporary war literature that trades on the traditional tropes of romantic suffering. As Yeats wrote, "It was easier to look at suffering if you had someone to blame for it" (xxxvii). Memoirs about war in Iraq and Afghanistan trade on this same idea, and the form of the contemporary war memoir has become so ubiquitous that some war narratives are nearly indistinguishable from each other. What Norris, McLoughlin, Yeats, Lewis, and Eliot all are suggesting is not that war is too extreme a subject to be captured in language, nor are they suggesting that the actual soldier on a Gettysburg picket line, in a World War I trench, or in a Humvee patrolling the streets of Baghdad has been misrepresented or will be misrepresented in popular historiography. No, they are discussing the inherent paradoxical issues that face war literature and the discourse it creates in criticism and the United States' wider war culture, issues that remain unanswered today. Or, to borrow Norris' words again, Yeats is touching on "art's inability to extend its power to express subjectivity—its power to make the interiority of lived experience available to its expressive media" (20). This inability can apply to any lived experience, but the experience of combat drowns out all other media that night try to express war's subjectivity.

Paul Fussell's Combat Gnosticism in Contemporary War Literature and Culture

Many critics note the primacy of personal narrative within the war literature genre, but few are interested in placing blame for combat gnosticism's dogmatic effect on contemporary war literature studies on any one author or scholar. The scholar who coined the term—James Campbell—does not restrain himself so. He finds fault with Paul Fussell's hugely influential study of war literature, *The Great War and Modern Memory* (1975). Fussell, Campbell rightly argues, focuses almost exclusively on the combatant and his irony-laden response to the mass slaughter of modern war during World War I. Fussell uses—as his primary source material—diaries, letters, memoirs, song lyrics, and poetry written mostly by men "who were there" in order to make his case that the soldiers who experienced the insanity of war ushered in a corresponding emphasis in popular storytelling, from the pieties of romanticism to the ironies of modernism.

Fussell points out that the war story is an often-blurred and often-confusing one no matter the similarities between the differing forms and motivations behind war reportage and art: "the memoir is a kind of fiction," he writes, "differing from the 'first novel' only by the continuous implicit attestations of veracity or appeals to documented historical fact" (*Great War* 336). On the surface, this seems reasonable and accommodating to all voices and all types of war experience. However, as he does throughout most of his books, Fussell makes assertions like this one in order to clear room in his valorization of the combatant's voice for those combatants who may have chosen to resort to imagination or artifice in their representations of war (one of his reference points is Siegfried Sassoon's George Sherston trilogy in which Sassoon adopts the Sherston persona for what many read as straightforward autobiography). As Fussell says in the afterword of the twenty-fifth anniversary edition of *The Great War and Modern Memory*, only the "re-readable memoirs and pseudo-memoirs" about "unforgettable military experiences" can faithfully represent war (363). An apologist for any type of fiction that manages to work its way into a combatant's representation of war, Fussell does indeed allow artifice into his methodology, but as he sees it, fictive works are useful only if they are accompanied with biographically supported attestations and appeals to actualities and facts, details that can be documented, verified, and cataloged. Then, and only then, Fussell suggests, can any fleeting worries over verisimilitude be dismissed.

In *Wartime: Understanding and Behavior in the Second World War* (1989), Fussell claims, "few novels of the war have succeeded in making a motive, almost a character, of predominant wartime emotion, boredom, or persuading readers that the horrors have not been melodramatized" (291). He also writes that the "best" reflections of war are those that avoid fictive elements like "significant dialogue" because such details are "almost always a sign of *ex post facto* novelistic visitation" (291). Fussell's observations and superlatives aren't necessarily improper or incorrect, but they indicate the ways that his entire project is designed to exclude other voices while elevating the combatant's. He also never bothers to address the fact that even a secret diary that is absolutely devoid of dialogue can still be untrustworthy as a primary document.

Who should produce art about war and how should one do so? Fredric Jameson poses a form of this question in his essay, "War and Representation" (2009). He doesn't necessarily provide an answer, but Jameson does suggest that war literature shares this debate—between experience and artifice—with many other "collective realities," categories of lived experience that Jameson lists as "group, nation, clan, class, general will, multitude" (1547). All of these collectivities, not just firsthand experience of combat, he says, "exceed representation fully as much as they do conceptualization and yet which ceaselessly tempt and exasperate narrative ambitions, conventional and experimental alike" (1547). Jameson discusses two "dialectics" of war writing, one that focuses on "sense-datum" and the other one that deals in "abstraction" (1547).

This categorizing is extremely similar to Fussell's arguments as well, the major difference being that Fussell regards the "gross dichotomizing" that happens in war's linguistic representation a somewhat necessary tool for combatant writers, the *only* authors, as he sees it, who can offer any epistemologically worthy version of war's reality (*Great War* 82). Fussell largely rejects the possibility that the conventions of literature written by anyone else can offer a "dialectic capable of synthesizing" diverging or converging experiences (*Great War* 88). Fussell wisely notes that "one of the legacies" of war is a "habit of simple distinction, simplification, and opposition" and that "ambiguity" and "truth" are war's "casualt[ies]" (*Great War* 87). He also correctly sees "simple antithesis everywhere" in the language of the combatant; however, he argues that this is *because* the traumatized men in the trenches needed an antagonistic response to combat in order to counteract the estrangement they feel from officers, staff members, and "everyone back in England" (*Great War* 94). Who should write about war and how should he or she do so? Fussell's answer is rather clear. The male combatant is the only one who can write it, and "gross dichotomizing" is the only way for him to do so, for "even if those at home had wanted to know the realities of war, they couldn't have without experiencing them" (*Great War* 95).

Thus, Fussell's version of combat gnosticism grows out of a rather cleverly crafted rhetorical device that Kenneth Burke called a "heads I win, tails you lose" mechanism (*Attitudes* 260). As Burke describes it, this is a "device whereby, if things turn out one way, your system accounts for them—and if they turn out the opposite way, your system also accounts for them" (*Attitudes* 260). Civilians may or may not want to know about combat, but even if they did want to know, Fussell argues that "civilian incomprehension" is inevitable, for war's "conditions were too novel, its industrialized ghastliness too unprecedented. The war would have been simply unbelievable" (*Great War* 95). Without entering into an argument regarding the ghastliness of one war compared with another, this is a difficult assertion to accept at face value.

As Campbell argues, Fussell conceives of war as synonymous with combat (204). Campbell says that Fussell doesn't so much "read texts about the war," as he reads "the war as a text" (208). This important distinction regarding realism, aesthetics, and any expectation regarding artistic truth through artistic expression accounts for the inherent problems in the war genre itself. Combat gnosticism describes, in essential terms, the trap of authority that drives nearly all aspects of the construction and consumption of the discourses of war. If war is the text to be read, combat gnosticism purports that it only can be read according to one order of that text's construction. Campbell doesn't say Fussell or combat gnosticism is wrong, per se; rather, Campbell argues:

> [T]his kind of formalist hierarchy signals a further gnostic development, for only the most unmediated statements are those which come straight from the heart of combat experience without the intervention of literary or poetic form, can be trusted. Fussell wants us to apprehend combat directly; he wants his combat memoirists to transcend language and give the Truth to us directly so that we too will have experienced what it means to know combat [207].

The issue that this brings to the forefront of the genre as a whole, as McLoughlin reminds in *Authoring War*, is one of authority manipulation according to an unwritten "autobiographical pact" between the messenger and the reader (42). As she writes, "First-hand experience or autopsy is indeed the crucial ingredient of authority, legitimacy and credibility in war reporting" (42). However, even though combat is indeed a unique experience, that might be all it is; it is, Campbell writes, "simply an experience among other experiences, a (gendered) voice among other (gendered) voices" (207). Thus, combat gnosticism and the obvious strands of solipsism behind it invite a number of conflicting issues if we lend autobiographical authority too much power in our consumption of war literature. This is the "epistemological trap" of combat gnosticism (Campbell 210). As a dominant ideology, it paves the way for writers and artists of all backgrounds to exploit McLoughlin's tropes of autopsy. This can have far-reaching and stunting implications for the development and growth of the genre as a whole.

Campbell's argument that Fussell's work entrenched the foundation of combat gnosticism in literary criticism was new in 1999, but he was not the first scholar to find fault with Fussell's work. Jonathan Marwill, in

1990, applauds Fussell for treating literature as a cultural artifact. As Marwill writes, Fussell's self-serving criticism lacks real "insight" because his works should really be read as "autobiography clothed as cultural criticism" (452). Fussell tended to "bully his evidence," Marwill points out, in order to shape it into conformity with an experience-first ideology (440):

> While some of the errors of either book may be due to sloppiness or naïveté, most are not. They are, instead, the product of a mind driven to confirm deeply-felt truths, the more deeply-felt because they are truths discovered in wracking experiences, not in books and talk. Once found, such truths are rarely questioned let alone surrendered, and the immediacy, their drama, and often their anguish can make for compelling stories.... But they are also imperious, intolerant truths, hearing echoes where none exist and blocking out dissonance by the hundred hollow strategies of denial [441].

Marwill isn't alone in his criticism of Fussell. In *Writing War: Fiction, Gender and Memory* (1991), Lynne Hanley dismisses Fussell's "stunningly narrow" study: "The locale of war literature is the front, the battlefield," she writes, "The author of war literature has to have been there" (30–31). Furthermore, she points out that Fussell's carefully selected war story is "tailored to obscure the causes of war and to assuage the consciences of the men who declare and fight wars" (30). This, she points out, "would not survive as the dominant account our literature offers of war if it were not the only account of war we recognize" (30). In her 2005 book, *Coming Out of War*, Janis Stout acknowledges that "Paul Fussell has already provided influential overviews of literary responses in English to the two [world] wars" (xix). However, Stout seeks to "challenge his interpretations," to include his "muting of the voices of women" and his "disparaging judgment that World War II did not produce any significant body of poetry of distinction" (xix).

It is rare, but some scholars of war literature have recently proceeded without paying Fussell and combat gnosticism any attention at all. Suman Gupta, in *Imagining Iraq: Literature in English and the Iraq Invasion* (2011), examines the ways the invasion and occupation of Iraq has been approached in contemporary fiction, blogs, and drama. Instead of focusing on works of literature written by veterans, Gupta focuses on "literary texts derived from and addressed to the civil and civilian sphere" (17). His reasoning is sound:

> Accounts of the invasion—including literary ones—given by US and UK soldiers in Iraq were often framed in terms of distinctive presuppositions (in terms of nationalistic agendas, heroism and cowardice, the technicalities of warfare) and *given* to readers as expressive of a kind of truth or from the moral high ground of lived professional experience.... Powerfully ensconced conventions now accord to "veterans"

> a somewhat sanctified status which seems to me questionable: often more to do with perceptions of having served and suffered for the state than to do with evidence of human and intellectual insight [17–18; italics original].

Gupta goes so far as to suggest that we should distrust "authentic" firsthand sources of war literature *because* they are "sanctified by experience" (18). He never suggests that this decision should be made because non-witness-based war literature is better or more accurate; it is simply more meaningful and trustworthy because it cannot be treated as hagiographical visions of unreliable reality (18).[6]

One might conclude, then, from these apparent high-water marks in recent war literature studies, that Fussell's epistemological celebration of combat exposure is on the wane, but this is far from the case. Michael Carson suggests that Fussell has been "derided by historians" for decades and that "the wealth of literature historicizing trauma compares roughly to that of literature surrounding war itself" ("Philosophy"). Even if this is true, no one has really figured out how to negotiate or balance Fussell's celebrated versions of historicized trauma. The genre, today, is as Alex Vernon describes it in his introduction to *Arms and the Self: War, the Military, and Autobiographical Writing* (2005); it is built by a "crossing, blurring, and transgressing of generic boundaries" (31). Yet, despite that blurring, Fussell—and his ideology of combat gnosticism—remains undeniably influential in the genre he helped solidify and perplex.

McLoughlin, for example, admits that the privilege attending the battlefield story confers an undeniable authority on such tales, but she doesn't take up the issue of whether or not that authority deepens war literature's efficacy or illuminating power as a cultural artifact. Rather, she writes, "whether this authority results in more insightful, accurate or useful accounts of war is here irrelevant as well as undecidable" (43). It might be undecidable, but it is most definitely relevant for most readers. McLoughlin's refusal to interrogate, discard, or qualify the impacts of combat gnosticism also somewhat accepts what Gupta's project eschews, the assumption that a "military account" is necessary in order to "tell civilians what's what" or to provide any "human and intellectual insight" into war and the nations that fight them (Gupta 18).

Vernon comments on the "interpenetration" of personal experience that is unavoidable for veteran-authors who produce creative works about their war experience *and* the veteran-critics who assess it:

> It should perhaps go without saying that when a scholar with significant life experience in or around war or the military turns to analyzing autobiographical narratives about war and the military, a certain personal investment obtains. Much is at stake [33].

One: Literature, Criticism and Fetishization of Experience   29

I am certainly not immune to this problem, but Fussell and other combat gnosticators somewhat unfairly capitalize on the personal investment they have made in war. Even Vernon, by claiming that "much is at stake" participates in a certain fetishization of combat experience. Is there anything more at stake in writing about war than for any other subject, in any other genre, in any other attempt to capture any other vision of reality in art?

It is important to remember a major disclaimer whenever one considers Fussell's writing and the many who hold combat gnosticism so dear. As Jonathan Marwill begins his essay, "Paul Fussell had a bad war" (431). That is, Fussell never managed a fully objective or academic approach to his own or anyone else's experiences in war, and this might be what Vernon is getting at with his comments above. Fussell says exactly that in "My War: How I got Irony in the Infantry" (1982). When he returned to the United States after serving in World War II, he was "a really pissed-off infantryman, disguised as a literary and cultural commentator" (40). The irony Fussell saw in firsthand witness accounts of both world wars served as his antidote to the dominance of other media that presented all soldiers as "white Anglo-Saxons, officers or aviators, with neat, short hair, clear eyes, gleaming teeth, and well-defined jawlines" (*Wartime* 128). I don't necessarily mind the claims of a pissed-off veteran merely because he is pissed-off. I actually admire what Fussell has to say about his particular approach to war literature, as he put it in the foreword of *Thank God for the Atom Bomb and Other Essays* (1988):

> Looking over these pieces, many of which are about war, I see that they propose another sort of battlefield, where the enemy consists of habitual euphemizers, professional dissimulators, inadequately educated academic administrators, censors, artistically pretentious third-rate novelists, sexual puritans, rigid optimists and Disneyfiers of life, writers who bitch about the review they receive, humorless critical doctrinaires with grievances (Marxist, Feminist, what-have-you), the sly rhetoricians of the National Rifle Association, exploiters of tourists, and, of course, the President [9].

This writing is, for one, quite provocative. It also describes the same battlefield my project enters. The problem, however, is that Fussell's antidote to popular hero worship is no universal panacea. We no longer can trust self-reportage of combat to stay off his list of enemies, if we ever could. Today, many still grab what Fussell grabbed—witness sourced fictional and nonfictional accounts about combat—and try to squeeze similar conclusions from them. Yet, these conclusions aren't necessarily always available. Irony doesn't always survive translation from the battlefield to the page. Disillusion is not a given byproduct of combat exposure. So, if the folks Fussell is trying to correct are, as he describes them, the "sentimental, the loony patriotic, the ignorant, and the bloodthirsty," today's veteran-turned-author might not be the best place to turn, if he or she ever was (*Wartime* ix).

The ideology of combat gnosticism doesn't suggest one answer to the tired but often-answered "what was it like?" question, but it refuses to admit that the factual nature of the answer doesn't matter. Not only is the phrase "combat experience" an extremely slippery one today, but it is becoming increasingly obvious that the very nature of the fighting in Iraq and Afghanistan (and now Syria) denies anything we may try to call an experience of war. Any attempt to do so beyond the legalistic rules of official military regulations falls apart as soon it begins. Even within the military vast confusion and animosity exists between those who call themselves combat-experienced and those who don't. Be it a persistent popular demand for immediate war recollection, a dominating (and often misguided) patriotism, or the abiding hatred and fear that still drives much of our post 9/11 scapegoating metanarratives—today's reading and writing public is determined to keep combat gnosticism exactly where Fussell put it in 1977. Fussell and other combat gnosticators might grant that there exists a "necessity of fiction in any memorable testimony about fact" (*Great War* 337), but combat gnosticism ignores the fact that many voices can speak fictionally about the facts of war and that they can come from any quarter of war's experience. Everyone has a narrative about war, and combat testimony is but one extremely focused way to translate one slice of war's experience into art. This is the power of combat gnosticism; it drowns out everything else by a manipulation of authority, one conferred by the dubious term "combat" while the epistemology it puts forward as superlative is no less suspicious than the loudest and unadorned pro-war propaganda.

Paul Fussell's Disciples

It is difficult to completely discard Fussell's observations, no matter one's critical or artistic stance. The entire corpus of Fussell's work can be read as a response to what he saw as the tendency of high-minded scholarship and wartime propaganda to sanitize the Second World War as he knew it. Ultimately, he sought to reveal war as it was rendered by its closest observers, and for these reasons his work is still extremely useful to any critic of war literature. Between 1977 and his death in 2012, Paul Fussell remained prolific and dominant in war literature studies circles, publishing book-length, interdisciplinary, first-person studies of war and war culture for four decades.[7] Moreover, his work was and is crucial in bringing attention to the literary worth of many works that had been marginalized previously as unworthy of critical attention. As W.D. Ehrhart noted shortly after Fussell's death in 2012, Fussell is still a "towering figure on the cultural landscape of modern American life" (1). In Fussell's *New York Times* obituary, Bruce Weber wrote, in no uncertain terms, "Fussell's influence was huge" (A29). In *The Cambridge Companion to the Literature of the First World War* (2005), Vincent Sherry notes, "[W]hether in spite of or because of the enormity of his assertions, Fussell has set the agenda for most of the criticism that has followed him" (267). John Wilson identifies what critics of Fussell's work often disregard:

> [Critics] fail to notice, or fail to mention, that Fussell is being read, in magazines and books published by Summit or Oxford University Press, while no one outside the academy read anything written by, say, Fredric Jameson. In his essayistic, unacademic, inexact way, Fussell is reaching a large audience, perhaps larger than that reached by any other American scholar [183–84].

Even Campbell, writing two years before 9/11, doesn't completely discard Fussell's scholarly contributions to the criticism of war literature. He is, as am I, particularly appreciative of Fussell's "iconoclastic stance toward received opinion" (206–07). As Emily Greenwood suggests, Fussell helped create a "meta-genre" of war literature that still today links "disillusionment" and "disenchantment" with "loss" and "tragedy."

A celebrated iconoclast, it is ironic that Fussell was never sacrilegious enough to avoid canonization. Today, Fussell and combat gnosticism are both experiencing a fresh resurgence in popular, scholarly, and artistic conceptions and receptions of war literature. The modern reader's taste for confession and vicarious experience drives interviewers and critics of war literature alike to beg for the real in all representations of wartime experience. Joseph Heller once claimed that "*Catch-22* is not really about World War II" ("Interview" 357). The "physical details," he said, "do come out of my own experiences," but, as Heller said, the novel is really about the Korean War, Joe McCarthy's political crusades, and the author's confessed "preoccupation with mortality" (356, 357). Fred Kiley and Walter McDonald argue, emphatically, that this wrinkle in the line between authorial intention and biography exempts *Catch-22* from any distracting inquiries into the link between the author's war experience and war art:

> Although [*Catch-22*] is set against the background of a major campaign during World War II, it is not *about* that war, and in that sense not to be pinned wriggling among the great and varied corpus of prose fiction called, unfairly, "war novels" [v].

Unfortunately, however, neither *Catch-22* nor any other contemporary war novel seems able to wriggle out from under the forces of combat gnosticism. In 2003, a fourteen-page essay appeared in *War, Literature, and the Arts* entitled "Joseph Heller's Combat Experiences in *Catch-22*" (Scoggins 213–27). Peruse the recent interviews of Kevin Powers or Phil Klay and it is clear how loudly Fussell's combat gnosticism resonates with audiences and critics today. One of the first questions these soldier-authors get is about how closely their fiction follows their real war experiences. Mainstream critics and online commentators of war literature have absorbed, often without critique, the ideology of their subject. What Fussell began as autobiography disguised as cultural criticism has become the critical standard for the genre.

One of the closest disciples of Fussell's combat gnosticism is Samuel Hynes, who, in his influential book *The Soldiers' Tale* (1997), makes no allowance for noncombatant or even combatant-but-fictive voices in his magisterial analysis of war literature. Hynes's book was, as Vernon notes, the "first critical work to attempt to shape a definition of the first-person nonfiction war narrative genre" though it "demonstrates the difficulties involved with and ideologies encountered in any effort to define the war narrative genre" (1). Even then, Hynes's book is still influential enough to be the most cited text in Vernon's 2005 collection of essays (1–2). Hynes does not cite Fussell often, but combat gnosticism is his book's entire design. Hynes writes, "I have avoided fiction that clearly *is* fiction, though I have included narratives that are obviously factual but adopt the transparent disguise of invented names" (xv; italics original). In short, Hynes's book is primarily interested in the lived "truths" that can be drawn from non-fictive-seeming first person accounts, what he calls "personal narratives," written by men who "were there" (4). In Hynes's conception, truth equals combat experience. Real combat is Hynes' only concern, and other kinds of war experience don't qualify as experience at all.

Hynes does admit that his overall purpose with *The Soldiers' Tale* is to provide an answer for the worn-out query "What was it like?" (87). This is, to be sure, Fussell's and many other combat gnosticators' main concern too, and while I concede that attempting to answer that question is a reasonable and worthy one, as a critical approach it is massively parochial and limiting. It is deceptive too. In its attempt to correct any popularly flawed perception regarding war, such an approach might even align quite neatly within any postmodern questioning of dominant metanarratives. But in Hynes' formulation, answering the question of "what was it like?" merely swaps one convention or one metanarrative for another one. Hynes had to make selections in order to carve out a subgenre driven by combat gnosticism, but once there, he never steps out of the cocoon of combat testimony, nor does he offer any allowance for any other mimetic source of war literature. He never allows that war's artistic representation could serve any other purpose than providing a palpable reflection of real combat. After all, his subtitle is *Bearing Witness to Modern War*, as if no one but those who felt "what it was really like to be there, where the actual killing was done" have anything to add to war's causes and impacts, as if a noncombat has nothing meaningful to which he or she might bear witness during war (xvi).

A number of book-length literary studies of war literature have recently capitalized on and reinforced the hardiness of combat gnosticism as a strategic literary construct. Three books of note are Wyatt Bonikowski's *Shell Shock and the Modernist Imagination* (2013), Ty Hawkins' *Reading Vietnam Amid the War on Terror* (2012), and Wallis Sanborn's *The American Novel of War* (2012). Hawkins' book, in particular, closely adheres to the tenets of combat gnosticism as he examines the "realist or naturalist aesthetics" of "traditional American War literature" that serve as "a means of bridging the gap between those who have experienced the horror of modern combat and those who have not" (181). Hawkins accepts—at face value—the truism that one had to experience combat in order to understand war, and, accordingly, he examines the ways five books about Vietnam conform to the shape of "Paul Fussell's innocence-experience-consideration structure" (91).[8] Ultimately, Hawkins suggests that, as Hynes does, that war literature's most important function is realized when it comes close to "collapsing the distance between the warrior-hero ideal and the reality of modern combat" for the folks back home (25).

Alex Vernon's introduction to *Arms and the Self*, entitled "No Genre's Land: The Problem of Genre in War Memoirs and Military Autobiographies," is an excellent assessment of the difficulties that attend any categorical assessment of war memoir and autobiography. However, he doesn't necessarily conclude, as I do, that combat gnosticism has a drowning effect on noncombatants' contributions to war literature. Indeed, he rather generously praises the scholarship of war literature for its inclusivity: "Literary scholarship," he writes, "consider[s] texts authored by combatants and noncombatants, by men and women, at the front and elsewhere" (5). Vernon does admit the tendency in war literature studies to focus on small categories of war texts, and he points to Lloyd Lewis's statement in *The Tainted War* (1985) that Lewis's study of "nonfiction narratives by American soldiers from Vietnam" captured "less than 5 percent of all the GIs connected with the tragedy of Vietnam" (3). However, Vernon stops short of clarifying why Lewis chose such a small sample size. As Lewis triumphantly announces in his own introduction, he purposefully excluded the 95 percent of Vietnam veterans and the narratives of high-ranking officers, sailors, airmen, "fliers," and any other military member who served in Vietnam in a support role based on the superlatives of combat gnosticism (13). Lewis is correct when he says that his chosen "lower-echelon ground troops experienced the war much differently than did sailors or fliers," but I'm not so certain about the uniqueness of his following claim, that these voices are collectively more valuable because these soldiers "were to a man thoroughly American, in their virtues as well as their flaws: idealistic, insolent, generous, direct, violent, and provincial" (14).[9] The same could be said about countless groups of Americans.

Today, combat gnosticism sometimes survives without Fussell anywhere near its helm, and the idea that combat experience is synonymous with war truth has often been accepted to the point that any questioning of it is utterly unfathomable. Geoff Dyer, in an essay titled "The Moral Art of War" (2010), flatly rejects the power of fiction in the wake of recent war reportage written by both soldiers and embedded, professional journalists: "Reportage, long-form reporting," he writes, "has left the novel looking superfluous" (216). With confidence, he continues, "Given the high quality of reportage about the current conflicts, it is difficult to see what the novelist might bring to the table except stylistic panache ... and the burden of unnecessary conventions" (217). Dyer doesn't mention Fussell in his blithe dismissal of imagination and fiction, but his appraisal of contemporary nonfiction about the wars in Iraq and Afghanistan rejects any artistic purpose that goes beyond answering the same old question, "What was it like?"

In a 2014 article for *The New Yorker*, George Packer provides what probably is the clearest and most well-known recent commentary on contemporary war literature, and he manages to re-entrench combat gnosticism in yet another generation of war fiction. Indeed, he begins his essay with a quote from Fussell: "Every war is ironic because every war is worse than expected" (69). This certainly holds true for our wars in Iraq and Afghanistan; yet, as Packer unpacks the "irony," he follows Fussell's celebration of combat gnosticism to the letter. Not only does he suggest that an author's combat role in Iraq is the only thing that gives war literature its requisite foundation, but he directly equates that experience with truth: "There's no truth in war—just each soldier's experience" (70).

Campbell summarizes the lasting influence of Fussell's work and combat gnosticism on scholarship:

[T]he scholarship in question does not so much criticize the poetry which forms its subject as it replicate[s] the poetry's ideology.... [S]uch an ideology has served both to limit severely the canon of texts that mainstream First World War criticism has seen as legitimate war writing and has simultaneously promoted war literature's status as a discrete body of work with almost no relation to non-war writing [203].

Packer shows us how, despite Fussell's many detractors, little urgency accompanies critical attempts to assess new war literature without capitulating first to the ideology of combat gnosticism, an ideology that remains deeply rooted in what Richard Rorty described as the "doctrine of truth as correspondence," one that ignores any notion that the link between physical reality and fictional discourse is unclear and indistinguishable (15).

The Anxiety of Authenticity in the Writing of War Literature

One of the biggest problems with combat gnosticism within the war literature genre is that it influences both readers *and* writers. It affects the way literature is received and which literature is published or adapted into movies or collected in anthologies, and it changes the way both veterans and civilians write—both creatively and critically. Norris writes: "The postgeneric condition, does not obviate the need of war writing to make generic choices nevertheless, even though these choices will be fraught with compromises and complicities, and with the danger of imposing significances preordained by genre upon historical experience" (23–24). She is right, of course. War writers and their critics face a long list of stumbling blocks, the least of which might be the decision to write about war in the first place. Norris notes that, in a Bakhtinian sense, war writers—perhaps even more so than readers—are prone to viewing "reality through the eyes of the genre," and the heavy generic hand of war literature, one held in place by combat gnosticism, makes what Norris calls the "intertexted process" of war writing an anxious one indeed (24). It is clear that novelists, poets, journalists, and scholars are all fraught with the generic choices they have to make.

Some of those anxieties are linked directly to the gatekeeping role that many veteran-authors or veteran-critics assume regarding war literature. Roxanna Robinson, a civilian, succinctly describes the situation: "the military is famously proprietary about war writing" (SR8). Candice Pipes reports that her students at the Air Force Academy "tend to invalidate 'fictional' accounts of war—one wrong use of a term, one inaccurate historical detail and they want to write off the author's efforts" (143). David Lawrence unapologetically agrees: "service members can be very persnickety when it comes to nomenclature, slang, uniform wear, etc." (96). As Randy Brown, a popular blogger who often discusses war literature, triumphantly puts it, "nothing breaks down the fourth wall for a veteran faster than a badly drawn tank."

Another blogger, a former professor of English at West Point and a retired Army officer named Peter Molin, crafts extensive and astute commentaries about contemporary war literature for his blog *Time Now*, but he rarely fails to note military minutiae that might be slightly off in a movie or a novel. In the film *The Messenger* (2009), Woody Harrelson and Ben Foster play casualty notification officers in the Army, and Molin writes that he "couldn't help noticing the goofiness with which the Foster and Harrelson characters wear their Army patrol caps" ("Don't"). In his review of Aaron Gwyn's *Wynne's War* (2014), Molin can't keep himself from pausing his otherwise penetrating review to point out that "it's inconceivable that the Green Berets wouldn't have 'TACSAT' radios and satellite phones to help them out of their jams" ("Grillin'").

In May of 2015, veteran-turned-author Matt Gallagher published a review of the one-person play starring Anne Hathaway—*Grounded*—that debuted in New York City. The play is about a pilot of unmanned aerial vehicles who flies her aircraft from a trailer in the middle of a Nevada desert and pushes buttons that unleash bombs on the other side of the globe. Gallagher admits to walking into the performance "still holding onto a ground soldier's sensibilities and stereotypes," but those sensibilities cloud his consumption of the play. Gallagher adopts a skeptical tone throughout, and he can't resist his otherwise reasonable review to note, "The play's devotion to military verisimilitude is admirable." Gallagher assures us that "the patches are in all the right spots" on Hathaway's flight suit and that "the raw, stunted lingo rings genuine" and that "Hathaway's pushups more than meet military regulation."

I'm no better; I groan every time a film turns the military salute into some sort of deeper-than-words-could-ever-express gesture of respect instead of its everyday, mechanical sign of greeting. The complaints and disapprovals above, however, are concerned with more than correctness. They are self-serving marks of combat gnosticism. Do readers of war literature and the viewers of war plays really need a military professional to tell them if a beret looks goofy or if a patch on a flight suit is the right color? The iconoclast in the field of war literature studies, today, might be the civilian or the combatant, the support troop or the critic, who ignores the urge to make such asides so that he or she can analyze war's representation rhetorically without becoming mired in irrelevant details of verisimilitude in a work's pursuit of reconstructing reality into art.

This type of critique might be why recent writers of war fiction have developed—as Emily Tredowe admits in an article for *The Daily Beast*—"insecurities around authority … when writing about war." The anxieties could come from any of the issues Norris references above, but combat gnosticism seems especially forceful here, especially when it is accompanied by a keenly felt fear of disrespecting military members, a fear of inaccuracy, or the artistic intent to create plausible characters and settings. Tredowe, a civilian war novelist, points out that among war fiction writers, the ideology of combat gnosticism drives a "hierarchy of 'how tough was your war,' a familiar if unspoken one-upping among" those who have (or have not) "been there." Ben Fountain, another civilian author whose work I examine in depth in Chapter Four of this book, notes the high stakes he felt were close at hand when he wrote *Billy Lynn's Long Halftime Walk*:

> A number of people have a problem with me writing about soldiers and veterans when I haven't had the experience. I have a lot more sympathy with their point of view than you might expect. It was a powerful thing in me to try to write that book. I did it for better or worse. It's not something to be taken lightly. It's an important thing and a necessary thing as a writer to always be reaching outside of yourself. They say write what you know. But what you know is rarely enough. You need to know more. But you've got to approach it with a lot of respect and humility [qtd. in North].

According to Tredowe, the anxiety even got to National Book Award winner Phil Klay, a former Marine and veteran of Operation Iraqi Freedom. Klay was no longer in the military during the second battle of Fallujah, but he wrote a short story set there anyway. During a public reading of that particular story, someone began laughing loudly in the back of the room. Klay's immediate worry was that the laugh was a "scoff" because "he'd gotten it all wrong" (Tredowe). Yet, as Molin relates on his blog, at a literature conference, Klay spoke of the "thick knowledge" he worked to gain before he was comfortable with writing war fiction that didn't come directly out of his own firsthand experience ("Minnesota"). Apparently, even with thick knowledge, the anxiety of authenticity never quite leaves a war writer. Roxanna Robinson mentions that during a radio interview she was doing to promote her novel *Sparta*, someone sent in an email that read, "This woman has never been in combat and knows nothing about it" (SR8). One wonders if she would have received the same comment if the circumstances of her life were withheld.

Burke says that different "strategies" can arise from any attempt to "remain realistic," and that some writers and readers forget "that realism is an aspect for foretelling" (*Philosophy* 299). Thus, war writers and their critics often search for the real and make the mistake of what Burke says is taking the idea of reality "as an end in itself":

> [The Author] is tempted to do this by two factors: 1) an ill-digested philosophy of science, leading him mistakenly to assume that "relentless" naturalistic "truthfulness" is a proper end in itself, and 2) a merely competitive desire to outstrip other writers by being "more realistic" than they [299].

Some authors of contemporary war fiction, like Ben Fountain and David Abrams, work very hard to check that box, the goal of seeming "more realistic" than other war writers. Other authors, such as Katey Schultz and Helen Benedict, politely sidestep the demands that the purveyors of combat gnosticism might demand from their work. Schultz—a civilian and the author of *Flashes of War* (2013)—reports that she understands "the desire to nit-pick, especially when someone's writing on 'your turf,'" but, she says, "ultimately, creative writing has nothing to do with the impulse to be perfectly accurate" (qtd. in Pipes 143). Benedict—a civilian and author of the war novel *Sand Queen*—suggests that "only two questions matter when it comes to reading or evaluating a war novel: is it honest? And does it glamorize war?" ("*Fives*"). I applaud both convictions, but an overarching unease among authors and critics remains regarding combat authority and accuracy that determines which writers write and the way they do so.

Heads I Win. Tails You Lose

In a 1989 essay for *The Atlantic*, Fussell speculated that, referring back to his lifelong thesis about combatant writing, "The troops' disillusion and their ironic response, in song and satire and silent contempt, came from knowing that the home front then (and very likely historiography later) could be aware of none of these things" ("Real" 34). The contempt that bruised and battered soldiers feel for those who remain safe and unaware at home is a common refrain in the military during war and peace; however, Fussell's parenthetical jab at "historiography later" is not only self-pitying, it is just plain wrong. Fussell seems to be well aware of this, but he follows one truism—*we are the only ones who know what it's like*—with another one—*it is impossible for us to tell you*. These arguments are horribly familiar within the genre, and such sophistic circular logic creates an insular place for combat gnosticism to thrive and grow. It allows people like George Packer to confidently assert that the "gap" between soldiers and civilians is "unbridgeable" (70). But why? Why should that gap of experience be any more insurmountable than any other lived experience?

I am reminded of a joke that my grandfather—a navigator in a World War II Navy dive-bomber—once told me:

> How many vets does it take to screw in a light bulb?
> You wouldn't understand; you weren't there.

In *The Great War and Modern Memory*, Fussell discusses this rhetorical device in detail:

> Logically, one supposes, there's no reason why a language devised by man should be inadequate to describe any of man's works. The problem was less one of "language" than of gentility and optimism; it was less a problem of "linguistics" than of rhetoric.... The real reason is that soldiers have discovered that no one is interested in the bad news they have to report. What listener wants to be torn and shaken when he doesn't have to be? We have made *unspeakable* mean indescribable: it really means *nasty* [*Great War* 184; italics original].

But is this truly the case? What nasty elements of war are we yet to encounter in war literature or personal narrative? Is anything truly unbelievable or indescribable? If art does anything, it can most certainly make the unbelievable believable. Marwill wonders the same thing about Fussell's assertions: "If it is unpreparedness, ineffectual weapons, blunders, harassment, booze and sex, deprivation, sadism, and brutality, most readers will be surprised by the claim. Have not these realities, or proximate versions thereof, come to our attention?" (435). Twenty-five years and at least three undeclared wars after Marwill wrote that, we are even more acquainted with these things. As the "autobiography" *American Sniper* has proven, plenty of people are interested in the bad news that a combatant has to report, even when that nasty news lacks any trace of irony.

In *Authoring War*, McLoughlin grants that such claims regarding the incommunicability of experience in war literature serves to "adumbrate catastrophe without articulating it," and she generously suggests that such a literary technique can be an important device, one of "adynaton," which she defines as the expression of "the impossibility of addressing oneself adequately to the topic" (152). But in a combatant tale designed to do nothing but provide vicarious experience, rarely are such philosophical concerns appropriate or applicable. As McLoughlin continues, "So what motivates these immediately belied disclaimers, these wordy disavowals of words? Some instances may be no more than conventional protestations of false modesty, decorous commonplaces of self-deception" (152). This is the most likely explanation to me, but McLoughlin does not relent. She goes on to offer that war writers use such disclaimers and diversions to indicate an exploration of "negative space" or to delve into the literary concept of the sublime (153). That might be true of *some* authors and *some* works of war fiction, but it is unlikely for the bulk of the material that now forms the latest iteration of combat gnosticism in war literature.

If a veteran-author or a critic argues that war writing is primarily useful as a tool to tell civilians "what it was like," then a writer's claim that he or she cannot or will not write about war is almost too convenient, excessively self-serving, clichéd, or otherwise meaningless. Maureen Ryan, in *The Other Side of Grief* (2008) calls this excuse-making tendency in war writing the "You Had to Be There" aphorism, one that is exhaustingly repeated by veterans who write literature about Vietnam: "You had to be there. Most of you weren't, so you can't understand. But we'll try nonetheless—over and over—to explain it" (17). This cliché is a curious byproduct and tool of combat gnosticism. It suggests a local epistemology that can only be accessed by the individual who graced a battlefield, but it also asserts that experienced knowledge lives in a liminal truth-space that forever will remain incommunicable, even though, of course, the veteran-turned-writer often goes right ahead and communicates that experience anyway. It is a Burkeian "heads I win, tails you lose" device again. As Ryan points out, "The withholding of the sacrosanct combat experience only reinforces the truism that you had to be there" (23). Such a device also completely disregards the reader. How is one supposed to respond but with a sympathetic nod?

New adherents to the tenets of combat gnosticism that trade on the "You Had to Be There" aphorism are appearing every day. In a recent essay for the website *Blue Force Tracker*, a freelance writer named Nolan Peterson, who publishes on a wide range of war-related topics, makes the reasonable observation that "talking about war is like trying to speak another language." It probably is, at least for some people. However, we the auditors can still hear them; all they have to do is speak. Still, Peterson (who leads his essay with a rundown of his own combat resume) goes on to state, "great writing about war can only come from those who have been there. Only they possess the personal experiences from which to draw to tell something about themselves they don't already know." Pronoun-antecedent confusion notwithstanding, his confident remark displays how silencing the rhetoric of combat gnosticism can be. Arguments in defense of it don't even need to make sense.

McLoughlin writes that "there is something counterintuitive about the literature of war," and that something is combat gnosticism and the popular suggestion that any extreme experience is un-writeable (Intro, *Literature* xiv). Writing is difficult, and, to be sure, writing about emotionally traumatic scenes rooted in experience is probably even more so. But both are possible. After all, learning how to write or voice the traumatic or extreme experience is the first step in the writing process. The reader's consumption and analysis of that representation is, many would argue, the one that matters. As McLoughlin notes, "Its readers also have significant responsibilities. Understanding how and why truths and lies about war are conveyed, perceiving the status of those who convey them, and appreciating the surrounding ethical issues are nothing less than necessary acts of global citizenship" (xiv). Still, even though Marwill reminds us that an "uncompromising naturalism is but one means for rendering reality," combat gnosticism and its goal of telling the uninitiated what war feels like remains dominant (444).

Fiction editors and publishers are at least partially culpable since capitalizing on the circularity of the You Had to Be There truism can be extremely fruitful. Readers want the easy redemption of titillating, pity-demanding tales of tragic heroism. Northup Frye summarizes how Wyndham Lewis developed a deep disdain for the popular veteran-penned war novels and war memoirs after World War I, what he considered vulgar approximations of the "new subject matter" of modern war (180). According to Frye, Lewis saw the artist of his day

> imitated by shrewd and clever craftsmen who swarm together in schools, movements, tendencies, groups, and generally in what Lewis calls phalanteries. These cliques, who are naturally on their guard to see that no real genius is given a hearing, vulgarized art into movements which become, like vulgarized science and philosophy, essentially political phenomena [*Northrop* 180].

Today, the reading public still wants the politically neutral or tragically palatable combat account, and the solider-become-writer is more than happy to oblige. New phalanteries have popped up online, in community-supported workshops, and in universities and writing programs across the country. As Michiko Kakutani explains, "M.F.A. programs, veteran's writing workshops and therapy-based writing programs used to treat post-traumatic stress disorder have tended to emphasize directness of expression and more naturalistic approaches" (A1). Indeed, as Sam Sacks outlines in a 2015 essay for *Harper's Magazine*, the modern creative writing program was borne out of the G.I. Bill and Wallace Stegner's idea to shape the Stanford writing program with the creative writing axiom that one should only write what one knows, an intentional mirror of an Army unit.[10] The explosion of creative writing programs across the country and a new post–9/11 G.I. Bill are no doubt good things for veterans who want to learn how to write, and publish, and heal.

I do not dispute any of this, but as Wyndham Lewis once wrote, "Truth has no place in action" (qtd. in Edwards 141). In *The Things They Carried* Tim O'Brien writes, "I did not look at my work as therapy, and still don't" (179). In a 2012 editorial that appeared in *Poetry* magazine, Yusef Komunyakaa agreed: "Poetry cannot serve as an emotional bandage for the blood and guts of warfare," he writes, "such an industry is doomed to dishonor the dead as well as the living" (145–46). Art may indeed provide vicarious experience, and creating it may provide writers a certain therapy for traumatic experiences, but combat gnosticism suggests that these purposes trump all others. The genre recently has witnessed an explosion in the number of literary outlets, venues, and contests that are exclusively open to veteran-authors. This definitely has allowed veterans who write war fiction access to a wider audience; it has helped me publish some of my own short stories. However, the insularity of these phalanteries results in an entirely myopic literary landscape, one that leads Sacks to argue that something is missing from contemporary war literature. Combat gnosticism's exclusionary model creates a civilian sphere that is either apathetic to what is written or reluctant to participate. I once asked a fellow graduate student at the University of Denver what he thought of a story I wrote about flying airplanes in Afghanistan, "What can I say?" he asked, "This is *your* world."

In 2006, the National Endowment for the Arts published a collection of creative work written by troops who were then deployed (a requirement for consideration in the collection) in support of the wars in Iraq and Afghanistan. The collection—entitled *Operation Homecoming*—is impressive in its scope and widely inclusive with its content, but the bulk of the works remains rooted in a collective goal of merely recording the event of war with the attendant stamp of authority that a veteran-author inherently lends such work. On the cover of the collection is a photo of three dirty soldiers in camouflage, leaning against a dirty tracked vehicle, reading letters from home. The message is clear: this art is only useful as a special communiqué between the home front and the war front. Another collection of war fiction—*Fire and Forget: Short Stories from the Long War* (2013)—packages its content just as *Operation Homecoming* does. While it contains a wide range of short war fiction from a variety of scenes from Iraq to New York, and while only three of them directly describe combat, the jacket and the preface pander to the same reading public that kept *American Sniper* on the *New York Times* Bestseller List for forty-two weeks in a row and made the cinematic adaptation of Chris Kyle's "autobiography" a box office hit: "What makes these stories even more remarkable is that all of them are written by men and women whose lives were directly engaged in the wars." Such résumé-parading is an example of what, in *A Toxic Genre* (2011), Martin Barker calls "reality guarantees" (118). Once such experience is established, the story can continue without demanding anything else from the reader beyond redemptive, vicarious-driven sympathy.

In the preface, the editors write, "Truth, *truthiness*, in this mass media cacophony we live in, comes up something for grabs. Well, here's some. Grab it. We were there. This is what we saw. This is *how it felt*. And we're here to say, it's not like you heard in the stories" (xv; italics original). That phrase—"whose lives were directly engaged in the wars"—screams historical mitigation, even with its intended vagueness. "Whose lives," you might ask, "aren't directly engaged in the wars?" Yes, the vast bulk of Americans have been insulated from the realities of the wars in Iraq and Afghanistan, but combat gnosticism is at least partially to blame for that. And yes, an all-voluntary military force means that many Americans have no personal or familial connection to war or the military, so a civilian-military divide that gets in the way of cross-cultural understanding probably does exist. But this problem is true of many cross-cultural exchanges. Kakutani observes the same thing: "the disconnect between life 'over there' and life 'back here' has emerged as a central theme in much of today's war writing" (A1). But how many different versions of that same story do we need? However effective fiction can be in resolving some, all, or none of these societal problems, the suggestion that understanding can only be achieved through a one-way transmission of experiential knowledge is unconvincing at best and ethically wrong at worst. I am not questioning the individual worth of any one of the stories in either collection. I also appreciate the playfulness on the idea that there may not be any representative truth—beyond truthiness—in any war story. I do, however, question the way that the preface claims the rewards of admitting the subjectivity of war truth while also eagerly claiming the benefits of combat gnosticism.

As Kakutani describes it, much of the recent war fiction that has been published in the United States has a "chamber music quality ... fable-like allegories or keyhole views ... to open small windows on these conflicts" (A1). Combat gnosticism might also explain why, as Kakutani points out, no "big, symphonic Iraq or Afghanistan novel" has been published to date (A1). While we all wait for the cycle of war literature's production to creak along, combat gnosticism determines (and hampers) how war literature is written and packaged and received. Meanwhile, experiential authority and personal wounding stand as the most important commodities to be debated and discussed while dissent and civilian perspectives on war are pushed to the critical background. Maybe this unflagging expectation for experiential authority in the contemporary American war story is why only four stories written by an American, in English, about Afghanistan or Iraq have appeared in *The New Yorker* since 9/11, despite the magazine's long history of publishing other types of war fiction.[11] Yes, it takes time for war fiction to appear, but the temporal distance between war's event and its representation in fiction may only be necessary so that the dominant cloud of combat gnosticism can disperse.

When *Operation Homecoming* appeared in 2006, it did draw a small number of unfavorable criticisms. Like Suman Gupta, poet and Vietnam veteran Yusef Komunyakaa distrusts the very nature of such testimony itself: "We had our soldier poets in Vietnam also; and for the most part, they penned what I call 'the boondock doggerel of blood and guts'.... The more immediate soldiers are to their acts of violence, the less creditable they are as witnesses" (144). Elliot Colla goes so far as to imagine a "military-literary complex" and an institutional conspiracy at work behind the collection. Hyperbole aside, Colla's point about soldier testimony in both fiction and non-fictive accounts of war (he calls it "embedded literature") is a sound one: "we accept embedded literature because we prefer stories about 'us' and not 'them.' We accept tales of combatant privilege because we would rather imagine ourselves being the ones holding the guns than those who are not."

Interestingly enough, Komunyakaa and Colla both sound a lot like Fussell. Here is Fussell in the afterword of the twenty-fifth anniversary edition of *The Great War and Modern Memory*: "I hoped that the effect of the book on [my American readers] might persuade them that even Gooks had feelings, that even they hated to die, and like us called for help or God or Mother when their agony became unbearable" (369).

Such is the surviving ambivalence that Fussell's contribution to the study of war literature pushes to the forefront of its creation, reception, and critical analysis. No readers or critics or artists should find fault with Fussell's hope that literature and criticism can combine and illuminate the common humanity that war destroys. The fact remains, however, that though Fussell helped to grow a genre linked by nothing but subject, and though he may have ushered in a focus on witness art, his influence and the ideology of combat gnosticism that survives him still unduly dictate what literature is allowed to emerge from the subjectivities of modern war and the way those subjectivities are discussed and accepted. This effect, I argue, is to the genre's detriment. Once the iconoclast, Fussell is now the dust-covered sage, the combat-experienced scholar who fostered an ideological inertia—combat gnosticism—that should be, but really isn't, waning.

In *If I Die in a Combat Zone*, Tim O'Brien asks, "Can the foot soldier teach anything important about war, merely for having been there?" (22–23). He answers his own question: "I think not. He can tell war stories" (23). So can everyone else. Fussell, Hynes, and other combat gnosticators force a boundary around one type of war's representation, but their source material never provides sufficient proof that such a boundary is necessary, representative, or superlative. Indeed, for every ironic song lyric Fussell cites and every diary entry he scours, one can just as easily locate similar songs and similar private expressions of experience that fall on precisely the opposite side of the disillusion he champions.

Fussell would probably agree with W.D. Ehrhart's pronouncement that "knowledge without experience is at best an empty thing, at worst a disaster" (6). The opposite is true too, and war's representation is its victim. As Kenneth Burke wrote about the often disregarded distinction between observation, art, and epistemology:

> Still, there is a difference, and a radical difference, between building a house and writing a poem about building a house.... There are practical acts, and there are symbolic acts (nor is the distinction, clear enough in its extremes, to be dropped simply because there is a borderline area wherein many practical acts take on a symbolic ingredient) [*Philosophy* 8–9].

This is the problem with war literature and any comprehensive approach to it as long as combat gnosticism reigns supreme. It isn't that all war writing deserves similar treatment because it all sits under the same generic umbrella; it's that much of it doesn't belong there in the first place. Ultimately, this is what Fussell and Hynes and others like them tried to fix. They worked extremely hard to sufficiently establish taxonomic boundaries for small categories; the problem is that they did so by trading in superlatives, exclusions, and certainty.

Hemingway once suggested that war literature should never seek to replace experience. This, he argues, is a foolish and ultimately useless expectation. What war literature can do, he said, is "prepare for and supplement experience. It can serve as a corrective after experience" for both the reader *and* the writer (Intro xxvii). Combat gnosticism ignores the forward-looking nature of this nuance. Or, as Jameson writes, the "dilemmas of representation" regarding war are "navigable only by formal innovation ... and not by any stable narrative convention" (1547). This leaves the critic of contemporary war literature in a bit of a bind. Norris describes the dilemma:

> Significant "truth" resides elsewhere than in facticity.... [T]here is an opening, then, for arguing that art's responsibilities might include the exposure of historical writing's own inability to totalize, whatever tonnage of facts it brings to bear on its telling of war, and to explore the status of history as historiography, inherently as textual, narrative, and metonymic as art itself.... Totalization—bringing the layers of war narrative together in a coherent whole—may be not only an impossibility but perhaps also, in some respects, and undesirability [22–23].

One is left wondering: Short of categorizing according to theme, authorial intention, authorial biography, or conflict, what is the literary critic to do? What are we to do if we fear minimizing the enormity and tragedy of war and the sacrifices of war's agents and the sufferings of war's victims? What are we to do if the dilemmas of representation Jameson speaks of tend to result in every expression of war's experience being treated as art just because it is has been expressed, over and over, by the ones who did the experiencing? What are we to do if combat gnosticism continues to demand that all war stories, not just personal narratives, memoirs, and autobiographies carry a flavor of authenticity or to be experientially true?

Two

Kenneth Burke
A Method for War Literature

> I have never seen anyone turn from *The Iliad* a-froth with desire for slaughter.—Kenneth Burke, *Philosophy* 239

Kenneth Burke wrote the following words more than seventy-five years ago, but they still resonate today:

> The great allurement in our present popular "inspirational literature," for instance, may be largely of this sort. It is a strategy for easy consolation. It "fills a need," since there is always a need for easy consolation—and in an era of confusion like our own the need is especially keen ["Literature" 298].[1]

Combat gnosticism and utilitarian concepts regarding the purpose of war literature have resulted in a genre that often feels stagnant, vapid, and repetitive. Likewise, criticism of contemporary war literature often has little to say about the social value of war literature beyond passing commentary on how close a work comes to accurately reflecting lived experiences of war. That, or the critic of contemporary war literature rests his or her commentary on the solace that accompanies tragic tales of war trauma, tales that are often praised for illuminating the human cost of war. These dominating critical poses are what make extensive scapegoat mechanisms such useful things to track in war literature. Burke's view of literature and poetry as symbolic action doesn't necessarily posit that authorial intent or experience are irrelevant to a popular or critical consumption of war literature, but it properly compartmentalizes these elements alongside other, more formal elements of a text and the culture in which they are created and consumed. War literature, then, when it is analyzed with Burke's scapegoat mechanism as a guide, counteracts the primacy of authorial claims of authenticity in the genre while it also accounts for distracting stylistic choices that work extremely hard (perhaps too hard) to establish a sense of the real in representations of war in order to unearth a work's potential artistic or propagandistic message.

Indeed, in an important essay that appeared in 2014 in *The New York Times*, Michiko Kakutani could do little else with her piece but note which voices of "soldiers and reporters" had managed to find publication homes for their work, work that succeeded because it was able to "slam home a sense of what the wars were like on the front lines" (A1). As Burke writes in his essay, "War and Cultural Life" (1942), "war does compel a people to conceive the reality of forces in much more realistic terms than need prevail under conditions of peace" (404). Kakatani's title—"Humans Costs of the Forever Wars, Enough to Fill a Bookshelf"—shows how, despite the growing number of fictional works that assess America's post–9/11 wars, criticism is hamstrung by literature that is hamstrung by the ideology of combat gnosticism.

Alex Vernon, in his introduction to *Arms and Self* (2005), remarks that since autobiography is not immune to fictive elements, "we are justified" in assuming a critical position of "considering both [fiction and nonfiction] as narratives simply, narratives that can only be treated as such" (31). Vernon goes on to add the significant caveat that we can only do so "*as long as we acknowledge and account for the author's generic intention*" (31; italics original). This suggestions is a reasonable enough one to make, especially since war literature criticism often ignores Michel Foucault's suggestion in "What is an author?" that, "In writing, the point is not to manifest or exalt the act of writing, nor is it to pin a subject within language; it is, rather, a question of creating a space into which the writing subject constantly disappears" (283). So, accounting for authorial intention may indeed resolve *some* of the problems that attend combat gnosticism and the genre of war literature. However, that may not always be such an easy or straightforward feat. Acknowledging intent alone doesn't necessarily account for the reigning epistemology that privileging a minuscule percentage of overall war experience (that of the combat soldier) creates in the genre as a whole. In Foucault's estimation, the driving force that continues to "pin" the writing subject in a work of fiction is "the old bipolar field of discourse" and the accompanying "oeuvre" of the author—the Author Function—that critics use to continue the very discourse the author began (286, 283). Thus, it would seem, at least as far as war literature is concerned, our dominant "man-and-his-work criticism" will, for the foreseeable future, continue to push the war writer in front of his art (Foucault 283). This is why I argue for a balanced and comprehensive approach to war literature, one that considers the text's scapegoating mechanism in its full context, a context that includes the author (in a manner similar to Foucault's concept of the Author Function) within his socio-historical moment. Indeed, as William Rueckert writes in *Kenneth Burke and the Drama of Human Relations* (1963), "when Burke says that the main ideal of criticism is 'to use all that is there to use' he literally means what he says" (74). However, this does not mean that we should become mired in questions of accuracy and authority regarding objective experience, concepts that become rather slippery when the topic is war.

To be sure, Burke does regard a poet and his purpose as key "dramatistic" elements in a poet's act of writing. His theory of dramatism places the poet (the "agent"), the poem (the "act"), and the poet's "purpose" in a "pentad" with "agency" and "scene" (*Grammar* xv). But while Burke does say that "purpose" plays a "major role" in the exegesis of discovering "'what is going on' in poetry" (*Philosophy* 124), he also says that purpose is

> by no means an exclusive role: it is merely one strong ingredient in the total recipe—and the critic must always be prepared to go beyond it, noting the ways in which it becomes interwoven with a much wider texture of motives [*Philosophy* 92].

In war, experience, artifice, and criticism are far too complex, and the interrelatedness of the three is far too complementary to justify any valorization of any author's biographical situatedness. Accordingly, Burke's dramatism is particularly apropos to contemporary war literature; it encourages a more dialectic or cooperative relationship between criticism and poetry:

> [I]n studying the full nature of a symbolic act you are entitled, if the material is available, to disclose also the things that the act is doing for the poet and no one else. Such private goads stimulate the artist, yet we may respond to imagery of guilt from totally different private goads of our own. We do not have to be drug addicts to respond to the guilt of a drug addict. The addiction is private, the guilt public. It is in such ways that the private and public areas of a symbolic act at once overlap and diverge [*Philosophy* 25].

My role, then, is to help make the guilt public, to show how the symbolic act of post–9/11 war literature overlaps with and/or diverges from the reader's.

Vernon recognizes that the biographical fallacy that attends war literature is a seductive and dangerous one, and he points out that "to assume and posit uncritically that a work of fiction accurately depicts the author's experiences of, or emotional response to, war and military is to make a rather gross interpretive error" (32). The key words in that sentence are "uncritically" and "accurately." They, yet again, highlight the appropriateness of tracing the Burkeian scapegoat mechanism in contemporary war literature, for, as Rueckert writes, Burke did indeed consider a poem or a work of prose fiction as "symbolic autobiography" (*Kenneth* 68). "In the course of the creative process," Rueckert posits, "there is a transfer, or transmutation" of the "poet's being" into "symbolic form" (68). Yet, neither Burke nor Rueckert suggests that the critic should rest in this place, aesthetically or ethically. It would be an "interpretive error" for any critic of any work of literature to, as Burke says, "cling to a kind of naïve verbal realism that refuses to realize the full extent of the role played by symbolicity in his notions of reality" (*Language* 5). Burke is the perfect counter to the ideology of combat gnosticism, for, as Burke writes, "Even if any given terminology is a *reflection* of reality, by its very nature as a terminology, it must be a *selection* of reality; and to this extent must function also as a *deflection* of reality" (*Language* 45). My rhetorical analysis of war culture, war language, and war literature accounts for that deflection by turning the lens onto the reader, by tracking the manner in which the elements of a given situation (literary or otherwise) interact in order to ascertain the underlying attitudes and motives behind the symbolic act.

In "War, Response and Contradiction" (1933), Burke includes a long discussion of what he calls the "mechanistic metaphor" as it applies to trends in literary criticism that are dominant, even today, in the genre of war literature (242).[2] Of the "put in/take out" "schema of stimulus and response" that is often used to "too literally" explain the way we perceive reality, Burke points out that, "returning to the issues of war," one doesn't "put in war-horrors and take out antimilitarism, put in 'human' pictures of war and take out war-spirit" ("War" 242). Burke doesn't privilege "human" representations of war over "war-horrors," but he does point out that the mechanistic approach to both versions of war damages both art *and* criticism:

> There is a kind of "one to one" correspondence between stimulus and response which is assumed in much contemporary criticism, and I believe that it is not justified. Does antimilitarism produce antimilitarism, corruption corruption, quietude quietude, acceptance acceptance, individualism individualism, etc.? I think that the entire issue must be broadened considerably ["War" 244].

Burke's words hold true for all genres and subjects of literature, but when we consider the vast Babel of voices that still competes for a "right" to represent war in literature, and when we consider that a preference for a naïve verbal realism may always abide in the ways that war literature is constructed and received, Burke's observation suggests that a close reading of the formal structures of plot and characterization that complete the scapegoat mechanism in a piece of war literature can forestall the easy vicarious redemption so common in tragically heroic war stories.

As Burke writes, though the "tiny sliver of reality each of us has experienced firsthand" is undeniably "important" to a writer and his or her audience, overemphasizing such concerns often means that we forget that the "the whole overall 'picture' is but a construct of our symbol systems" (*Language* 5). Grasping the "whole overall picture" of any situation requires remarkable resourcefulness from a critic, and this may be one of the reasons why the critic of war literature relies so heavily on the biographical circumstances of the veteran-author when he or she seeks to weigh authorial purpose. After all, Burke writes, "if you look for a man's *burden*, you will find the principle that reveals the structure of his unburdening; or, in attenuated form, if you look for his problem, you will find the lead that explains the structure of his solution" (*Philosophy* 92; italics original). When the writer is a veteran, the burden sometimes overshadows the structure of the unburdening.

In a 2013 essay for *The New York Times* "At War" blog, Brian Van Reet displays a dire need for a method like Burke's. In his essay, "A Problematic Genre, the 'Kill Memoir,'" Van Reet explains the major problem he finds with the glut of combat memoirs that were flooding the publishing market. Specifically, Van Reet argues that these works do little to expand our understanding of war and its effects on humanity. Van Reet calls these books "kill memoirs," witness-based stories of violence and self-congratulation that trade on combat resumes, high body counts, and the appeal of "real-seeming" tales based on experiential accuracy. These "kill memoirs," he rightly notes, follow a two-part formula. First, they make a "claim to authenticity" generically, by stating clearly that they are to be read as autobiography, memoir, or firsthand testimony. Second, kill memoirs "assure the reader the he will learn the intimate details of taking human life." Van Reet is, in some respects, doing what Vernon encourages above. After noting the authorial intention of such narratives, he goes on to suggest that these kill memoirs fail in that they reinforce the military-civilian divide. He writes, "Rather than complicate the question (did you kill anyone during war?) or subvert it or implicate the American public as a party to what was done in its name, these books simply answer in the most spectacularly affirmative way possible." Van Reet is right, of course. Such works probably do confirm the worst stereotypes of the typical American military member. The problem, though, is that his response is driven by a morally indignant attitude that can be easily dismissed or ignored; indeed, some civilians and military members may not consider the stereotypes negative at all.

The memoirs Van Reet is concerned with perpetuate the cycle of what Roy Scranton, in the *Los Angeles Review of Books*, termed "the myth of the trauma hero," a master narrative in the war literature genre that "frames and filters our perceptions of reality through a set of recognizable and comforting conventions," conventions that grant a reader voyeuristic redemption drawn from the reader's access to a hero's movement from wounded to healed ("The Trauma Hero"). This well-worn path is essentially what Van Reet notices and bemoans in these kill memoirs, and I agree with almost everything he has to say about popular war literature and its questionable ethics. I also join him as he directs praise toward the recent war fiction about Iraq that, as of the writing of his essay, was just beginning to appear in increasing numbers. As Van Reet suggests, fiction allows a more ethically responsible vehicle by which a veteran-writer can draw upon experience and "create something greater and truer than the sum of its parts." I further agree that the works Van Reet attacks are problematically opportunistic, boastful, sensational, and—in some cases—full of fabrications.[3] The most popular contemporary kill memoirs often celebrate what should remain uncelebrated. For all of these reasons, Van Reet is right to alert, as he does, to the way many veterans write about war. However, once Van Reet makes his point about the appropriate way that aesthetics and ethics should affect war literature (an argument he makes quite well), he misses the chance to step out of the cloud of combat gnosticism and instead closes with an empty plea: "Those of us veterans who are writing about these wars," he writes, "can do better than that. And the publishers should, too." Sam Sacks makes a similar complaint in the final sentences of his essay, "First-Person Shooters: What's Missing in Contemporary War Fiction": "One of the jobs of literature is to wake us from stupor. But in matters of war, our sleep is deep, and the best attempts of today's veterans have done little to disturb it."

This stupor is what follows when combat gnosticism determines what works reach the reading public. The kill memoirs he criticizes rely far more on conventional narratives and vicarious victimage than they do on experience. What Van Reet's analysis needs is a method by which he can examine these crude tales rhetorically, to reveal the easy redemption that draws complicit war enthusiasts to these books. What he needs is a methodology that treats all literature and symbolic constructions of unreliable reality as propaganda and art. I'm not arguing that the popularity of the kill memoir is a necessarily a good thing, generically and politically speaking, nor am I suggesting that Van Reet is wrong to object to the prideful boastings of men who kill. The problem is that his analysis never quite escapes the constricting trends of the genre, trends that lend excessive epistemological authority to authors merely because they were the ones pulling the triggers or ducking bullets. Van Reet makes the dubious assertion that war literature's sole value is to be an "arbiter of truth," but for him, that "truth" is still exclusively rooted in the experience of combat. Thus, he somewhat misses the opportunity—through his overriding indignant motive—to analyze the symbolic elements that these kill memoirs use to cleanse from the reader any sense of humility when he or she faces death in such stark terms.

I point out the compounding issues behind Van Reet's essay not to necessarily dispute his conclusions but to highlight Burke's reminder that, "to an extent, books merely exploit our attitudes—and to an extent they may form our attitudes" ("War" 235). Van Reet and other critics like him come to war literature with attitudes preformed by combat gnosticism, and they are rightly offended when war writers exploit those attitudes. A plea for ethical writing from veterans is, to be sure, a worthy pursuit, but as long as combat gnosticism remains, there always might be a popular desire for the triumphant combat memoir that, of course, reflects our preconceived attitudes about war right back to us. What the genre needs is a method that rescues the contemporary war story from the generic impulse to delineate war literature according to poetic, scientific, or rhetorical ends, which, Burke says, are not mutually exclusive; rather, they all overlap and blend through "the substance of the literary act" as it affects an audience (*Philosophy* viii). Or, as Burke writes, "whereas poetic language is a kind of symbolic action, for itself and in itself, and whereas scientific action is a preparation for action, rhetorical language is inducement to action (or to attitude, attitude being an incipient act)" (*Rhetoric* 42). By examining war's language and representation, together, as "symbolic action," Burke says, we can reveal "the fact that invective is an intrinsic resource of language," and we can simultaneously avoid the "genetic fallacy" ("Dramatism" 328).

As Burke writes in his 1966 essay that defines "Dramatism," all language is essentially a system of symbolic substitution that follows a simple series of if/then statements: "If action, then drama; if drama, then conflict; if conflict, then victimage" ("Dramatism" 342). Therefore:

> A dramatistic view of human motives thus culminates in the ironic admonition that perversions of the sacrificial principle (purgation by scapegoat, [congregations by segregation]) are the constant temptation of human societies, whose orders are built by a kind of animal exceptionally adept in the ways of symbolic action [343].[4]

This brings me back to the issue regarding the brute reality of war and the role that art plays in the intricate interconnectedness of war's reality and the aesthetic/propagandistic values that a work uses (or misuses) to complete its rhetorical goals. As Burke's work reminds, art is a learning tool but not inherently so. It requires a savvy auditor to track the symbolic action in a given work and reveal how a symbol (or a racist proverb, or the appropriation of "Geronimo," or a boastful "kill memoir") can "by its function as name and definition, give simplicity and order to an otherwise unclarified complexity" and complete the human cycle of order, guilt, and redemption through vicarious victimage (*Counter-Statement* 154).

In "War, Response, and Contradiction" (1933), Burke essentially shows us how one might negotiate opposing attitudes regarding the way war is represented in art. This essay is, ostensibly, a response to two separate book reviews, short analyses that were published earlier in 1933, side by side, in an issue of *The New Republic*. In these paired columns, Archibald MacLeish and Malcolm Cowley responded to a collection of World War I photos—*The First World War* (1933)—edited by Laurence Stallings. Each critic takes an entirely different approach to Stallings's collection, and Burke steps in to, above all, point out that critics of literature and other forms of art (but most obviously critics of war literature) often fall prey to the "assumption that people are quite as direct as machines in their responses" to representations of war ("War" 241). Again, the focus is on the response to the representation, not the representation itself. Thus, Burke's essay stands as a useful model for the contemporary critic of war literature who might object, on aesthetic or ethical grounds, to the way a veteran or a civilian writes about war. Since Burke considered war a massive symptom of the failure of verbal debate in popular and political culture, his essay serves the critic today, as a criticism *of* criticism. He gives us a perspective on a perspective. Before discussion of the opposing positions of MacLeish and Cowley, in what Burke calls the "battle of the books," he writes:

> Aesthetical values are intermingled with ethical values—and the ethical is the basis of the practical. Or, put more simply: our ideas of the beautiful, the curious, the interesting, the unpleasant, the boring are closely bound with our ideas of the good, the desirable and undesirable have much to do with our attitudes towards our everyday activities ["War" 234].

With this guiding thesis, Burke assumes a particularly reasonable stance regarding the debate over the type of photos Stallings included in his collection, and he manages to remain equally charitable to both men (Burke was good friends with Cowley).

MacLeish is upset that Stallings's book of World War I photos is not comprehensive enough, that it ignores that the war was wholly a picture of "parades, speeches, brass bands, *bistros*, boredom, terror, anguish, heroism, endurance, humor, death" (159). And, above all, MacLeish says, portraying the "truth" of the war means portraying the fact that it was "a human war" whose "adversaries were men" and whose "stories were stories of men" (159). Or, as Burke summarizes MacLeish's position, MacLeish objects to the idea that Stallings's collection only "pictures the repellant side of war" ("War" 236). Such a collection, MacLeish argues, is not art at all; rather, it is utter propaganda that operates as "one of the most anti-war tracts every produced" (160). He firmly believes that art about war should record "those things, seen or unseen, which have actually occurred ... regardless the effect upon the minds of the young or the minds of the old" (160).

On the other side of the debate stands Malcolm Cowley whose piece is more of a response to MacLeish than it is to Stallings. He doesn't as much take issue with Stallings's selectivity as he does with MacLeish's impassioned anti-propagandistic argument about what art should and should not do. Cowley writes:

> What (MacLeish) says in effect is that other artists, out of hatred for propaganda, ought to do their best to bring about that very disaster which they and he most want to prevent. This is either nonsense, or else it is mysticism too deep for most of us to understand [161].

Burke says that the argument is a "vital" one because both men, essentially, are agreeing with the central tenet of Burke's methodology, that art is "designed to elicit a 'response' of some sort" in an audience ("War" 235, 236). Thus, Burke emphatically reminds us that, despite the intent of the artist, all art is propaganda, or, at a minimum, all art is "by its very nature an abstractive process, a simplification" that "has an interpretive or 'philosophic' consistency which events in actuality do not have" ("War" 237). As Burke writes, "MacLeish seems mainly concerned with the poet's response to experience, and Cowley with the public's response to the poet" when both should be concerned with the auditor's response to the photos ("War" 235). Van Reet, for his part, makes both arguments in his essay as well; he is concerned with contemporary war memoirists' responses to experience *and* with the public's positive response to the actions they report. Burke shows how limiting both concerns can be.

As Burke negotiates the MacLeish-Cowley debate, he shows in glaring detail how both scholars' rhetoric is ultimately distracted by the reality the photos symbolically represent. Van Reet makes the same mistake. Of MacLeish, Burke asks, "Where indeed can MacLeish point to the authority of the events 'as they actually occurred,' when the occurrence is still confined to the poet's symbols themselves?" ("War" 237). And then he goes on to respond to MacLeish's appeal for objective "truth" in war photography with a wonderful metaphor regarding the Rosetta Stone, which, he reminds us "was carved for the purpose of conveying certain information local to the times" ("War" 237). So, too, are the memoirs that make up Van Reet's "kill memoir" genre. Yet, just as the Rosetta Stone "became important to (modern linguists) as a key for deciphering Egyptian," the value of a war memoir or a collection of photos as documented "truth" pales as far as the work's rhetorical purpose or motive is concerned later ("War" 237). Like the stone, we use a war memoir "for our purposes, for a 'truth' which did not exist at the time of its erection" ("War" 237). And so, for that reason, "we owe the stone no allegiance" ("War" 237).

"Are not wars what we make of them?" Burke asks, "Why must we attempt to uphold, by strange canons of 'truth,' the '1916 character' of war?" ("War" 238). We could ask the same question of combat gnosticism and any suggestion that war literature should accurately illuminate the so-called human cost of war or provide a vicarious experience of war to any reader without recognizing the cheap redemption that vicarious experience offers. A glance at my bookshelf proves how seductive such tales are. On the top of one stack I can see Sebastian Junger's documentary *Korengal: This Is What War Feels Like*. I might echo Burke and ask, "Why must we attempt to uphold, by strange canons of 'combat-based-truth,' the 'post–9/11 character' of war?"

In what is probably Burke's most famous essay—a review of Hitler's *Mein Kampf* first published in the *Southern Review* in 1939[5]—Burke practices what he preaches. That is, in "The Rhetoric of Hitler's 'Battle,'" Burke considered it his job, as a critic, to "find all available ways of making the Hitlerite distortions of religion apparent, in order that politicians of his kind in America be unable to perform a similar swindle" (21). The lasting applicability and power of his analysis, thus, relies on the fact that Burke doesn't merely outline Hitler's use of an extensive scapegoat mechanism. He doesn't merely respond to a "poet." Instead, he shows us how susceptible all people are to such simply symbol mongering, manipulation that is especially effective when a nation is full of the resentment that follows a national trauma. Almost eighty years ago, Burke described *Mein Kampf* as "the well of Nazi magic; crude magic, but effective," pointing out that "A people trained in pragmatism should want to inspect this magic" (2). Today, considering that unrest, conquest, imperialism, terrorism, murder, and war continue to spread and morph across the globe through "magical" systems of hierarchy and scapegoating, it is rather urgent for us to continue Burke's project, to inspect other "wells," other "fonts" for similarly "crude magic."

Burke not only discusses the way language can be used by a poet like Hitler, but he also shows the literary critic how, through rhetorical analysis, he or she can remove some of the power of such language. First, Hitler essentialized the "international Jew" as the "international devil" according to "two keystones" of "opposite equations" that highlighted "Aryan 'heroism' and 'sacrifice'" as opposed to "Jewish 'cunning' and 'arrogance'" (13). Whereas the Aryan pursued "self-preservation" based upon "the sacrifice of the individual to the group, hence, militarism, army discipline, and one big company union" the threatening Jew sought "self-preservation" based on "individualism" which "attain[ed] its cunning ends by the exploitation of peace" (14). Since any number of "bad features" can be loaded up onto the symbolic "devil" or "scapegoat," war and murder and destruction follow close behind (4). And, with the help of a "sinister secularized revision of Christian theology," Hitler seamlessly put a "sense of dignity upon a fighting basis," one "requiring the conquest of 'inferior races'" (9). While Burke shows us the "exasperating, even nauseating" ways that Hitler managed to goad an entire country into ritually purging an entire race through murder and genocide, his essay is eerily predictive of bin Laden's war against America *and* America's military response (1).

Burke shows us the intricate yet frighteningly simple steps that Hitler's scapegoat mechanism involved. First, out of the symbolic fog of words, Hitler deliberately crafted a "unification device" that featured the establishment of an "inborn dignity" within his "Aryan" race (9). Next, he followed with a "projection device," one that enacted the need for a cleanse, or a "curative process" that included "hand[ing] over one's ills to a scapegoat, thereby getting purification by dissociation" (9). The cultish killing of the scapegoat, then, results in a "symbolic rebirth" for any who may choose to subscribe to the tenets of the unification device (9). "The projective device of the scapegoat," Burke writes, "coupled with the Hitlerite doctrine of inborn racial superiority, provides its followers with a 'positive' view of life. They can again get the feel of *moving forward*, towards a *goal*" (9). With the contemporary war narrative—fictive or non-fictive—it is quite easy to trace the same mechanism's potential to affect a reader in a similar manner:

> [I]f one can hand over his infirmities to a vessel, or "cause," outside the self, one can battle an external enemy instead of battling the enemy within. And the greater one's internal inadequacies, the greater the amount of evils one can load up on the back of "the enemy" [9].

The astute reader can observe, assess, and construct a guard against (if necessary) similar medicine of the contemporary war story.

Tracing the Burkeian scapegoat, as the rest of this book will show, allows the critic of war literature to "lie on the bias across the categories of modern specialization" ("Literature" 303). It also "automatically breaks down the barriers erected about literature as a specialized pursuit" ("Literature" 303). In other words, it breaks down the barriers of combat gnosticism. As Elizabeth Weiser writes in "Burke and War," "Dramatism encourages a poetic dialectic—the celebrations of differing perspectives—and transcendence—the search for points of merger—in an effective parliamentary debate" (287). Thus, this book considers all works of war literature as providing audiences "strategies for selecting enemies and allies, for socializing losses, for warding off evil eye, for purification, propitiation, and desanctification, consolation and vengeance, admonition and exhortation, implicit commands or instructions of one sort or another" ("Literature" 304).

Burke passed away in 1993, and the bulk of his rhetoric was aimed at World War II and the Cold War, but his philosophy resonated throughout his life and continues to do so today. This resilience is, yet again, what makes Kenneth Burke's methodology such an important tool to bring to war literature. In his 2009 *PMLA* essay, Fredric Jameson identifies elements in "representations of war that are content to confirm the stereotype" of traditional literary aesthetics:

> Indeed one often has the feeling that all war novels (and war films) are pretty much the same and have few enough surprises for us, even though their situations may vary. In practice, we can enumerate some seven or eight situations, which more or less exhaust the genre [1533].

Jameson goes on to conclude that, because war writers often recycle tired and repetitive tropes and plot forms, the genre is rather limited by the popular "suspicion that war is ultimately unrepresentable" (1533). I covered this issue in the previous chapter, but I bring Jameson up again because he is one of the few scholars of war literature who suggests that Kenneth Burke's methodology can offer the critic a useful guide by which he or she can parse any work of war literature—despite the limiting issues of repetitive "situations" or the aphorism that "You Had to Be There." With Burke, one can analyze war literature with full awareness of the ideology of combat gnosticism and the persistence of a naïve verbal realism in popular expectations regarding war and artifice.

Jameson writes, "What may prove most helpful here, then, is Kenneth Burke's 'dramatistic pentad,' which differentiates between act, agent, agency, purpose, and scene as so many distinct media through which the narrative material can be focused" (1533). Jameson continues:

> [N]arrative semiotics, by identifying Burke's first three categories with one another—an act always somehow implying an agent and the agent in turn implying an agency—suggests a differing ordering of these perspectives, in which purpose somehow withdraws (as a feature of interpretation rather than of representation) [1534].

Jameson's point that "there is no correct or true photographically accurate rendering of such multidimensional realities" during war describes my ultimate reason to focus on war literature's impact on the reader instead of focusing on its therapeutic or trauma-healing service to the author (1534). Such an analysis, based on narrative semiotics, could allow us to promote tolerance, embrace difference, and avoid legitimizing pictures of war or the glorification of state-sponsored violence without becoming mired in distracting issues of accuracy and contests of seeming real.

So, let's return to that day in 2005 in Saudi Arabia when that young Marine told me to "watch out" so "I don't get scalped by no Injuns," the story that I mentioned in the introduction. Kenneth Burke would likely respond by pointing out that that young man was responding to a recurring situation type (Americans at war) by simulating reality through proverb ("don't get scalped by Injuns") because he lacked any other way to express his own socio-historic situatedness. Yes, the racist proverb I heard in Saudi Arabia reflects a common American attitude that has proven disastrous for large swaths of cultures, nations, and peoples across decades of war and violent conflict, and it continues to have disastrous effects today, not only on native Americans and their cultures, but also on enemy populations anywhere the United States exerts itself militarily. So I am right to alert to the use and misuse of Native American stereotypes and symbols in contemporary war discourse. Burke would likely add that the critic has an important role to play in such linguistic situations; for, as he argues, language is best conceived as "stylistic medicine," and "the poet is, indeed, a medicine man" (*Philosophy* 61, 64).

When certain social phenomena recur with frequency, proverbs and symbols become very clear linguistic expressions of man's (the symbol-using animal's) medicine. Burke had a strong affinity for proverbs, and he used them, as I do, to show how that mistaken Marine had little recourse when he found himself in "a certain social relationship" that had recurred with such frequency in his country's past, that he was able to find a convenient "word for it" ("Literature" 293). It is on this "social relationship" that I focus my analysis. The need for a scapegoat via plot or phrase is obvious in contemporary war literature, a body of literature that—for the last fifteen years—has been left mainly to the combat soldier. Therefore, it is worth returning, one last time, to the benefits of analyzing war literature according to Burke's scapegoat mechanism. It essentially does the very thing Margot Norris, Kate McLoughlin, and other leading scholars of war literature seek to do in their work. Thus, the separate chapters of this book heed C. Allen Carter's admonition in *Kenneth Burke and the Scapegoat Process* (1996) that the responsibility of disentangling the scapegoat mechanism falls on the critic:

> The problem is that when we scapegoat those unaware of the ubiquity of scapegoating, we scapegoat nonetheless; when we use a rhetoric of opposition, we rhetorically set the stage for new oppositions; and when we try to plot a better world, we entangle ourselves in new plots. From the zone of these tensions we can never escape, but through systematic criticism of narrative we can limit ourselves to relatively benign forms of victimage [53].

Or, as Burke says, by tracing the scapegoat mechanism in contemporary war fiction, we can "help some of the rawness to abate, by including a much wider range of man's symbolic prowess under the heading of the fearsomely appreciated, and thereby providing less incentives to be overprompt at feeling exacted with moral indignation" ("Linguistic" 301). Burke writes in *A Grammar of Motives*,

> What we now most need is to perfect and simplify the ways of admonition, so that men may cease to persecute one another under the promptings of demonic ambition that arrive in turn from distortions and misconceptions of purpose [305].

As Samuel Hynes reminds us, "War is not an occasional interruption of a normality called peace; it is a climate in which we live" (xii). Burke would agree with that assessment, but instead of normalizing war through unquestioned symbol systems of sacrifice, pity, and hero worship, his critical method—and the critical method of this book—seeks to undercut the "tyrannous ubiquity" of "strife, enmity, factions, as a characteristic motive of rhetorical expression" in contemporary war literature (*Rhetoric* 20). Thus, my approach to contemporary war literature remains culturally rooted, but it also correctly repositions combatants and noncombatants as equal agents in the discourse of war, a discourse that insists on creating scapegoats. Art may never be as powerful as we want it to be, and the same is true of art's criticism. Still, I join Burke in his hope that criticism such as mine can bridge the gap between war experience and the discourse that it creates so that humans, everywhere, might "cease to persecute one another."

Three

Confounding Expectations in Kevin Powers's The Yellow Birds

> War may be treated as an agency, insofar as it is a means to an end; as a collective act, subdivisible into many individual acts; as a purpose, in schemes proclaiming a cult of war.—
> Kenneth Burke, *Counter-Statement* 144

One of the first critically acclaimed works of contemporary war fiction to emerge from the United States' invasion and occupation of Iraq was Kevin Powers's novel *The Yellow Birds* (2012). The novel was met with dozens of positive reviews, and it has rightly garnered an impressive list of major awards, including being named a finalist for the 2012 National Book Award for fiction.[1] The work is a fictive tale of one soldier—Private John Bartle—and his struggle with guilt before, during, and after his combat experience in Iraq. It isn't necessarily a unique work as far as a narrative arc is concerned, but it is remarkable since it fully examines the ways that the ghosts of war and memory can be reconstructed in language. With a disjointed style, a meticulously controlled form, and a tone dripping with guilt, Powers delivers a work of artifice that places unique demands on a reader, a reader most likely accustomed to mere chronicles of war experience. As such, the novel is especially ambitious and necessary.

Much of the novel's emotional tenor is captured in the thought process of this young veteran named Bartle who uses long passages of self-reflection to process and examine his past war experience. Here is his line of thinking as he walks through an airport upon his return home:

> The ghosts of the dead filled the empty seats of every gate I passed: boys destroyed by mortars and rockets and bullets and IEDs to the point that when we tried to get them to a medevac, the skin slid off, or limbs barely held in place detached, and I

> thought that they were young and had girls at home or some dream that they thought would make their lives important [104].

As this passage indicates, Powers's war novel contends with the side effects of experience and death and the ways memory can haunt and implicate those survivors (the hero *and* the reader) who try to remember the unpleasant particularities of war. As Doug Stanton writes in a review of the novel for *The Daily Beast*: "We don't need anymore 'information,' 'facts,' 'reality,'" he writes, "We need story, and fewer pixels. We need crisp canvas, a brush." *The Yellow Birds* is that story, that living dream, or better yet, it is one man's living nightmare about war, a nightmare the reader shares and Powers challenges us to examine further.

The novel tracks the disintegration of three soldiers—John Bartle (our protagonist and narrator), a scarred sergeant named Sterling, and an unblemished idealist named Daniel "Murph" Murphy. It begins conventionally enough, with a dust covered Iraqi war scene full of dirt, blood, profanity, bullets, and a dead man, but we quickly learn that none of these elements cause Bartle's nightmare, and so tracking down the full mechanism of his burdening and unburdening becomes our mission for the rest of the novel. Early on, Powers establishes three things, all of which become extremely important for the structure and form of the novel as a whole. We learn through the opening narration that Bartle and Murph are closely bound together, that Bartle hates Sterling, and that Murph is going to die. As Bartle announces, "I didn't die. Murph did" (14). Bartle survives Iraq, but he *barely* survives war.

Bartle does not relate the circumstances of Murph's actual death until the novel's end, and this is one of the many formal elements that keep us reading. Eerily reminiscent of Bowe Bergdahl's capture in Afghanistan in 2009,[2] "Murph" submits to the stress of war and walks into an enemy-controlled village in Iraq, unarmed and undressed (ostensibly an act of suicide). He is killed, and his body is mutilated and thrown from the top of a mosque's minaret. When Bartle and Sterling find Murph's tangled body, they decide that they have no choice but to "fix this like it never happened" (208). In an attempt to both cover-up the circumstances of Murph's death and to exact a certain amount of revenge, Sergeant Sterling shoots an innocent Iraqi man in the face (after the man helps them move Murph's body) and burns the minaret—and, presumably, the attached mosque—to the ground. Sterling and Bartle then float both corpses down the Tigris River.

Since we learn none of these details until the very end of the novel, the book as a whole has less to do with Daniel Murphy's death than it does with the consequences of the survival of Bartle and Sterling and the social order that asked them to go to war in the first place. Powers rebuilds one man's war experience into a harrowing reckoning of guilt, a reckoning that extends to the reader. In this way, the reader must assume an active role in Bartle's reconstruction of the ghosts of war into a usable story, and in that exercise we reveal a deep scapegoat mechanism therein. In the end, healing is possible for both the reader and the hero, but it only comes when we remove the enemy from the drama and render war as its own agent, a formal feat that strips from the violence of war any legitimizing purpose.

Bartle closes the opening chapter with a simple statement: "We had lived, Murph and me" (24). This setup tempts us to turn the following pages: we want to know how Murph dies and how Bartle survives, but we also need to discover the nature of their friendship. As the scapegoat mechanism progresses and Bartle begins collecting requisite doses of guilt, Powers balances traditional tropes of war literature inside a disjointed style that disrupts a conventional, linear chronicle of war experience. He keeps us invested in the examination of these two soldiers' lives. It begins with a battle scene in Iraq, but then it moves to a training exercise and a predeployment picnic in New Jersey, two flashbacks that firmly establish the conflict to be examined in this war novel: Bartle's burdening through the acceptance of an untenable obligation, an agreement that I call Bartle's "war promise." Bartle makes his war promise twice, and it forms both the foundation of his friendship with Murph *and* the central conflict of the novel. Sergeant Sterling tells Murph, "I want you to get in Bartle's back pocket and I want you to stay there," and Bartle accepts the burden with a quick "Roger, Sergeant" (33, 34). Later, Bartle has a similar exchange with Murph's mother Ladonna, a well-meaning lady who begs Bartle to bring Murph home alive. Again, Bartle reflexively agrees, "I promise. I promise I'll bring him home to you" (47). Immediately after this, the suffering begins, and people begin dying. Thus, the war promise becomes Bartle's hamartia, and as Bartle and Murph fight to maintain contact with their own humanity in the responsibility-free war zone of Iraq, the reader is asked to do little else beyond balancing culpability, guilt, and punishment.

The war promise is a fairly common trope in American war stories, and it serves Powers well. In *Saving Private Ryan* (1998), Tom Hanks' character (Captain Miller) promises to bring Matt Damon's character (Private Ryan) back home safely, and Miller's successful completion of his war promise (followed by his death) allows the movie to end with a cathartic, redemptive conclusion for both the hero and the audience. Leslie Marmon Silko's *Ceremony* (1977) displays the war promise in an entirely different manner as Tayo's failed promise to bring Rocky "home safe" from World War II allows Silko a way to explore the interconnectedness of individual experience and the spiritual healing one can access through community (73). Indeed, when Tayo makes his war promise to his grandmother, Tayo notices that his pledge carries with it massive, yet inscrutable, implications. As Tayo reports, "he could see that she was waiting for something to happen; but he knew that she always hoped, that she always expected it to happen to him, not to Rocky" (73).

In *The Yellow Birds*, the war promise allows Powers a way to chronicle the manifestation of war's guilt in three vastly different soldiers as each one flows to, through, and from the war in Iraq. Among other things, this war promise asks us to regard, in close detail, the nature of the social contract that got these soldiers to Iraq in the first place, to make what Paul Berlin, in Tim O'Brien's *Going After Cacciato* (1978) calls "acts of consent" (319). In a long passage toward the end of O'Brien's novel, Paul Berlin identifies the way that war complicates the soldier's reincorporation into society by a blending and bending of social obligations and individual promise making:

> I don't pretend to be expert on matters of obligation, either moral or contractual, but I do know when I *feel* obliged. Obligation is more than a claim imposed on us; it is a personal sense of indebtedness. It is a feeling, an acknowledgement, that through many prior acts of consent we have agreed to perform certain future acts. I have that feeling. I make that acknowledgement. By my prior acts—acts of consent—I have bound myself to performing subsequent acts. I put on a uniform. I boarded a plane.... These were explicit consents. But beyond them were many tacit promises: to my family, my friends, my town, my country, my fellow soldiers. These promises, too, accumulated. I was not misled. I was not gulled. On the contrary, I believe.... I *feel* ... that I am being asked to perform a final service that is entirely compatible with what I had promised earlier. A debt, a legitimate debt, is being called in [319].

Like O'Brien's novel, *The Yellow Birds* examines these issues and the various conflicts that arise around "obligations" and "acts of consent" when a soldier volunteers for war and recognizes, too late, that he or she still is indebted for something afterward. That is, the war promise in *The Yellow Birds* asks us to join the object of our observation and make a full, dialectic reckoning of war's cost (or moral burden) so that no one character or reader escapes implication when the legitimate debt of war (war's guilt) is called in. Bartle's survival becomes our own survival but so, too, does his side of the deal, his guilt.

Though he grudgingly acquiesces, Bartle knows what he is accepting.

When he promises Sergeant Sterling to look out for Murph, he reflects that he "didn't want to be responsible for [Murph]" (36). When he promises Ladonna Murphy, Bartle thinks to himself—in a subtle echo of Bartleby's "I would prefer not to": "I barely knew the guy. Stop. Stop asking me questions. I don't want to be accountable. I don't know anything about this" (46). This reluctance is part of the mechanism by which Powers is able to spread around the guilt of Bartle's war promise. Yes, he ultimately agrees to bring Murph home alive, but Ladonna Murphy allowed him no other response. Bartle volunteered for service in the U.S. Army, but someone or something else created the social environment that made his specific service in Iraq compulsory and attractive. In both cases, Bartle knows what he is getting into, but many, many others contributed to the order that made his obligations necessary, that made Bartle feel as if he "had no alternative," no "other paths to take" (24).

The reader has to piece together many of the hinted at promises, secrets, and crimes of the three protagonists slowly. As Bartle concludes toward the middle of the novel, recollecting traumatic experience is "like putting a puzzle together from behind: the shapes familiar, the picture quickly fading, the muted tan of the cardboard backing a tease at wholeness and completion" (139). Disjointed temporally, the narrative jumps from Iraq to New Jersey to Germany to Virginia and then to a military prison, and so the reader must help Bartle fit the puzzle back together again. To do so, we need answers for many questions. Why is such an innocuous promise such a transgression? How does Murph die and why does his ultimate sacrifice cause Bartle such guilt? Why is Bartle in prison? Why does Bartle hate Sterling? Because we need to know and because we need to purge the guilt that begins building from the very first word of the novel, we keep searching for answers. We share the protagonist's examination of his own culpability and his quiet desire for redemption. We become party to war's guilt and that guilt's imperfect redemption, and in that redemption we find that that effort, the attempt "to piece the war into a pattern," probably is a fool's errand (216).

Kevin Powers's Philosophy of Form: Packaging the American War Novel

Powers was a machine gunner in the U.S. Army, served two tours in Iraq, and then, after leaving the military, completed an undergraduate degree at Virginia Commonwealth University and then a Master's of Fine Arts at the University of Texas at Austin where he was a Michener Fellow in Poetry. The novel benefits from its author's training as both a soldier and a poet, though neither experience ever manages to fully hijack the narrative or its style. As Elizabeth Samet summarizes in a review for *The New Republic*, Powers's "military experience clearly taught him many things, yet his book feels less like a thinly veiled autobiographical fiction than like a fully realized work of the imagination" ("War Lies"). The most remarkable thing about Powers is this fact, that instead of first publishing a war memoir or autobiography, he chose to first craft a fictive treatment, not of his own experience, but of, as he describes it, "the cartography of one man's consciousness" ("Author's Note" 156).

This is a fairly vague description of the novel, but Samet's observation that Powers's novel is no "thinly veiled autobiographical fiction" is an astute one, and this quality is ultimately what allows Powers's novel to transcend the limits of his war experience. Powers isn't the first veteran-author to turn to war fiction first, but like many of his famous war fiction writing predecessors he still penned a tale at least loosely based on his own experience. After leaving his short stint as a pilot-in-training with the Royal Canadian Air Force, William Faulkner's first novel was *Soldier's Pay* (1926), a novel that closely parallels his own career as a pilot that the armistice cut short. Following his six days of work with the Red Cross canteen service and his subsequent wounding, Ernest Hemingway used both experiences to create Nick Adams (*In Our Time*), Jack Barnes (*The Sun Also Rises*), and Frederic Henry (*A Farewell to Arms*). This should come as no surprise; authors write what they know, but other war veteran-authors who have risen to the top of the canon of more recent war literature tended to go straight to the combat memoir. Tim O'Brien penned a memoir first with *If I Die in a Combat Zone, Box Me Up and Ship Me Home* (1973) as did Philip Caputo with *A Rumor of War* (1977). Celebrated Iraq war poet Brian Turner published two collections of autobiographical poetry and a memoir first. Many Iraq war memoirs and blogs-turned-into-books appeared before *The Yellow Birds*, but Powers most likely is the first Iraq war veteran to successfully create a work of war fiction devoid of *obvious* elements of autobiography.

As such, then, it is illuminating to examine this novel's packaging, that extra push it needed to establish its rightful and authentic place among the other subgenres of war writing that appeared first. On the cover of the first edition, three exclamatory blurbs from Colm Toibin and Ann Patchett (endorsements from established, award-winning fiction writers) and Anthony Swofford (the endorsement of the successful veteran-author) primarily are concerned with situating the novel as literary, or as a more artistically serious work of fiction. These authors describe Powers's novel as "Compelling" and "Inexplicably beautiful" and "Powerful." Perhaps because the cover art displays two small soldiers with guns, in silhouette, transposed over a setting sun, the publisher only included one generic reference to war or war literature. Right below Powers's byline, Tom Wolfe calls *The Yellow Birds* "The *All Quiet on the Western Front* of America's Arab wars."

The back jacket and Powers's website, however, overtly control the reader's expectations with longer testimonials from other established writers and critics, ranging from Philip Caputo to Robert Olen Butler (both veteran-authors of Vietnam and Vietnam War fiction). Caputo, the author of the Vietnam War novel *Indian Country* (1987), writes, "War has been a subject of literature ever since *The Iliad*. The best books transcend their time and circumstances to say something enduring and truthful about war itself. *The Yellow Birds* belongs in that category." Philipp Meyer also uses the word "category" in his praise and adds Tim O'Brien and Norman Mailer to the list of comparable authors: "*The Yellow Birds* belongs in the same category as Tim O'Brien's *The Things They Carried* and Norman Mailer's *The Naked and the Dead*." Anthony Swofford, the author of *Jarhead* (2003), does the same genre assignment on Powers's website: "This book will endure," he writes, "Read it and then put it way up on that high rare shelf alongside Ernest Hemingway and Tim O'Brien" (Powers, "Reviews"). Such an effort speaks to the wide range of expectation that needs to be managed when the war writer is a war veteran. Powers chose to write fiction before he wrote a memoir. Since the public lacks a record of Powers's relationship with war in an autobiography or some other documented personal chronicle, these blurbs acknowledge the power of combat gnosticism while they also account for why the cover isn't stamped with the label, "Based on a true story."

It will be interesting to see how Powers views *The Yellow Birds* a few decades from now. Tim O'Brien didn't move on to the war novel until his memoir, *If I Die in a Combat Zone*, allowed him a way to empty his imagination of the heavy baggage of war experience. As Alex Vernon points out, "Had he not done so, his first novel about Vietnam, *Going After Cacciato*, would have been a different and lesser work, as his mind would not have been free to re-imagine the war" (30). Or, as O'Brien told Eric Schroeder, he used the memoir to get his combat experience "out of [his] system" so he could create art (148). It also might have allowed him time and space to practice, to hone his writing skills. Norman Mailer often suggested he got lucky with *The Naked and the Dead* (1948). In the introduction to the 50th anniversary edition, he discusses the author in the third person:

> [H]e was naïve, he was passionate about writing, he knew very little about the subtler demands of a good style, he did not have a great deal of restraint, and he burned with excitement as he wrote.... The book was sloppily written in many parts ... and there was hardly a noun in any sentence that was not holding hands with the nearest and most commonly available adjective [xi].

Powers was wise to learn from Mailer and O'Brien's example, jumping as he did directly to the fictive narrative of war following a period of formal writing training at the University of Texas.

Still, auditors constantly try to force Powers's experience into the pages of his novel. A purview of the interviews he has granted suggests that many consumers of his work still prefer—or, at a minimum, expect—the witness account of reportage to a more imaginative examination of war. They want the vicarious experience. In 2012 when Powers was interviewed on PBS, the interviewer's second question was, "How much of the book, the novel, is based on your experience?" A couple months earlier, on C-SPAN, it took the interviewer three minutes to ask, "Is this based on your experience?" In both cases Powers answers in the negative, making the point that "the emotional core" is a part of the novel that he "identifies with strongly." You can almost feel each interviewer's disappointment.[3] As Hemingway's Nick Adams reports in the short piece, "On Writing," "Everything good he'd ever written he'd made up. None of it had ever happened" (237). But, no matter what, "That was what the family couldn't understand. They thought it was all experience" (238). Powers seems to have met the same expectations.

Kenneth Burke delineates the insistence for truth in art along two lines: "scientific truth" and "aesthetic truth" (*Counter-Statement* 42). Tim O'Brien does the same in *The Things They Carried* when he privileges "story truth" above "happening truth" (203). This is the double bind of the war veteran who writes war fiction: experience provides the subject material upon which fictive accounts of war can be built, but the reader of contemporary war literature remains rooted in his or her desire for documentary verisimilitude. Art, Burke says, results whenever a writer "has converted his pattern of experience into a Symbolic equivalent" (*Counter-Statement* 157). That conversion suffers when we demand too much scientific truth in aesthetic representations. As Burke says, "it would be a great mistake to see art merely as a weak representation of some actual experience" (*Counter-Statement* 41). In "How to Tell a True War Story,"

O'Brien examines the same idea when he writes: "You can tell a true war story by the questions you ask. Somebody tells a story, let's say, and afterward you ask, 'Is it true?' and if the answer matters, you've got your answer" (79). As O'Brien suggests, when the subject of fiction is war or any other extreme or traumatic experience, the impulse to ask "is it true?" is a reasonable one. The auditor of that tale fails his or her critical role, however, if the answer matters (of course, what O'Brien means by "matters" is open to discussion).

The ubiquity of experience-tracing questions might be why Powers added an "Author's Note" to the 2013 paperback reprint of *The Yellow Birds*. In it, he sounds much like Kurt Vonnegut in the opening chapter to *Slaughter-House Five* and Vonnegut the returning soldier who—initially—wished to report back on what he had done and seen. Vonnegut writes:

> When I got home from the Second World War twenty-three years ago, I thought it would be easy for me to write about the destruction of Dresden, since all I would have to do would be to report what I had seen. And I thought, too, that it would be a masterpiece or at least make me a lot of money, since the subject was so big. But not many words about Dresden came from my mind then—not enough of them to make a book, anyway. And not many words come now [3].

Powers writes, "*The Yellow Birds* began as an attempt to reckon with one question: What was it like over there?" (156). Like Vonnegut, though, Powers recognizes that that is an unreasonable, limiting, or impossible goal. As Powers coyly explains, "war is only like itself" (156). This is a noteworthy perspective for a veteran to assume. Whereas it took Kurt Vonnegut twenty-three years to change his post-war writing goal from reportage to the masterpiece *Slaughterhouse-Five* (1969) and it took O'Brien an entire memoir in order to create art, it only took Powers four years to acknowledge that fiction offers something that memoir and autobiography do not.

Powers writes:

> Though I hope I've told one small part of the truth about the war, what I've written is not meant to report or document, nor is it meant to argue or advocate. Instead, I tried with what little skill I have to create the cartography of one man's consciousness, to let it stand, however briefly, as my reminder [156].

In 2013, Jonathan Ruppin asked Powers if fiction is a better mode than "reportage" for "portraying the reality of combat?" (159). Powers responded, "I wouldn't say that it works better, only that it works in a different way. The benefit is that it can confound expectations, particularly in the case of these wars that have been going on for so long" (159). This is a curious response to a common question: Fiction can "confound expectations" within a genre that is dominated by non-fictive combat narratives or fictive combat narratives penned by veterans with the appropriate level of combat experience. Authorial intention aside, Powers's work asserts a rhetorical stance regarding war's experience, war's memory, and the resulting war guilt that should be carried back to a reading public.

Regardless, the marketing strategy made apparent in the relentless name-dropping and generic categorizing of the blurbs implies the expectations that must be confounded and the depths of meaning that must be plumbed when a veteran crafts a purely imaginative work of war fiction. Such blurb-praise points to the fact that war fiction—particularly a war novel like Powers's—demands such genre and peer alignment. In a marketplace glutted with witness testimony regarding combat's experience, the audience needs to be specially prepared. The generic qualifications listed in the blurbs aren't necessarily unwarranted or ill-conceived. Quite the contrary, *The Yellow Birds* perhaps needs them, both to sell its "emotional truth" and to properly situate it amid the panoply of other voices of war that precede and follow it.

These ubiquitous blurbs of praise are far from being the final word on Powers's novel, but they are the most visible marks of what I find most fascinating about *The Yellow Birds*: its negotiation of what Kenneth Burke calls the psychology of form. For instance, it may be easy to compare *The Yellow Birds* with *All Quiet on the Western Front* (1928), as Tom Wolfe does at the bottom of the book's cover. But this little blurb becomes a massive part of *The Yellow Birds'* management of form when we consider that Remarque's World War I novel was trumpeted as "anti-war" by pacifists while also being banned and burned by the Nazis as "the literary betrayal of the soldiers of the Great War" (Barker 32–33). It carries even further when we recognize that the author of that comparative blurb is the author of *The Right Stuff* (1979), a hero-worshipping non-fictive chronicle of NASA's first astronauts and test pilots, men Wolfe repeatedly describes as "single-combat warriors" throughout his book (97).[4] Burke first built his ideas about the psychology of the audience and form in his book *Counter-Statement* (1931). Drawing from his example of *Hamlet* and the "assiduously prepared for" ghost, Burke argues that form is more about the psychology of the audience than it is about the psychology of the hero (30):

> Or, seen from another angle, form is the creation of an appetite in the mind of the auditor, and the adequate satisfying of that appetite. This satisfaction—so complicated is the human mechanism—at times involves a temporary set of frustrations, but in the end these frustrations prove to be simply a more involved kind of satis-

faction, and furthermore serve to make the satisfaction of fulfillment more intense ... it involves desires and their appeasements [*Counter-Statement* 31].

With Burke's ideas as a guide, the critic can approach war fiction like *The Yellow Birds* and avoid the common complaints that face readers of war literature, namely, the debate between authentic representations of real experience and artifice. Just as Shakespeare's play forces his audience to wait and anticipate—consciously or unconsciously—until the fourth scene of the first act for the ghost of Hamlet's father to appear, the reader of *The Yellow Birds* is made equally ready for the common tropes of war literature before he or she even reaches the first page. Thus, from a Burkeian point-of-view, the blurbs are linguistic alarm bells that call us to look more closely at the work's form and construction. They direct us to look for the war novel's scapegoats.

"Desires and their appeasements" separated by artful "frustrations": if we analyze *The Yellow Birds* accordingly, Powers's "symbolic prowess" becomes quite clear (*Language* 297). His management of form extends the project that began with the blurbs; the publisher and the blurb-contributing fiction writers whet the appetite without, and Powers continues it within with the war promise and the guilt that obligation carries. And Powers does it all without suggesting that this book is in any way a documentation of one man's actual experience. Or, as Burke would describe it, Powers's symbolic "eloquence," as he employs various methods of "maintaining interest" qualifies it as "pure art" (*Counter-Statement* 37). If we accept the scapegoat principle as "a device natural to language" then we can witness the function of such literature as Powers's serving a weakening effect on the spell that the scapegoat ritual casts ("Dramatism" 451). Analyzing the novel's form also allows us to reveal how Powers develops the scapegoating process in complex ways and, ultimately, to redirect the moral implications of waging war back on the reading public.

Managing Appetites and Appeasements in the War Novel

In *The Yellow Birds,* Bartle's burden (his war promise) is fairly easy to identify, but the "structure of his unburdening" (the scapegoat mechanism) allows a more complex message regarding Bartle's war. As C. Allen Carter writes,

> Burke does not simply give us a theory of the multidimensional message and warn us about the ominous direction our messages can take us. He urges that we strengthen those linguistic purposes that might enable us to redirect the scapegoat process [133].

When we trace the curative victims that Powers's novel creates and then disposes, one is left with more than a mere cartography of one man's consciousness. That is, Bartle's war promises and the guilt that follows them, since they are only tangentially related to Murph and Sterling's suicides, display the full spectrum of how obligation and guilt interact during and after war for both the agents and auditors of this war story.

Burke writes in *The Philosophy of Literary Form*:

> When you begin to consider the situations behind the tactics of expression, you will find tactics that organize a work technically *because* they organize it emotionally.... Hence, if you look for a man's *burden*, you will find the principle that reveals the structure of his unburdening; or, in attenuating form, if you look for his problem, you will find the lead that explains the structure of his solution. His answer gets its form by relation to the questions he is answering [92].

War literature like Powers's operates much like classic drama. Burke points out that Aeschylus, Shakespeare, and Racine were "dealing with material which was more or less a matter of common knowledge so that the broad outlines of the plot were known in advance" (37). Powers's contemporary audience comes to his war novel and the war promise in much the same way; it is the fiction writer's skill and management of surprise, suspense, and eloquence that can lend to its status as what Burke would call "pure art." It is up to the scholar to parse the purity, however. As Burke puts it,

> Truth in art is not the discovery of facts, not an addition to human knowledge in the scientific sense of the word. It is, rather, the exercise of human propriety, the formulation of symbols which rigidify our sense of poise and rhythm. Artistic truth is the externalization of taste [*Counter-Statement* 42].

Thus, Powers confounds the expectations of what Burke calls the "racial appetites" of the auditor, and he does so immediately (*Counter-Statement* 41).

When we open *The Yellow Birds*, two epigraphs greet us. The first one is a "traditional U.S. Army Marching Cadence," which essentially is Powers's first attempt to manage form in his novel (the title has limited meaning without it)[5]:

> A yellow bird
> With a yellow bill
> Was perched upon
> My windowsill
>
> I lured him in
> With a piece of bread
> And then I smashed
> His fucking head ...

I never was in the Army, but I remember well the exact same "marching cadence" during my own Air Force basic training in 1995, though we called such chants "Jodies."[6] My "flight" of fellow basic trainees sang these rhythmic call-and-response songs (each line is called by a leader and then repeated by the group) everywhere we went; they kept us in step as we marched, and they made us laugh.

As for the term "Jody," Bruce Jackson points out in his book on Southern blues that the name "Jody" comes from "Joe the Grinder," a central character in a series of old blues lyrics dating as far back as 1939 (169).[7] Pronounced as "Jody Grinder," with "Grinder" operating as a metaphor "for a certain kind of coital movement," Jackson explains that the character traveled from a blues song recorded in Gould, Arkansas, in 1939 to Southern penitentiaries before moving on to Jody Grinder's place in military marching chants. The reasons for the common character in the blues, in prison, and in military life are central to Powers's decision to include a Jody as an epigraph. As Jackson observes, "life in an army during wartime and life in prison anytime have a number of aspects in common" (167). That is, prisoners and troops share a common anxiety about the woman left at home, an easy prey for a wife-stealing citizen like Joe the Grinder, or "Jody." As Burns explains, Jodies not only "bring soldiers together as a disciplined force," they also give voice to the collective frustrations of individuals "in limbo" who "will remain so until they die in combat or return home" (81, 83). Above all, Burns argues, Jodies function as a "safety valve that only insiders understand. In overtly complaining about what the free-world cuckolder is up to, soldiers are covertly registering resentment at those who keep them unfree and therefore unable to defend themselves against Jody" (84). Many of the Jodies in circulation inside the military aren't always about the cuckolder back home, but they often deal with agency or the lack thereof in often crude, obscene, violent, sexist, profane, racist, and homophobic ways, including the one Powers includes as an epigraph. Such self-pitying celebrations come at the expense of other groups of human beings, mechanisms that military members use to achieve unity and solidarity through demonizing or belittling linguistic descriptions. Thus, the modern Jodie somewhat accurately reflects the dialectic nature of a soldier's existence: He is an agent of hegemonic violence; but he comforts himself with the idea that all of his acts lack agency.

In this way, Powers's Jody establishes the work's authenticity as a war novel and begins to build the novel's scapegoating process. If the yellow bird of the title is killed off before the novel even begins (as it is in the Jody), the reader must be on the lookout for a character that will symbolically stand in for the dead bird. However, Powers doesn't complete the Jody; he eliminates the final stanza in an exceedingly fascinating manipulation of form that trades on both the authenticity implied by an insider's song and the scapegoating device implied within it. If we are looking for a stand-in for the yellow bird, we are also on the lookout for a stand-in for the killer of that yellow bird. In other words, the Jody dares us to find someone to blame, but the ellipses of the missing stanza make us search elsewhere for a target.

I remember that particular "Yellow Bird Jody" as concluding with a crassly humorous twist:

> The moral of
> The story is,
> To get some head
> You need some bread.

Powers's decision to leave this stanza out of his novel is probably a sound one. If form unifies symbol and motive, such levity would be out of place. Alone, the first two stanzas situate the work within the war novel genre, and they begin building suspense with the common themes of a typical war story: innocence is going to be shattered, and violence is going to become so commonplace that it will be expressed as another banal detail of war. The reader then must locate symbolic substitutions for the bird on the windowsill and the killer of that bird; the excised stanza calls into question the identity-erasing (or should we call it unifying?) indoctrination inherent to military training. One could propose Bartle's opening musings about war as another reason why this final stanza simply doesn't fit: "I'd been trained to think that war was the great unifier, that it brought people closer together than any other activity on earth. Bullshit. War is the great maker of solipsists: how are you going to save my life today?" (12). The full Jody would not match such an attitude.

Including the final stanza would also lessen the first epigraph's syllogistic strength when it is considered alongside the second one. That is, the second epigraph announces a project common to other war literature while it also suggests a deeper message and a complication of our appetite for a scapegoat. A quote from Sir Thomas Browne's 1658 work *Hydriotaphia*, the epigraph reads:

> To be ignorant of evils to come, and forgetfull of evils past, is a mercifull provision in nature, whereby we digest the mixture of our few and evil dayes, and our delivered senses not relapsing into cutting remembrances, our sorrows are not kept raw by the edge of repetitions.

So, on the one hand, this passage's place as an epigraph suggests that *The Yellow Birds* will serve the war-art-as-treatment-for-war-trauma paradigm

Three: Confounding Expectations in Powers's Yellow Birds

that remains extremely common in the genre. Is this not what so many works of war literature seek, to inscribe the "cutting remembrance" and in so doing somehow blunt the "raw edges" of traumatic memories? However, Browne's work, *Hydriotaphia* (which translates as "Urn Burial"), is an extensive meditation on the burial practices of ancient cultures. In a long march through these various practices, Browne repeatedly concludes that each one is a pathetic human gesture of futility built in response to the finality of death.

I can hear an echo of this same sentiment in Powers's "Author's Note" when he writes about his aborted attempt to create a "real" monument to experience and memory. "War is only like itself," Powers concludes (156). This position falls in line with the combatant-first solipsism Bartle describes above while it dances dangerously close to normalizing war. Yet, that position—"war is only like itself"—is a difficult one to maintain if the reader considers the same war from the perspective of an Iraqi civilian. Browne's epigraph could be taken as both a confirmation of and challenge to any argument about the singularity of war or war's experience. While Browne judges man hopeful in his attempts to create such "dying mementos," he also judges humanity as ultimately pitiful in our universal impulse to use that memento to create lasting monuments to any fleeting moment of existence (136). So where is Powers's swerve with this epigraph? Perhaps one doesn't exist, but the second epigraph at least partially counteracts the solipsistic attitude of the narrator while it never quite fully negates it.

Browne's quote almost replaces the missing final stanza of the "Yellow Bird Jody." Shortly before the passage that is Powers's second epigraph, Browne writes that our memories are "the entelechia and soul of our subsistences" (134). He continues, writing that, sadly, "There is no antidote against the Opium of time, which temporally considereth all things; Our Fathers find their graves in our short memoires, and sadly tell us how we may be buried in our Survivors" (134). Thus, if we look at the epigraphs together, we can reduce them to the following elements: innocence symbolized by the yellow bird is violently scapegoated (the act) in a military setting established by the Jody (scene) by the typical, indoctrinated military member (agent) through trickery (agency). The only element missing is the purpose, the final accounting for why the agent (the "I" voice in the Jody) acted as he did, why he killed the bird. This is, possibly, another reason why Powers did not include the final stanza. Had he, it would provide a purpose and would fix blame through a crude pun on the bird's head and a sexual act, a motive that doesn't implicate the reader at all. Leaving it out also implies that there may be no reasonable purpose for such violence and that such action without judgment is utterly impossible. It acts according to Derrida's concept of "trace," the meaning left by the erasure that serves to distinguish readers into two camps—the experienced insider and the vicarious outsider (61). Thus, the second epigraph prevents the missing stanza from the Jody operating as an insider's wink. As William Rueckert writes, for Burke, "there are no purposeless acts, only an act the purpose of which is not yet known, or not yet fully understood" (*Kenneth Burke* 178). With the second epigraph, Powers's novel proposes through symbolic implication that such an attitude about killing and violence, no matter how blithely it is represented or how grudgingly the culpability is accepted, is most likely humanly unmanageable, as well. Better yet, the epigraphs suggest that carrying such an attitude to any motive cannot occur without incurring massive amounts of guilt. As the epigraph from Browne indicates, the human agent will invariably "relapse" into the "mixture" of his "few and evil days."

It's worth commenting here on the term "entelechia," since Browne and Burke both use it in their philosophies and Powers demonstrates it in his novel. Browne uses it in the Aristotelian sense; in *De Anima*, Aristotle formulates the term *entelekheia* as a description of physical matter as it is realized in the soul. In Aristotle's formulation, the soul is the actuality of matter's potential and eventual embodiment. In *Dramatism and Development* (1972), Burke explains: "the resources of symbolic action culminate in a possibly non–Aristotelian application of the Aristotelian 'entelechy'" (36). Or, as Burke expands, it is through symbolic action that "man might (not so successfully) actualize his potential as a rational animal" ("Why Satire?" 314). Thus, Burke stretches Aristotle's concept and applies it to all aspects of human verbal structures, including our impulse to create art, and he clarifies "entelechy" to mean "tracking down the implications of a position, going to the end of the line" (314). Entelechy, then, is one of Burke's defining ontological conditions, one that he roots within his rhetorical scapegoating concept and his definition of man.

Burke's definition of man includes entelechy as a crucial motive for all human drama, especially since all language is appropriately conceived as symbolic action: "Man is goaded by the spirit of hierarchy (or moved by the sense of order) and rotten with perfection" *(Language* 16). Thus, man cannot avoid being moved (or "goaded") by this "rotten" entelechal principle, "a principle of perfection implicit in the nature of symbol systems" and "central to the nature of language as motive" (*Language* 17). The urge to achieve perfection—through art, technology, or military might—

drives every human or political impulse, including the need to create monuments, to invade other countries, or to craft a work of fiction that attempts to render memory into some transmittable confessional form. Thus, through the terministic screen established by the epigraphs, we are "goaded" to track violence visited upon innocence and the eventual reckoning with the resulting guilt (Browne's "mercifull provision in nature").

The reader of *The Yellow Birds* hasn't even reached the first page of the novel, but the dramatistic structure in in place. As Burke writes, "For the so-called 'desire to kill' a certain person is much more properly analyzable as a desire to *transform the principle* which that person *represents*" (13; italics original). Both scapegoats in *The Yellow Birds* commit suicide in reflexive acts of death, and we therefore observe the principles that their self-killings transform (or purge). As the Jody of the epigraph suggests, Bartle is going to fail to maintain order (in the form of his war promise), for who can keep a promise? Murph's suicide leads to Bartle's collection of massive amounts of guilt, and we join him as he seeks redemption through various avenues, first in his fantasies of suicide and then, through vicarious victimage, in the suicide of his superior, Sergeant Sterling. So this novel is not only Bartle's confession as we are not asked to grant him absolution. We are, however, asked to join him there by accepting our own proper quota of guilt.

Powers's epigraphs are much more than token witticisms or well-turned phrases that lend their authority to the words that follow. They suggest a structure while simultaneously confounding our expectations. Since any sense of order, driven by entelechy, implies an overarching hierarchy, the epigraphs suggest that the following novel will be an antidote against the agency-erasing hierarchical psychosis inherent to the military, to traumatic experience, and to the easy redemptions that often accompany narratives of war.

Tracing the Scapegoats' Demise

As we move into the text, we know that the protagonists are at war, suggested by the cover art, the blurbs, and the epigraphs, but we don't yet know exactly where that war is taking place. We get it on the first page, though, announced quietly in the first chapter's title. Actually, it is less of a title and more of a label, a tag of war's particular setting: "September 2004, Al Tafar, Ninevah Province, Iraq." With the biblical implications of "Ninevah" and the 9/11 implications of "September," this title bears comparison to the following oft-quoted passage from Hemingway's *A Farewell to Arms*:

> There were many words that you could not stand to hear and finally only the names of places had dignity. Certain numbers were the same way and certain dates and these with the names of the places were all you could say and have them mean anything. Abstract words such as glory, honor, courage, or hallow were obscene beside the concrete names of villages, the numbers of roads, the names of rivers, the numbers of regiments and the dates [185].

Abstractions like "glory" and "honor" and "courage" pale in their ability to capture the depth of human tragedy in war—they decline into cliché as their symbolic capabilities lose strength—especially when they are aligned with the synecdochic complexities captured with the name of a battlefield, a massacre site, or of a unit. Think of a few and Hemingway's point is immediately clear. Sand Creek, Dresden, Chosin Reservoir, My Lai, Fallujah, Seal Team 6: each one stands for so much more than the actions of war or massacre they reference. They become sign-carrying symbols that capture the full emotional power of each contextual situation. In a post–9/11 America, "September 2004, Al Tafar, Ninevah Province, Iraq" does the same thing. Given our prior knowledge that this is indeed a war novel, all we need to establish war's location is a cluster of words like "Iraq" and "September" and, well, any word prefaced with the Arabic article "Al." We don't even need "Tafar" or "Ninevah Province, Iraq." After September 11, 2001, *Al* somewhat equals *Iraq*, and *Iraq* equals *war*. With this date and location, then, the novel launches us into war, and we will stay there though less than half of the novel actually is set in Iraq.

"The war tried to kill us in the spring": thus begins this war novel, but Powers denies "war" its expected rhetorical function as the scene of the opening pages (3). The title and these first few words throw us into war, and what follows is a clarification of much of what I just teased out of the epigraphs in the previous section. "Iraq" is the scene instead of "war" (since each word implies the other one), so war becomes an agent of the novel right alongside the soldiers who move around within war. Akin to war gods in Greek mythology, war becomes what Burke calls a "super-agent" (*Grammar* xx). Not only is war the first noun in the entire work, the first subject, it is the catalyst that motivates Bartle and Murph and Sterling to act. Symbolically, it will kill them and allow them to kill, and like Ares, it is ubiquitous, overwhelming, and insatiable. And so the protagonists wallow here under the comforting assumption that the war god mutes their own agency; they enjoy the idea that war alone wields all the power in this place and therefore deserves all of the blame.

Their war is what Burke would classify as "super-scene, super-act, and super-agent" all in one (*Grammar* 71). As such, Bartle immediately shuffles it to the top of the symbolic hierarchy of the novel:

> While we slept, the war rubbed its thousand ribs against the ground in prayer. When we pressed onward through exhaustion, its eyes were white and open in the dark. While we ate, the war fasted, fed by its own depravation. It made love and gave birth and spread through fire [3].

And in this way, war becomes symbolically effective. That is, it *acts*. As Burke says,

> The objective writer attempts to make effective Symbols; the subjective writer attempts to make Symbols effective (that is, constructs a Symbol as the replica of his own pattern of experience, and having constructed it, schemes to find ways of making it effective) [*Counter-Statement* 195].

The first person plural pronoun is all we know of the human beings, but the audience is asked to equate war with everything else that could potentially express or enjoy a sense of agency. War is the only agent in sight, synecdochic for everything else, including death, violence, dust, and fear. Since war is the only thing that can act, then, it performs functions denied the human beings. It makes love and gives birth, but the living humans act intransitively. The soldiers don't fight an enemy; they "moved" and "slept" and "pressed onward" and "waited" (3, 5). And this makes perfect sense because Bartle and his comrades have long used this kind of construction to assuage their own guilt and responsibility. This distinction allows them to claim powerlessness; they are nothing but passive objects that flow according to the super-agent's whim. So Bartle finds it difficult to atone for the guilt he feels, and we must join him there. It isn't until he (with our help) is able to look back from his "position of safety in a warm cabin above a clear stream in the Blue Ridge" mountains that Bartle can see that his previous attitude worked well as a coping mechanism, one designed to mitigate his (deserved) feelings of guilt (11).

In the second paragraph of the novel, war the super-agent is as present and undeniable as the seasons. It is as inescapable as the sun:

> Then, in summer, the war tried to kill us as the heat blanched all color from the plains. The sun pressed into our skins, and the war sent its citizens rustling into the shade of white buildings. It cast a white shade on everything, like a veil over our eyes. It tried to kill us every day [3].

Interestingly enough, war and the sun are both defined by their negative.[8] We tend to mark the sun by its shine, but an equally appropriate marker is the shade it casts. War casts a "white shade on everything," and Bartle recognizes himself there so that war becomes a soothing thing, a blanket under which he can hide. Thus, it is only in this dialectic construction of war that the narrator exists anywhere in the dramatistic pentad. Grasping at the assertion that they lack all agency, Bartle and his fellow soldiers comfort themselves by noting that they are not among the "bloating piles in the troughs of the hills outside the cities, the faces puffed and green, allergic now to life" (4).

We know what they are *not*, but what *are* they? Stuck in war's shade, these soldiers, these non-agents, think that they exist as the negative of war and nothing more, and this precedence is crucial to establish early on, before we meet the hero and before we meet any of war's victims. War, we are supposed to assume, is an undeniable force of nature, and since the audience faces it right up front, we can then more easily accept the extent of its drug-like effects on the soldiers and therefore prepare for any victims who may appear to serve as a curative for Bartle's guilt (and our own). In most war narratives, a demonized enemy fills this roll, but Powers directs that vicarious purging elsewhere.[9] Considering that war is oftentimes measured empirically by a count of casualties (rhetorical value marked by rhetorical sacrifice), war's negative is noted by accounting the many who have not become its victims yet, war's unclaimed scapegoats. Bartle and Murph encounter dead people everywhere, and so they make a game of marking the empirical accounting of war's casualties: "the war had killed thousands by September" (4). They identify themselves among the merely not-counted-yet: "But it had killed fewer than a thousand soldiers like me and Murph" (4). Meanwhile, the reader must admit that the negative of war is not peace and that the opposite of "soldiers like me and Murph" is not "Iraqi civilians" or "insurgent fighters."

The "thousands" is the way Murph and Bartle track and recognize and order the super-agent. It is the clear and definite number Murph and Bartle avoid; they do not want to be the one-thousandth American soldier killed in Iraq. Both soldiers are more than aware that the number is arbitrary and meaningless; they both know the war has killed way more than a thousand "others" already. Bartle counts up to the number when he is in the desert, and he remembers later how important it seemed then. Sergeant Ezekial Vasquez from Laredo, Texas, is #748 (12). Specialist Miriam Jackson, aged nineteen, is #914 (13). Bartle's post-war narration, however, allows him to look back and recognize the foolishness in his counting: "We didn't know the list was limitless. We didn't think beyond a thousand" (14). Bartle recognizes too late that his self-conception in Iraq was completely occluded by the massive symbolic presence of war. It isn't until he is out of prison and in his warm cabin in the Blue Ridge Mountains that he can see—

something we can see all along the way—that he and Murph always were more than agency-free numbers that hadn't been counted yet.

If any doubt remains in the reader's mind that he or she should keep reading in order to locate the novel's curative victims and the war's guilty perpetrators, the god-term *war* removes all doubt immediately. The seasons, the weather, the sun, the landscape, the human beings, the threat of death: all of these things are known only through the screen of war. War does rub "its thousand ribs against the ground in prayer," like a Muslim prostrate on a prayer rug, but this symbol unifies more than it indicates difference or draws a dialectical border between the subjective American soldier and an objectified enemy (3). "Pioneers" and "citizens" people this space, not Americans and *hajjis* (3). Since Bartle and Murph are obsessed with the number one thousand, the metaphor above might even suggest a different supplicant: the American dead (one-thousand ribs' worth) pray at war's altar. This leaves Bartle with one chore when he returns home with his burden of guilt: to mark the difference between himself and the scapegoats.

Bartle's narration doesn't return to the idea of being the one-thousandth American soldier to die in Iraq until the final chapter, when he is in prison, marking the wall of his cell for each event he thinks he "remembers":

> My first few months inside, I spent a lot of time trying to piece the war into a pattern. I developed the habit of making a mark on my cell wall when I remembered a particular event, thinking that at some later date I could refer to it and assemble the marks into a story that made sense [216].

The guards think he is marking time until he is released, and one of them asks, "Must be nine eighty-three, nine ninety, right? Almost a thousand?" (218). Then, and only then, does Bartle think of Murph in such a manner; "[Murph] was not counted for a while" because Bartle and Sterling covered up the circumstances of his death (218). Neither Bartle nor the reader will ever know if Murph was the one-thousandth. But, by this time, Bartle can draw a certain relief from this ambiguity; he has reached a place where he can admit that Murph's rank on that arbitrary list means nothing. It mattered when he was a deluded soldier, but now he has matured just enough to both comfort and punish himself with the fact that neither he nor Murph will be on any accurate list of the war dead. Indeed, if that list accurately accounted for dead Iraqis and Americans, it would number in the hundreds of thousands.

We empathize with Bartle's dilemma as the surviving, coping soldier, but we can see something that he doesn't. We can see that, in his world, the super-agent war masks culpability, a construction that might allow Bartle to survive but also one that prevents access to any sort of consciousness-expanding cathartic release. For Bartle, war only confines and deadens. The opening pages ask us to treat war as the only actor, as the only perpetrator, but that system falls apart as soon as it is erected. Like the yellow bird lured to the windowsill by a piece of bread, Bartle asks us to see him in a similar light. He wants us to recognize that his wartime acts may not have been entirely noble, but he had to consider them "necessary" in order to survive (11). We are left wondering if this logic will hold up to scrutiny.

America's culture lured Bartle and Murph and Sterling to the windowsill of war, but Bartle takes longer than his peers to understand none of them easily fit as the symbolic victim in this war. Indeed, his delayed awareness of that fact is essentially what saves him. On the other hand, Murph understands his symbolic role in war (his agency) and commits suicide by walking into enemy territory, naked. Sterling follows suit when he returns to the United States and puts a bullet through his own head. Unlike Bartle, they assert themselves dramatically in the super-agent's wake: they die by their own devices (agency), to cope with their own guilt (purpose), alone (scene). Thus, Bartle's narration essentially asks us to witness the aftermath in the one soldier who does not succeed in purging his own guilt in similar manner.

In this way we can accept Bartle's insistence on maintaining his agency-free perception of self with trepidation. We understand why, when he looks back, that he remembers not being "surprised by the cruelty of [his] ambivalence then" and how "nothing seemed more natural than someone getting killed" (11). We can see why he needs to remember carrying a rifle and pointing it at human beings and pulling the trigger and seeing dead people "lying in the courtyards of the city or in its lace of alleys" without locating himself anywhere therein as the causal agent (15). And it makes a certain twisted sense for him to count "X number of enemies lying dead in a dusty field" (15). After all, when Bartle remembers pulling the trigger on his rifle and firing a bullet for the first time in combat, he describes the act not as "firing" his gun but as "releas[ing]" the bullet "into the field," as if the bullet and the gun operated with minds of their own (20). When he shoots at a man behind a "low wall in a courtyard" with the rest of his unit, he does think, for a moment, "What kind of men are we?" (21). But then he quickly recognizes how helpful it is to refrain from assigning responsibility:

> [The man he shot] may have been frightened, but I didn't mind that so much because I was frightened too, and I realized with a great shock that I was shooting

at him and that I wouldn't stop until I was sure that he was dead, and I felt better not knowing we were killing him together and that it was just as well not to be sure you are the one who did it [21].

Powers avoids the emotional hypertrophy and atrophy of other more formulaic chronicles of war stories by complicating the mere naming and labeling of how one object lies against another. Bartle's obsessive concern with numbers and his dialectical self-identification is part of Powers's intricate development of what R. G. Collingwood calls "the constructive imagination" (242). As Bartle concludes, history is "imagination or it's nothing"; it can be "unwoven," like "the threads of a rope" (100, 101). As Hayden White suggests, "no historical event is *intrinsically tragic*; it can only be conceived as such from a particular point of view or from within the context of a structured set of events of which it is an element enjoying a privileged place" (84). *The Yellow Birds* unbraids Bartle's war experience and places his war promise in a privileged place so the auditor cannot avoid seeing that many more deserve blame for this war's tragedy alongside the hero.

White calls such placing "emplotment," or, as he defines it, the "encodation of the facts contained in the chronicle as components of specific *kinds* of plot structure" (83). Thus, when Powers delivers the first scapegoat, early on in the novel, we can easily accept him as a vessel of purgation:

> It never happened. I didn't die. Murph did. And though I wasn't there when it happened, I believe unswervingly that when Murph was killed, the dirty knives that stabbed him were addressed "To whom it may concern." Nothing made us special. Not living. Not dying. Not even being ordinary [14].

With Murph's death, dirty knives kill, not an insurgent or an enemy. As Yossarian says in *Catch-22*, "The enemy ... is anybody who's going to get you killed, no matter *which* side he's on" (120). *The Yellow Birds* suggests the same thing. One agent rises above all others—war—and everyone else is collectively the war's enemy; they are all enemies (and victims) of war instead of each other.

We do encounter references to an enemy early in the second chapter, but that enemy remains description-free and unnamed, euphemistically referred to with this war's label for the feared enemy Other: the misappropriated *hajji*. Bartle and the rest of his platoon learn to use the term to describe the enemy, and—fittingly—they learn the nomenclature from Sergeant Sterling, the speaker of the term for its first three appearances in the novel (17, 19, 39). During the opening battle scene when Bartle fires his rifle for the first time, he refers to the enemy with nothing but the third-person plural pronoun "they." Bartle remembers the battle:

> And *they* did come, shadowed in window. *They* came out from behind woven prayer rugs and fired off bursts and the bullets whipped past and we'd duck and listen as they smacked against the concrete and mud-brick and little pieces flew in every direction. *They* ran through trash-strewn alleys, past burning drums and plastic blowing like clumps of thistle over the ancient cobblestones [20; italics added].

Bartle strips the enemy of identity, essentially removing the enemy from the dramatistic scene and making it easier to kill and disregard, and Sergeant Sterling is the one to teach him this linguistic trick. As Sterling says, "It's their idea every time. They ought to kill themselves instead of us" (42). This strategy teaches Bartle how to claim an agency-free observer's role, an omniscient perspective that subtly invalidates the motives of fighters who hide behind a religion that uses prayer rugs. In all its subjective glory, Bartle deploys war as the only thing that can threaten or destroy, but we can tell that this perspective will never lead to a healthy or lasting truth after his war ends. At one point, Bartle pauses long enough to mention, "I wasn't sure who 'they' were" (43). He blames war for everything, but it's a question he never really needs to bother answering.

In his "Author's Note," Powers says that fiction can "confound expectations." He could have said, fiction allows the emplotment of scapegoats in such a way that it confounds the very process of scapegoating itself. In *Permanence and Change*, Burke writes:

> In referring to the curative totality of the perfect sacrifice, as modified by the predominantly secular nature of modern civilization, we would suggest that the kind of victimage most "natural" to such a situation would be some variant of the Hitlerite emphasis (which put the stress upon the idea of a total cathartic enemy rather than upon the idea of a total cathartic friend) [288].

Whereas Hitler scapegoated the international Jew, Powers's scapegoating mechanism redirects victimage away from *hajji* or the wholesale Othering of an enemy and onto Bartle's comrades in arms.

We direly need their victimage as much as Bartle. Not only do they purge all of the baggage of Bartle's failed war promise, but we need antecedents for the "us" of the first line of the novel, for the "I" of the Yellow Bird Jody, and for the yellow bird itself. Bartle isn't named until the end of the first chapter (17), so it is fitting that the first name we encounter is Murph (3). The second named character we meet is Sergeant Sterling (6). We do meet a few named family members (like Ladonna Murphy) and a few named ancillary characters, but most of the other characters only carry labels of rank or function (a Lieutenant, an embedded reporter, a priest in a German chapel, a glory-hounding colonel, a war-crime investigator). And so, since Bartle, Murph, and Sterling are the only significant characters with names, the audience's appetite for the mortification and/or redemption of these men develops quickly. As the plot unfolds, the audience's help remains necessary to complete the purgation by scapegoat. Burke writes in his definition of "Dramatism":

> If order, then guilt; if guilt, then need for redemption; but any such "payment" is victimage. Or: if action, then drama; if drama, then conflict; if conflict, then victimage.... A dramatistic view of human motives thus culminates in the ironic admonition that perversions of the sacrificial principle (purgation by scapegoat, congregation by segregation) are the constant temptation of human societies ["Dramatism" 342, 343].

Following Burke's if/then statements, we could go so far as to make some simple substitutions from *The Yellow Birds*: if Iraq, then war (entelechy driven order); if war then death (and attendant guilt); if guilt, then scapegoating (through Murph and Sterling's self-mortification). This equation works for soldiers and civilians alike, or, in this case, for Bartle *and* for the reader of *The Yellow Birds*.

As C. Allen Carter reminds, "Some stories, however, are better left unperfected, for inevitably what is perfected is a story of victimage. The troubling fact is that our myths tend to 'go scapegoat'" (46). *The Yellow Birds* is one of those unperfected stories of victimage. It goes scapegoat, but when we trace the development and disposal of the scapegoats in this war story, we can partially confound the process of easy redemption. When the critic reveals the scapegoat for what it is, he or she can slightly confound the process and therefore achieve something that is extremely difficult in war literature: a withheld redemption for both the hero and the audience so that a nagging culpability remains, spread appropriately across all sectors of war's drama.

"Getting Deviant": The Scapegoating of Sergeant Sterling

The Yellow Birds is a flashback that covers nine years of Bartle's life, but actual war only occupies ten short months following Bartle's first meeting with Murph at Fort Dix (30). Thus, Bartle's quarrel is with his own accountability and the scapegoating process that Powers establishes in the opening pages of the novel. Bartle transgresses by making a promise, but he also writes a letter. Eventually, we find out that he is an accomplice for a war crime and that he covers up the truth about Murph's death. So yes, he mourns Murph, but his guilt actually is rooted in his acceptance of his own agency, something he never has been able to do during war. Symbolized with two inertia-driven byways—the Tigris River in Iraq and the James River in Richmond—Bartle's service has little direct causal relationship with his guilt. He remembers "struggling to find a sense of urgency that seemed proportional" to his preparation to go to war, and he locates that lack of urgency at the very beginning of his military career in basic training (a time when he sang blithely about mindless violence in the "Yellow Bird Jody" from the epigraph) (35). And it feels great, as he recalls: "it had dawned on me that I'd never have to make a decision again" (35).

The assumed lack of agency was liberating at first, but as he concludes, "I had to learn that freedom is not the same thing as the absence of accountability" (35). He doesn't kill Murph, nor does he directly or indirectly cause Murph's death, but he does act (or as he puts it, he experiences "freedom") to establish order and a hierarchy. Bartle knows he made a mistake trying to force order onto Murph's life:

> I know it was a terrible thing to write that letter. What I don't know is where it fits in with all of the other terrible things I think about. At some point I stopped believing in significance. Order became an accident of observation [31].

Like the circumstances of Murph's death, we don't know anything about this letter's contents. But as far as Bartle's purgation is concerned, neither the letter nor Murph's death really matter. We do know that Bartle sent this mysterious letter to Murph's mother after Murph died, and we know that Bartle used it to impersonate her son, a ruse she easily sniffed out. But this primarily satisfies our need for a carefully built suspense. We keep reading because we need to know why Bartle lies in the letter and why he feels such guilt over an innocuous promise. More importantly, we need to know why he is in prison. In the jumbled temporality of the novel's structure, however, Bartle's redemption comes first. That is, the entire novel is a first person reflection from somewhere beyond war. Before we even have a victim, we know Bartle eventually is to be redeemed by the cult of the kill because, at a minimum, he survives long enough to tell this tale we are reading, which stands as his final and incomplete purging.

The reflective nature of the narrative allows Bartle to go back and trace his failures and crimes, and we go with him, to examine the scapegoat mechanism that follows. He is full of pain and grief over Murph's death, but he cannot place himself in its causes. In Iraq, when Murph begins falling apart emotionally, Bartle remembers:

> [H]ow desperately I wanted to measure the particulars of Murph's new, strange behavior and trace it back to one moment, to one cause, to one thing that I would not be guilty of.... I couldn't think of anything else. I thought a lot about that ridicu-

lous promise I'd made to Murphy's mother. I could even remember what I'd said, or even what had been asked for. Bring him home? What, in one piece? At all? I couldn't remember. Would I have failed if he wasn't happy, if he was no longer sane? [155].

Murphy is dead at no fault of Bartle's, so we must find another site for Bartle's vicarious victimage, and Sergeant Sterling fits the role perfectly. This man will carry all of Bartle's actual war sins all the way back from Iraq, and then he will put a bullet through his own head and thus become Bartle's scapegoat and the bringer of Bartle's (partial) redemption.

The victimage of Sterling is the most poignant development in the entire novel, and as such, Bartle's catharsis is delayed and delayed, layered between his experience, its recollection, and Murph's slow unraveling. Though Bartle and Murph try to fill the role, Sergeant Sterling is the first and only candidate to fully qualify as the speaker of the Yellow Bird Jody. He is the model soldier, the example these young men are ordered to follow and mimic. Bartle lays out the case for Sterling's appropriateness as his eventual and convenient scapegoat. He is an excellent non-commissioned officer who leads well but also skillfully panders to his officers: "Sterling seemed to know exactly how hard to push the LT so that discipline remained" (17). He is humble. He wins medals and awards, but Bartle notices that he never wears them (35). When the men are all awarded medals after the harrowing firefight from the opening pages, they all cynically ignore the reading of the citations while "only Sterling kept his military bearing and remained attentive" (152). He is the "tall and trimly muscled" perfect soldier, with "blond hair and blue eyes" (35). The captain in charge of their company even introduces Sterling, literally, as the poster child of war: "Sergeant Sterling," the man exclaims, "will be put on the fucking recruiting posters, men" (35). Sterling confirms all the negative stereotypes of a soldier too: He reads porn magazines; he abuses a girl in a German brothel; and he is very good at killing. A less-deviant Iago, Sterling creates a "tinge of malice vaguely diffused through the texture of events and relationships [that] can here be condensed into a single principle" ("Othello" 169). Burke wrote those words in an essay about *Othello*, but they easily apply to *The Yellow Birds*, as well.

Bartle went to war and, for a moment, became the speaker of the Yellow Bird Jody, an agency-free—but necessary—soldier who responds to the demands of war according to training and rote practice and an entelechy-driven desire to "be good." He wanted to be a good soldier, and he wanted to be a good man and a keeper of promises. He also wanted to survive. However, all of these desires prove difficult to reconcile due to his conflicting notions of guilt and powerlessness. When he was asked if Bartle's guilt is fueled by Murph's death or some sort of survivor's guilt, Powers told an interviewer,

> I would not be able to separate the two. The root of his guilt is that he wanted to be good, and he tried to be good, but he failed. His conflict is between his desire to redeem that failure and his acceptance of complete powerlessness [qtd. in Ruppin 160].

Bartle wanted to be like Sterling, who instructs Bartle and Murph to "stay deviant in this motherfucker" and "dig deep. Find that nasty streak" in order to survive war (156, 42). The problem is that Murph's underlying humanity causes him to fail in that digging almost immediately while Bartle succeeds. It isn't until later that he is able to collect all the appropriate attendant guilt and all the baggage that properly goes with staying deviant, with finding his nasty streak. Tim O'Brien touched on this idea in a recent interview:

> I worry that there's not enough trauma.... It feels to me as if we as humans tend to heal too well and too quickly and too thoroughly. The scabs are too thick so we don't feel too much.... If you don't have anger issues inside of you, I think you're crazy, that you're not human.... I feel that one of the ways to deal with trauma is to be traumatized, to acknowledge that I was hurt, that I'm still hurting, and that I hurt other people [Wolff].

Bartle accumulates huge amounts of guilt for being like Sterling, for forcing thick scabs over the trauma of his experiences and actions. At first, he manages to construct his experience of war so that it mitigates his own agency, but then, after he returns home, he is forced the see the truth of the matter, that one cannot act as he did without collecting massive amounts of guilt, guilt that must be purged.

It takes a long time for Bartle to recognize this since he and Murph both understand that arguing with Sterling's example would be nothing more than redrawing the lines of a map one isn't even using. For, as Bartle ponders, a map is less a "picture of facts and more a poor translation in two dimensions" (225). Indeed, Ladonna Murphy visits Bartle in jail and brings him a map of Iraq. At first, Bartle thinks, "it was an odd gesture" (224). He folds and unfolds it, "struggling with the arrangement of the arbitrary lines that it would fold itself along when I went to put it up at night.... The grid seemed so foreign and imprecise. Just a place scaled out of existence on a map" (224). This map symbolism runs parallel to Sterling's scapegoat role. Bartle remarks that, during war, men like Sterling are "necessary" (19). But he still hates him. He hates Sterling for "the way he excel[s] in death and brutality and domination" (19). He hates Sterling's bravery, a "narrowly focused" bravery that was "pure and unadulterated" (43). Such bravery is, Bartle admits, almost obligatory in war, but it is "a kind of elemental self-sacrifice, free of ideology, free of logic" (43). As Bartle's familiarity with war deepens, he comes to embody everything he hates in Sterling. He hates Sterling's mindless commitment to war, but he needs it, and for a moment, so do we: "I needed him to jar me into action even when they were trying to kill me, how I felt like a coward until he screamed into my ear, 'Shoot the hajji fucks!'" (19). Bartle explains, "[I]t wasn't just the fact of his having been there that caused us to respect him. He was harsh, but fair, and there was a kind of evolutionary beauty in his competence" (33). Bartle struggles with his need to imitate what he both loves and hates, and, of course, we do too.

Sterling is exactly what his society demanded he be, and as such he is the origination of all ritual violence. Bartle describes Sterling from his prison cell:

> I'm not sure he would have realized he was permitted to have his own desires and preferences.... His life had been entirely contingent, like a body in orbit, only seen on account of the way it wobbles around its star. Everything he'd done had been a response to a preexisting expectation [188].

And in this contingent role, he abuses a woman in a German brothel and murders an Iraqi "cartwright" who helps move Murph's body. He also burns down the minaret Murph was thrown from and kills an old couple in a car in the opening combat scene (221, 22). Bartle places no explicit moral judgments on these acts, but in making Sterling a bit of a maniac soldier with criminal tendencies, the audience can easily accept or even forget Bartle's similar transgressions. We are tempted to accept, as Bartle reflects later, the idea that Sterling *and* Bartle are merely completing the order that society (or better yet, the reader) has set for them.

Sterling's eventual suicide affects a number of cathartic functions. René Girard's concept of "mimetic desire," from *Violence and the Sacred* (1977), accounts for Bartle's dilemma (143). He wants to imitate Sterling, but to do so, since he both despises and admires the man, Bartle must ritually eliminate and replace him. When the unit leaves Iraq, it stops at a base near Kaiserslautern, Germany—this tale's scene of purgatorial reckoning—and the two men argue about their murders and cover-ups in Iraq. Sterling threatens: "Me and you. Like we're married. I've fucking got you, Private Bartle. UC motherfucking MJ, anytime I want" (68). We aren't quite sure what Sterling is referring to at this point, and Bartle tepidly suggests that he can reveal their secrets, but vengeance and justice-free punishment are unavailable in this scapegoating process. That would merely perpetuate the order that the novel encourages us to identify, track, and protect ourselves against. As Lawrence Coupe summarizes, Girard's concept of "mimetic desire would, if fulfilled, result in the collapse of the social order, with chronic aggression the norm" (136). Thus, we suspend our judgment of Sterling and Bartle's crimes until Powers completes the killing off of the poster child. By the time we learn of his crimes (in the final two chapters), our desire for retribution already has been fulfilled. Or, as Bartle puts it, "Sterling never made it back to be accountable" (186). That is, he shot himself first. He held himself accountable so we didn't have to. We are left only marveling at the crimes, and we almost forget that Bartle is party to them as well.

Girard's concept of the scapegoat is slightly different from Burke's, but both philosophers agree that the scapegoat mechanism is the most important ritual in myth and language (Coupe 137–138). As Girard points out in *Violence and the Sacred*, reprisal and vengeance have no place in that ritual:

> The desire to commit an act of violence on those near us cannot be suppressed without a conflict; we must divert that impulse, therefore, toward a sacrificial victim, the creature we can strike down without fear of reprisal, since he lacks a champion [13].

War provides Bartle and the reader with the champion-free sacrificial victim in the form of Sergeant Sterling. Bartle will ponder suicide, but Sterling succeeds, and this is as it should be. Had Sterling survived long enough to accept his own prison sentence alongside Bartle, or if Bartle had also purged his own guilt through self-killing, the novel would have fallen into disarray.

Bartle does make a half-hearted attempt to drown himself in the James River, and there he finds a sort of dialectical rebirthing, a rebirth that is allowed following a long, two-page diatribe of purging questions, questions that many purveyors of violence face but very few bother answering. In this passage, Bartle begins with a desire "to be asleep forever" (144), and he closes with the same impulse, of just wanting "to go to sleep and not wake up and fuck 'em all" (146). Slipping into second person, he manipulates the second-person pronoun and its referents in a series of turns and shifts that move from accusation to commiseration and antagonism. He talks about "making up" for the men and women he has killed and has seen killed and about his urge "to kill everything you saw sometimes because it felt like there was acid seeping down into your soul" (144). He connects his "mother's pride" when he comes home with the way he and his rifle made "people crumple" (144). Bartle admits to his crimes, though at this point we still don't quite know what he is talking about: "everyone is so fucking happy to see you, the murderer, the fucking accomplice, the at-bare-minimum bearer of some fucking responsibility" (145). And then, in what is probably the most powerful passage of the novel, he talks about the inherent conflict between volunteer military service—O'Brien's "acts of consent"—and service's aftermath: "but then you signed up to go so it's all your fault, really, because you went on purpose, so you are in the end doubly fucked, so why not just find a spot and curl up and die" (145). This stream of consciousness reveals Bartle's conflicted recognition of the hypocrisies and regrets of military service and the tacit obligations they require. He has survived, but an excruciating humanity remains, and so we watch. We watch Bartle's symbolic act of attempted self-killing as he slips underneath the water, and we share his guilt. He survives, though, and we recognize that he maybe never intended to commit suicide; he is painfully abandoning an old self, a self who "wanted to be a man" by joining the army (145). Bartle's abandonment of that old self suggests, along with the various metanarratives of military service, that we should follow the same path.

Thus, Bartle is not even surprised when the news of Sterling's suicide finally arrives. Before the investigator can finish saying the word, "accident" (188). Bartle closes his eyes and imagines the purgation, his ultimate cathartic release:

> When I closed [my eyes] I saw Sergeant Sterling on the side of a mountain. Saw the rifle barrel in his mouth. Saw the way he went limp, so limp in that impossible moment when the small bullet emerged from his head. Saw his body slide a few feet down the mountain, the worn soles of his boots coming to rest in a clot of pine needles [188].

Bartle imagines the bullet exiting Sterling's brain and taking a portion of his guilt with it, but no eyewitness description of the carnage exists in the book. This scene is built in his imagination only, so the purgation happens off stage for the reader. No red-handed Medea rushes onto the stage after the deed is done, so the off-stage, self-inflicted violence deepens while the cleansing effect of the self-killing stops short of fully completing Bartle's and the reader's complete redemption. Again, this is as it should be, for Bartle must be rightly punished even though we never quite learn which action in particular landed him in prison. Is it the accomplice role he played in the murder of the Cartwright? Is it the fake letter and the cover-up of the true nature of Murph's death? Bartle has so thoroughly compartmentalized his wartime actions as being agency free that it doesn't really matter. Bartle recognizes this nuance as well:

> I knew the C.I.D. investigators would find me eventually, and I was pretty sure I knew what they wanted. Someone had to be punished for what happened to Murph. It probably wouldn't matter what our level of culpability was. I was guilty of something, that much was certain [179].

The remaining guilt is a general byproduct of loving men like Sterling who, of course, never "made it back to be accountable" (186). As Coupe writes, in the ritual of "mimetic violence," the "arbitrary persecution of a victim becomes in the myth the just punishment of a crime" (137). Sterling is, for Bartle, a sort of arbitrary victim. Both men are guilty of crimes, but Sterling's suicide fulfills both needs (Bartle's purgation and our desire for just punishment for his slightly more heinous war crimes). His suicide and Bartle's prison sentence therefore restore all demands for social order. A combat-scarred, mindless, killing machine, Sergeant Sterling is the sacred cow of this war and this war novel. It is his death that allows Bartle to conclude: "I do feel ordinary again" (224).

That cycle, the one that allows the public to create a soldier, use a soldier as a tool of aggression, and then "feel ordinary" again after that soldier's death is what the scapegoating process in Powers's novel reveals. We *should* feel uncomfortable with Sterling's existence and death, not necessarily because he committed suicide, but because he existed at all.

"Something happened": The Scapegoating of Daniel Murphy

Bartle's redemption allows the audience a parallel catharsis of sorts, but we participate voyeuristically, as curious observers who simply want to know why Bartle is in jail and why he hates Sterling so much. As for our full postcathartic redemption, it doesn't arrive until the second-to-last chapter (Chapter 10). Unlike Sterling's death, so much depends on the specific events and vivid details of Murph's self-killing. For us, Daniel "Murph" Murphy is an aesthetic object, and we never forget that his character is imitating something. And despite how much we may discount his role as nothing but an authorial invention, Murph's life and death pose many questions regarding our previously held beliefs and apprehensions about war. A modern-day Billy Budd, not only does Murph's death drive Bartle from scene to scene and haunt his every recollection of war, he also traps the audience within the novel's yellow bird metaphor. In this way, Murph serves double duty as a scapegoat and a goad, an unstable cluster of motives that urge us to reexamine war, the soldiers we create, and the war blame we often refuse to accept after we send them off to kill and die on our behalf.

The audience need not harbor a desire for Murph's death because Powers maintains our morbid curiosity about it throughout the novel. Murph's death, as Burke describes Othello's, "goads (tortures) the plot forward step by step, for the audience's villainous entertainments and filthy purgation" ("Othello" 170). If Sterling is the speaker of the "Yellow Bird Jody" and Bartle is alternately the speaker and the bird, Murph never is anything but the Yellow Bird until he realizes, too late, that he was convinced that he should try to be the speaker as well. And we are almost happy to see him go even though his peripeteia makes us all mourn his death, for the grief is, quite literally, the audience's own. We knew it was coming; so when it does finally arrive, it satisfies the suspense first and does little to cleanse the order (American war culture) that results in this poor kid's suicidal surrender. Through Bartle's narration, it is clear that he and Murph differ vastly in their attempts to stay deviant. Whereas Bartle survives long enough to be redeemed by Sterling's self-kill and to accept a measure of prison time for his crimes, Murph suffers a slow but definite descent into his inescapable humanity. Here is the closing paragraph of Bartle's penultimate run-up to Murph's scapegoating scene:

> What happened? What fucking happened? That's not even the question, I thought. How is that the question? How do you answer the unanswerable? To say what happened, the mere facts, the disposition of events in time, would come to seem like a kind of treachery. The dominoes of moments, lined up symmetrically, then tumbling backward against the hazy and unsure push of cause, showed only that a fall is every object's destiny. It is not enough to say what happened. Everything happened. Everything fell [148].

What happens, in Murph's case, is that he steps out from beneath the shade that Bartle's super-agent war casts and accepts his own accountability and agency. It literally kills him.

His death follows a slow unraveling. First, he misses the "unasked-for ceremony" (the same one that Sterling quietly attends) that bestows medals on the unit for their actions during the fight that opened the novel (153). He starts avoiding Bartle, and we join Bartle in becoming increasingly concerned with his fate as he clearly becomes unable to "stay deviant" (156). Bartle describes his behavior after following the opening battle scene, "We were unaware of even our own savagery now: the beatings and the kicked dogs, the searches and the sheer brutality of our presence. Each action was a page in an exercise book performed by rote" (159). Yes, Bartle claims to be unaware of his own savagery, but Murph does not so easily mitigate his own culpability. He fails to sustain his part in the barbarity of war, and it is clear that he is going to have to pay for that failure. He throws away his "casualty card" and then he tosses a picture of his girlfriend (159). He starts marking graffiti all over the base with the tag, "Murph was here" along with "two eyes and a nose peering over one thin line" (159). Dating to World War II, the "Kilroy was here" marker typically tracked a unit's anonymous movement from one place to another. Or, as Paul Dickson suggests, "Kilroy was a mischievous outsider, staring at, and probably laughing at, the world" (182). Murph subverts that meaning, though; his graffiti marks the FOB as a place he will soon depart. His markings are no morale-boosting symbols of encouragement; rather, "Murph was here" darkly foreshadows his desertion, his self-purging.

That self-mortification comes after a mortar round kills a medic Murph had been watching for days:

> Murph, gape-jawed and crying, was gone. He left after finding the medic's body sprawled in a spot of sunlight that fell through a hole the mortar made in the broken chapel's roof. He wasn't at her ceremony.... He'd already left through a hole in the wire by then, his clothes and disassembled weapon scattered in the dust [193].

Thus, Murph becomes a rather straightforward version of a modern, self-appointed biblical scapegoat from the book of Leviticus. From this vantage point, Murph's death scene—at least partially—resembles the Mosaic ritual of the Day of Atonement in which a goat is ritually driven off into the wilderness in order to symbolically cleanse the rest of the community. But he is no martyr; he is a scapegoat. Whereas the horns of the traditional Judaic scapegoat were wrapped in red cloth, Murph (the incompetent soldier who failed to stay deviant) walks into Al Tafar, naked, an offering of public atonement for the "sheer brutality" of his society's "presence" (159). Girard explains the ease with which it is possible to accept a secular symbolic scapegoat in place of a traditionally religious one:

> When we exclaim: "the victim is a scapegoat," we resort to a biblical expression that no longer has the same significance as it had for the participants in the ritual of that name.... Every explicit reference to the Passion has disappeared, but the Passion is always juxtaposed with representations of persecution from the perspective of the persecutors. The same model serves as a cipher for decoding, but it is so well assimilated that it is used mechanically without any explicit reference to its Judaic and Christian origins [202].

Murph's death problematizes any easy redemption for the reader through the scapegoat mechanism. It challenges the audience to question the necessity of his obligations in the first place and wonder if it is truly possible to stay deviant and to survive unscathed. Murph was not as deviant as Sterling, nor was he able to mitigate his own agency like Bartle. As Girard says of Oedipus, Murph is our perfect scapegoat because he "combin[ed] the marginality of the outsider with the marginality of the insider ... the more signs of a victim an individual bears, the more likely he is to attract disaster" (25).

Still, the filthy purgation of this war story cannot be concluded until we learn the particularities of Murph's death. Whereas war, as we are trained elsewhere in American war literature, is often localized into individual threats disposed of by one more pull of the trigger, in *The Yellow Birds*, the menace of war is generalized enough that the mirror of blame can only be turned inward. Something haunts in *The Yellow Birds* that we fear and hate. It isn't the enemy; it isn't the hero; it isn't even Sergeant Sterling. It most certainly isn't Daniel Murphy. It is war and the culture that builds a hierarchy and an order that asks men like Sterling and Bartle and Murphy to make such destructive acts of consent, to make war promises.

When we pick up the novel and allow Powers's negotiation of form to pull us through the various stages of the scapegoating process, we implicate ourselves in that exchange. We are mournful when we find Murph's dead body, but we also are relieved, nonetheless, to be given the partial redemption we so desperately need. As Bartle describes it,

> We found Murph, finally, covered in a patch of lifeless hyacinth, resting motionless in the shade of the grass and low branches.... Laid up hard and broken-boned in the patch of vegetation that was his journey's end, his body was twisted at absurd angles beneath the pink and shimmering tower [205].

The sad reality is that Murph's "fall" could, if it is not examined with the proper lens, fail to goad further action from the audience. As Bartle says, "the body had fallen, the boy already dead, the fall itself meant nothing" (205). Thus, the floating of Murph's body down the Tigris River is quite appropriate. A twenty-one-gun salute or a flag-draped coffin has no place in this drama. If Murph is the carrier of the reader's guilt, it is right that our shame be carried away in a secret, shameful manner. The Burkeian pentad is complete: *The Yellow Birds* (*agent*) depicts the well-worn and expected soldier-fighting-an-enemy-and-himself structure (*scene*). This is a traditional convention of the genre, but Powers redirects the scapegoat ritual (*act*) through the deaths of Murph and Sterling with a masterful negotiation of what Burke called "psychology of form" (*agency*), all in order to reassess the proper assignation of guilt from the Iraq war (*purpose*) onto the surviving perpetrators of war's violence (Bartle *and* the reader).

Four

The Comic Corrective and Ben Fountain's Billy Lynn

> Artists do not load power kegs—they light fuses.... The artist is like the man who cried "Fire!" in a theater. The "brilliancy" of the fellow arose out of the fact that he shouted the word best adapted to "touching off" a stampede under these particular conditions.—Kenneth Burke, "Auscultation" 137

In the fall of 2013, I attended a lecture delivered by Ben Fountain, the author of *Billy Lynn's Long Halftime Walk* (2012), at the Air Force Academy in Colorado Springs.[1] As he took the stage and began talking, Fountain seemed pleased to be speaking to a large group of cadets and Air Force officers, and as one of those officers (and a student of war fiction) I was eager to hear what he had to say about his wildly popular book, one of the first extended fictional treatments of the Iraq war to be written by a civilian. His talk, though, had little to do with *Billy Lynn*; instead, Fountain focused on *Billy Lynn*'s underlying politics, something he described as the "Fantasy Industrial Complex." His description of the concept sounded a lot like Kenneth Burke's observation, in a preface to the 1952 edition of *Counter-Statement*, of the "motivational tangle that besets our nation, plaguing political leaders who would unite nationwide parties" (xiii). Indeed, in fascinatingly similar terms, Fountain's "Fantasy Industry Complex" covers much of the same entanglement that exists today in post–9/11 American culture. As Burke posits, a "tangle of motives" in the United States "affects the temper of even our artistic spokesmen who are not specifically concerned with such problems" (*Counter-Statement* xiii). Fountain is one of those artistic spokesman, and his temper is most certainly affected by the manipulation of public sentiment that he sees in nearly every aspect of life in a post–9/11 United States that thoroughly uses and abuses its symbols.

Whereas Burke's catalysts for his ideas regarding symbolic action were the depression, two world wars, and the looming menace of nuclear war, Fountain's "Fantasy Industrial Complex" grew out of the trauma of 9/11 and the American responses to it. The bubble created by improper symbol use, Fountain says, has become the controlling factor in American motivations and reasoning. Like Burke did decades earlier, Fountain suggests that language and rhetoric have both caused—and can be potential saviors of—failures in the sociopolitical realms of human existence. Fountain conceives an American culture that is entirely dominated by a virtually agent-free simulacra of "electronica, entertainment, and media" in the years following 9/11 (3). Much like Jean Baudrillard's compelling arguments that the first gulf war "did not take place"—or, rather, that war would be known and conceived primarily through its "rotten simulation" in representations in the media (59)—Fountain observes that "we often don't know what's real anymore" in any realm of American life (3). Thus, war has become one more item in a long list of faked and simulated experiences that are mainly desired for their titillating or comforting purposes. Instead of genuine engagement, Fountain suggests, the product-driven version of reality we consume and demand is one based on "fantasy, triviality, and materialism" (3). The American soldier is today just one more effective prop—or scapegoated symbol—in the Fantasy Industry Complex's vast arsenal. He or she has become a manipulated sign carrier—stripped of agency—for all of our post–9/11 anxieties, and the "Fantasy Industrial Complex" uses him or her for vicarious reassurance that we still live in a sound and just society.

In addition to all this talk about the "Fantasy Industrial Complex," Fountain did, of course, discuss his novel. He summarized by saying that it is "about football, cheerleaders, sex, death, war, capitalism, the transmigration of souls, brothers and sisters, parents and children, the movie industry, Destiny's Child, and the general insanity of American life in the early years of the 21st century" (1). Yes, that is quite the list, and he wasn't exaggerating. The novel presents all of these elements, which, taken as a whole, form the basis of his Fantasy Industrial Complex and confront the eponymous hero Billy Lynn. In fact, these encounters shape the plot of *Billy Lynn*, action that follows a group of U.S. soldiers—"Bravo Squad"—as they are plucked from combat and draped with medals following a televised firefight in Iraq. This group of heroes is paraded across the country on a "Victory Tour," and the novel picks them up on the last day of this tour, a day spent in Texas Stadium, on Thanksgiving Day in 2004, as the guests of honor for a Dallas Cowboys football game and a halftime show with Beyoncé and Destiny's Child. In luxury suites and VIP lounges, the conspicuously rich bathe in the glow that follows these fighting men around. The civilians fawn and praise, and as the soldiers float through this brush with adoration and money, they realize that the battle in Iraq that made them momentarily famous did nothing to prepare them for a slightly different battle in America.

Packaged and sold as heroes to a starving public, these soldiers are tepidly trying to sell their stories to Hollywood before they return to Iraq. But a movie deal for these soldiers is not to be. Instead, the rich and the powerful beckon and manipulate these lower and middle class citizen-soldiers, but in Fountain's formulation, the collision of these two groups serves mainly to highlight their underlying differences, differences that determine each individual's rather firm place amid the hierarchies and social strata of American society. Every American in this stadium shares much—Fountain seems to say—but not quite enough to ever achieve consubstantiality. No, something in American culture prevents empathy; something gets in the way of a healthy sharing of experiences across the borders drawn by capitalism and entertainment. The Fantasy Industrial Complex ensures that no true identification, no lasting merger, can ever happen between those who fight the wars and those who ask them to do so on their behalf. Simply put, the Fantasy Industrial Complex is built on the back of the scapegoated soldier.

The soldiers of Bravo squad enjoy the game and the fleeting fame, though. They mix with football players and football fans, but they never are quite invited to emerge from the cocoon of their small group. And as the movie deal they seek falls apart and their return to Iraq draws near, Billy Lynn and his sage leader, Sergeant Dime, slowly realize that fame, gratitude, and sacrifice *all* are necessarily hollow gestures. In the America to which these soldiers have returned, a place peopled by the insulated rich and the equally insulated drunken masses, these socioeconomically disadvantaged civilian-soldiers are desired as passive objects in a game of consumption and disposal. Iraq, then, is maybe the one place where these soldiers can truly become themselves, the only place where they can achieve unmitigated agency with their guns, their brotherhood, and their heroics. Thus, both places—Texas and Iraq—come across as locations we don't really want to be, worlds that aren't necessarily worth fighting for.

For all of these reasons, Fountain's satire is ripe for Kenneth Burke's guilt-purification-redemption methodology, for the novel is shaped and controlled by Fountain's unmistakable comic frame and a scapegoat mechanism that closely follows Burke's concept of vicarious victimage. Like

The Yellow Birds, the measured redemption that *Billy Lynn* affords readers is preceded by two types of "mortification"; that is, catharsis is available through the "homicidal" slaying of a scapegoat (the hero, Billy Lynn), and, as Burke writes, through the scapegoat's suicidal mortification of himself (*Rhetoric* 223). Billy doesn't die in this novel, but by its end, after the Cowboys lose the game, the fans go home, pleased with their patriotic exertions, while the soldiers voluntarily—almost eagerly—return to Iraq. Or in terms of Burke's scapegoat mechanism, the guilty public unburdens itself with thank-you-for-your-service platitudes and vicarious cathartic engagement with the video of Bravo squad's firefight; meanwhile, Bravo squad voluntarily returns to possible death in Iraq. And America is glad to see this group go so the ritual of America's war in Iraq can continue, uninterrupted and unexamined. The war goes on, and culpability is left floating somewhere in the air above Texas Stadium, adhering to neither the soldiers nor the citizens.

Maintaining a Perspective by Incongruity: Fountain's War on War Porn

A bit of that guilt sticks to us though. In many ways, Fountain creates a comic version of war's consumption in popular culture through what Kenneth Burke calls a "perspective by incongruity" (*Attitudes* 308). The "comic corrective," and the "comic frame," Burke elaborates, are effective tools that build up a perspective by incongruity, which is, as he defines it, "a method for gauging situations by verbal 'atom cracking'" (308). Or, as Burke refined the term in a 1983 interview, a "perspective by incongruity is a way of seeing two ways at once. It's the whole principle of an ironic approach to something" ("Counter-Gridlock" 350).[2] Much like the economist Thorstein Veblen's concept of "trained incapacity," Burke says, a perspective by incongruity assesses a situation in terms that allow us to see through incompatible perspectives of a contextual situation in order to identify the "trained incapacity" in the dramatic scene's agents ("Counter-Gridlock" 350).

The agents—the characters—of a novel like Fountain's are not necessarily equipped to view all perspectives of their contextual situations at once, but we are. Billy Lynn, the fans, the rich: all of these agents are trained to remain incapacitated by their debilitating levels of awareness, a clarity occluded by limiting experiences, prejudices, and desires that in no way leave them "competent to look at a situation otherwise" ("Counter-

Gridlock" 350). Billy and the other members of Bravo squad lack the cultural competence needed to view themselves as the rest of the world does, and the citizens at the football game lack the generosity required to fully empathize with Bravo. The dialectic blending of subject and object might not be available for the characters of *Billy Lynn*, but we, the novel's auditors, are not so restrained. Since we are privy to some or all of the soldier perspectives in the novel, we can construct a corresponding metaperspective, one that is built by the novel's incongruent motivations. We can track Fountain's ironic juxtaposition of agents, acts, agency, and purpose in one massive scene.[3] These elements, and Fountain's "ways of placement," help us understand, as Burke says, "what people are doing and why they are doing it" (*Grammar* 3). As Burke writes, the audience occupies a special vantage point that allows us to see "the operation of errors that the characters of the play cannot see; thus seeing two angles at once, it is chastened by dramatic irony; it is admonished to remember that intelligence means *wisdom* ... it requires fear, resignation, the sense of limits, as an important ingredient" (*Attitudes* 42).

This concept is an important one to keep in mind when we read *Billy Lynn* and any other work of contemporary war literature. The typical American citizen (to include war veterans)—entertained and intoxicated by the symbols of war—is not competent at viewing war; he or she sees the spectacle, the images of war only. Even a Navy S.E.A.L. is crippled by his first-person shooter perspective on war. A perspective by incongruity, then, allows a sophisticated reader to see multiple perspectives at once, to determine which dramatistic element—act, agent, agency, scene, or purpose—is emphasized over the others in each war story so that we can track the ruptures in the various narratives that these elements form when they come together. We can also recognize that civilians are not the only ones with perspectives clouded by experiences and expectations for the way war is shared by a hungry public.

A perspective by incongruity resists, as Debra Hawhee concludes, "the notion of one truth or one 'right' interpretation" (134). As Hawhee says, this allows a critic to instead "adopt different 'slicing styles'—read, different perspectives—as mutually informing, and more importantly, as a conscious—and ever artificial—shaping" (135). In these perspectives' "incommensurability," says Hawhee, the reader is best prepared with satire and with a comic frame "for the maximum Perspective by Incongruity" (135). Burke would approve of Fountain's novel, I think, for it uses irony and satire and mockery to highlight American symbol abuse by all of its citizens and citizen-soldiers, and it does so with a relentless rewrite of one slice of reality enacted on Thanksgiving Day in Dallas, Texas, in 2004. It brings together the many in a massive stadium in order to highlight popular culture's alienating but dominant power over us all.

Fountain's novel, therefore, offers the reader the benefit of a "comic synthesis" of "antithetical emphases" that ultimately stresses "*man in society*" (*Attitudes* 170; italics original). This is yet another reason why Burke's forensic methodology is such a useful tool for war literature; it suggests that a synthesis of war and war's agents can lead to understanding, not through a mere vicarious cathartic experience, but through an examination of a comic frame that "could not, and should not, offer recompense" for anyone (*Attitudes* 175). Instead of easy redemption, a comic frame like Fountain's lends itself to a work's overall comic corrective function. Thus, we can transcend Fountain's propagandistic purposes and reveal the scapegoat mechanism as a guiding trope. The reader then can assume, as Burke says, a "polemical-debunking frame" that works to balance other readings of war literature, readings that "have unintentionally blinded us to the full operation of 'alienating processes'" (*Attitudes* 167).

As Burke sees it, comedy and tragedy share much in terms of their dramatic structures and the scapegoat mechanisms they both employ. He writes, "Like tragedy, comedy warns against the dangers of pride, but its emphasis shifts from *crime* to *stupidity*" (*Attitudes* 41; italics original). Analyzing *Billy Lynn* with Burke's comic corrective in mind can allow us to distance ourselves from reinforced binaries, no matter how they are drawn, because assuming a comic frame brings the reader "spiritual wealth, by making even bad books and trivial remarks legitimate objects of study" (173). It does this by mitigating the "difficulties in engineering a shift to new symbols of authority, as required by the new social relationships that the revolutions of historic environment have made necessary" so that one may eventually find a way to accommodate "the structure of others' lives" (173). In other words, tracing the scapegoat via the comic frame maximizes the empathetic resonance of any work of literature since we are encouraged to favor healthy ambivalence over easy resolution. And, since comedy allows us to see men as "fools" instead of as "villains"—as Burke puts it— we can complete the "comic circle" of Fountain's satire; we can see "that *all* people are exposed to situations in which they must act as fools" without excusing ourselves for the same foolish behavior (*Attitudes* 41). In the case of Billy Lynn and his fellow soldiers, redemption only arrives through the complicated and ironic re-coupling of soldier with war, the only relationship that makes sense—twisted though it might be—in today's Fantasy Industrial Complex.

Billy Lynn was well received when it appeared in 2012, and like *The Yellow Birds*, it also was a finalist for the 2012 National Book Award. It won the National Book Critics Circle award, and it currently is being adapted into a movie by Oscar award winning director, Ang Lee.⁴ Much of its success has to do with the overall conception of the novel and the propagandistic message within. In an interview with *The Huffington Post*, Fountain explains the moment of inspiration that drove him to adopt what Burke would call his "propagandistic (didactic) strategy" (*Attitudes* 166):

> The initial impulse came from watching the halftime show of a Dallas Cowboys Thanksgiving Day game in the mid–2000s. The show was very much like the one I describe in the book, this surreal and patently insane—to me, anyway—mash-up of militarism, pop culture, American triumphalism and soft-core porn. At one point during the show the camera flashed on a group of soldiers who were marching along with everyone else down on the field, and they looked like actual combat soldiers. They were in desert camo, and looked lean and tan; my sense was that they'd been over there fighting in Iraq or Afghanistan. And I wondered what it would do to your head, to have been over there immersed in daily life-or-death situations, then you return to the U.S. and get plunked down in the middle of this very artificial situation. How, in other words, would you keep from going crazy? [Wayne].

Fountain inserts Billy Lynn and Bravo squad wholesale into that same Texas Stadium on that exact same Thanksgiving Day in 2004. In this way, *Billy Lynn*'s fan fiction conception just slightly changes the camera angle of history. This is a significant construction for a war novel. It only takes a couple of seconds online to discover that the Bears and the Cowboys did indeed play on that day in 2004.⁵ A quick internet search also is all it takes to find the very footage that Fountain describes above. So precisely located, it is very easy to accept the fictional Billy Lynn, his corresponding viewpoint, and the propagandistic message Fountain relates. *Billy Lynn* is both a *roman à clef* and a work of historical fiction that allows Fountain to capitalize on the gravitational pull of a specific context surrounding an event that was viewed live by 11.3 million people across the nation on a Thanksgiving Day twenty months after the United States invaded Iraq.⁶ It will be interesting to see how Ang Lee manages to work all of this reality into his movie version of the novel, but in the novel, Fountain overtly overplays that hand as he puts this "real" scene and its easily recognizable celebrities to good use.

This contextual grounding is both the novel's crowning achievement and its greatest liability. Fountain would probably agree with Burke's reminder that "literature must always have its 'gravitational pull'" and that literature "must always be directed towards some worldly situation" ("Auscultation" 55). Fountain would also likely agree with Burke's argument that all literature is propagandistic or political to a certain extent. As Fountain puts it in an interview with Edan Lepucki:

> Everything is political, if we're living among other human beings. Certainly everything in a society is political, right down to what we do in bed with other people.... And war is perhaps the ultimate political sphere. Some presentations of the Iraq war—Hollywood movies, especially—have tried to be neutral, to simply present the soldiers' experience on the ground without political commentary. Well, what you get then is a video game.... Any realistic exploration of the war is going to have to include the political element; otherwise it's just not worth the time.

What Fountain seems to intend with this video game metaphor is, as I see it, that he wants to avoid falling into the pattern of the typical war story, one that is conceived from and designed to perpetuate an ideology of combat gnosticism. He disdains the idea that much art about war is designed to normalize war through vicarious experience, and while he definitely hopes to create a realistic exploration of war, he rejects the common artistic purpose of much of war literature that seeks to answer the clichéd question, "What was it like?"

While it is worth noting that many actual video games are overtly obvious with their political commentary, Fountain's metaphor can be well-taken, especially if we consider that he likely is referring to the mass market desire for first person presentations of combat experience.[7] He suggests something close to Roger Stahl's argument in *Militainment, Inc.* (2010) that "video games are increasingly both the medium and the metaphor by which we understand war" (112). Therefore, the line Fountain is concerned with is the fine one that lies between "war porn"—a term popularized by Jean Baudrillard to describe the disturbing photos American troops took of abused prisoners at Abu Ghraib—and reality-based representations of war. Indeed, Baudrillard's description of the Abu Ghraib photos resonates especially loudly in *Billy Lynn*:

> The degrading images of something that is the opposite of an event, a non-event of an obscene banality, the degradation, atrocious but banal, not only of the victims, but of the amateur scriptwriters of this parody of violence. The worst is that it all becomes a parody of violence, a parody of the war itself, pornography becoming the ultimate form of the abjection of war which is unable to be simply war, to be simply about killing, and instead turns itself into a grotesque infantile reality-show, in a desperate simulacrum of power.

While Fountain keeps the soldier's banal experience at the top of an epistemological hierarchy of the war (Billy's firsthand knowledge of the battlefield is *the* one we are to assume as the most pure and unadulterated by the Fantasy Industrial Complex), and much of Fountain's stylistic choices were driven by the ideology of combat gnosticism (the inscription he wrote in my book reads, "I hope I got it right"), the scapegoat mechanism in *Billy Lynn* most certainly eschews political neutrality as Fountain uses it to highlight and criticize the public's pornographic fascination with war.

At one point in Fountain's novel, a richly dressed and intricately manicured woman accosts Billy in a luxury VIP lounge so she can tell him about the night the video of Bravo squad's famous firefight broke on the evening news:

> I thought that [my husband] had lost his *mind*. I hear him *screeeeeming* in the media room and I *ruuuussshhh* downstairs to find him *standing* on my good George Fourth library table, in, my *Gohd*, his *cow-boy* boots, doing this *Rocky* thing [193; italics original].

The husband, a man named March Hawey, listens along, nodding, and then simply adds, "It was cathartic" (193). These are the type of people we are supposed to judge as fools, to consider with contempt, as horribly misguided and controlled by the spectacles they desire and consume with orgasmic gratification. Billy reluctantly sees them so, as well, pausing in his narration long enough to emphasize that word: "*cathartic*" (193). For Billy—and for us—March Hawey is a clown; he is little more than a "craggy-faced granddad," a Texan who is "famous mainly for being rich and famous" with a "kindly rumpled sag of his narrow features" and an "elfin tweak of his eyes and ears" (192). This is the strength of *Billy Lynn's* comic frame and the perspective by incongruity it invites. We can see how this man and his wife turn Billy's war into one of Baudrillard's "grotesque infantile reality-show[s]," but we are not encouraged to despise either one as a villain. They never become more than clownish fools following self-serving motivations.

Billy quickly notes this, and he notes that his televised war heroics provide little more than a "titillatory chill" for people like Hawey, his wife, and the growing group that forms around him during this pregame gathering (194). The recorded firefight includes video of Billy running through a hail of gunfire to save a wounded friend—Hawey uses "John Wayne" as a verb to describe it (193)—so the group pumps Billy for more information. Ironically, however, the video, a visual documentation of experience, isn't enough to tell them everything they need. They want what Billy has. They say they want to know how war feels, but Billy's version of war offers nothing more to the crowd than the video; thus, as he says, he has no choice but to give them the easy out, what he calls "the payoff" (194). He thanks his training, and he makes a joke about not running out of ammo, and everyone explodes in an orgasmic release of laughter and a "vigorous round robin of socializing" (194). It takes much more than the "real" video or the "real" warrior's firsthand combat testimony to replace experiential ignorance with the clarity of empathetic understanding. The setting, the mode of communication, the adulatory atmosphere: none of these contribute to an appropriate manner by which one can ask or answer questions about war, death, and state-sponsored violence. Billy may be desired and needed, but just far enough for civilian consumers to achieve a visceral, bodily response to *their* war, not his. They all have seen what he saw (via video), but in that consumption, the actual witness of war is rather irrelevant to the cathartic exchange of war experience when it is translated into entertainment. As Billy muses, the footage of Bravo's firefight can be located online by searching for "Bravo snuff movie" or "America's throbbing cock of justice" (288).

Billy clearly is sullied by the experience, but he is well aware of his role:

> In a way it's so easy, all he has to do is say what they want to hear and they're happy, they love him, everybody gets along. Sometimes he has to remind himself there's no dishonor in it. He hasn't told any lies, he doesn't exaggerate, yet so often he comes away from these encounters with the sleazy, gamey aftertaste of having lied [194].

Fountain's satire explores this distance between the banality of the experience and the banality of its consumption. Still, though the novel has been reviewed dozens of times in print and online, there seems to be little agreement on how one should generically align *Billy Lynn's Long Halftime Walk*. On the cover, Karl Marlantes calls it "the *Catch-22* of the Iraq War." This clever blurb is not particularly illuminating, but a number of critics grab it and use it to situate their own reviews of the novel. David Lawrence, for one, suggests that *Billy Lynn* is not satire because *Billy Lynn* differs from Heller's work as far as the target of critique is concerned (90). Heller's target, Lawrence says, was the bureaucracy of war, whereas Fountain's is contemporary American society. Lawrence is right of course, at least partially, but the distinction he marks between the two works doesn't necessarily mean Fountain's work is best read as unsatirical realism. Just because their targets are different does not mean the authors use radically different satirical techniques, though, of course, they do indeed use different satirical modes. Khaled Hosseini agrees with Lawrence, but he doesn't completely discard the label of "satire" as it applies to *Billy Lynn*. He says, "I feel like it's a book that's grounded in reality, with scraps of satire, whereas *Catch-22* was satire, with scraps of reality." Matt Gallagher, in his *Daily Beast* review, writes—essentially—the same thing: "No, *Billy Lynn* isn't satire topped with sprinkles of realism. It's the exact opposite." Carolyn Kellogg, comes down—reasonably—on the other side. In her *Los*

Angeles Times review, she points out that "Fountain's novel is not a work of realism; it's an über-story, defined by irony and metaphor."

One might suggest that all of these critics really are saying the same thing, that *Billy Lynn* conveys its propagandistic message with a blending of satire and hyper-realism. And in that sense, they all would be right. Both satire and realism ask us to suspend our disbelief and accept the constructed world of the text instead. And both satire and realism insist that, in that suspension, a lasting rhetorical goad can invade a reader's psyche. Given that the vast difference between "realism," the literary style, and the objective fact of "reality," satire can absolutely seem as real (or even more real) as a work of realism. This balance is difficult to maintain, as Burke reminds us in his essay "Realisms, Occidental Style" (1982): "Though the realism of literature does give us the *feel* of reality, as non-literary documents cannot, it can provide no assurance that the *verisimilitude* of a fiction is the same as the *truth*" (47; italics original).

But what *is* this novel? Since *Billy Lynn* is most notable for this unique pop-culture conception and targeted critique of popular culture (unique, at least, as far as contemporary war fiction is concerned), ridicule seems to be its defining trait. The hero Billy Lynn is haunted by the death of a close friend in combat. Yet, it is most certainly *not* a tragedy or an accounting of the human cost of war, though tragic elements are shot throughout the narrative. It isn't a chronicle of a battle or the redemption of a disillusioned soldier or the examination of one fighting man's conscience, though all of that happens at varying degrees during the narration. *Billy Lynn* redirects our gaze as we reobserve various spectacles: a televised football game, a televised halftime show, a televised firefight. Everything in the book has its cheerleaders: the NFL, Beyoncé, war. Yet, the difference between these agents and their auditors is only a matter of degree. The implication of their commonalities, as Fountain establishes it, is that spectacles, not reality, exert the ultimate control in any attempt we may make to understand our post 9/11 war-fighting world. Thus, Fountain resorts to a ratcheted-up, real replication of Thanksgiving Day in 2004, and a varied perspective by incongruity—coupled with a standard scapegoat mechanism—becomes the crutch on which he leans all of his propaganda.

Ben Fountain's War Burlesque

Fountain's work *can* contribute to Burke's project of *ad bellum purificandum*, perhaps despite itself. Consider three of Fountain's chapter titles:

"Dry-Humping for the Lord," (139), "Jamie Lee Curtis Made a Shitty Movie" (155), "Raped by Angels" (226). Fountain's themes are serious, but his tone is irreverent (and bordering on ridiculous) as he deconstructs public adoration for war heroes as a means by which a complicit society ritually purges social guilt for war itself. At times, however, Fountain's style prevents a full or maximum perspective by incongruity. The result is a loss of effectiveness and emotional resonance due to what I see as a somewhat frantic attempt to establish authenticity and authority on the topic of war in fiction written by a civilian. Or, to put it another way, Fountain often panders to the demands of combat gnosticism, stylistically and thematically.[8] Interviewers often ask Fountain about any accounting he might have done to make up for, as David Lawrence puts it, any "experiential gaps" in the writing of his novel (96). Fountain's response is understandable: "This is a serious question," he says, "and one I've thought about a lot. Given that I've never been in the military, did I even have the right to attempt a book like this?" (96). He repeated that worry to Edan Lepucki: "I felt like I had to earn the right to write this book, and the only way I could do that was by working very hard to imagine myself into the soldier's experience, and hopefully write it correctly." (For this reason, I contend that *Billy Lynn* often distracts from building a maximum perspective by incongruity in its burlesque treatment of America's military response to 9/11. "Correctly" writing an experience: there are very few topics of fiction that create such anxiety among its writers.) Fountain even says that writing about war and the military involves a sacrosanct right that must be earned. Meanwhile, there is hardly any other aspect of American life that avoids his eager and confident censure. His respectful concern for soldierly correctness and a deference to some sort of witness-based authenticity not only excuses the American military and the individual soldier from his satire, but it also results in a style that comes across as more anxious than real, a comic frame that often is more contrived than corrective.

Still, because of Fountain's wit, his comic rendering of dialogue, and his acerbic use of humor, the novel is distinctive and worth reading. Considering that war literature is often dominated by pious, triumphant tales of combat and trauma that usually are received as hagiographic representations of soldiers at war, Fountain's approach is fresh and different. As Burke writes,

> The important distinction between comedy and humor, that is disclosed when we approach art forms as "frames of acceptance," as "strategies" for living. Humor is the opposite of the heroic. The heroic promotes acceptance of *magnification*, making the hero's character as great as the situation he confronts, and fortifying the non-

> heroic individual vicariously, by identification with the hero; but humor reverses the process: it takes up the slack between the momentousness of the situation and the feebleness of those in the situation by *dwarfing the situation*. It converts downwards, as the heroic converts upward [*Attitudes* 53–54].

Indeed, Fountain's treatment of the many actual references in his novel takes us behind the scenes of a carefully controlled performance (a televised football game) and a chaotic one (a televised war). Billy Lynn is the hero of both situations. He is our witty narrator, and he is the public's Silver-Star-wearing protagonist during a battle caught on tape. So intertwined humor "takes up the slack" between the two situations. Billy confronts both, and his character is adequately great in the face of both violence and entertainment so that the reader and the football fan are allowed vicarious identification with Billy's greatness.

Billy provides a cathartic purging for every person he encounters as both the hero and the scapegoat, and by the end, Billy is almost happy to accept the role of the martyr. Of course, as Burke reminds us, "martyr" is the Greek word for "witness" ("Variations" 178). So, at first, Billy is the heroic agent through which the American public can enjoy a vivid, near-first-person vicarious purging. He bears witness to war, but since the public has the video of his heroics, they don't even need him for vicarious reassurance. As Billy describes the people in his hometown:

> Nice people but they did go on, and so *fierce* about the war! They were transformed at such moments, talking about war—their eyes bugged out, their necks bulged, their voices grew husky with bloodlust. Billy wondered about them then, the piratical appetites in these good Christian folk [86–87].

Satire allows Fountain's comedy to convert the hero scapegoating process downwards. Billy may be comforted with the idea that he is a martyr for American war culture, but these people's bodily responses to his presence baffles him; sometimes, the citizens he meets are such big "fans of Bravo," they "break wind, so propulsive is their stress" (37). However, these tiny cathartic purges—the farts, the bulging veins, the voiced exclamations—are not enough to assuage the public's need for Billy to return to Iraq so that he can carry with him all the filth and guilty admiration they lump on his shoulders during his Victory Tour.

Like Destiny Child's halftime show, *Billy Lynn*, too, is a spectacle. Since it is also part of the Fantasy Industrial Complex, we must accept it in its own terms if it is to resonate with us or convince us at all. Delivered in a rushed colloquial language, much of Fountain's plot relies on an uncomplicated mockery of easy targets (rich Texans, intoxicated citizens quick with "thank you for your service" platitudes, NFL football players). Replete with hyperbolic archetypes and experimental renderings of font and text, the storyline, at times, nears the absurd. In the end, however, Fountain's comic frame and the popularity of his "context of situation" (again, millions watched that game and halftime show) might be all that prevents Fountain's novel from sliding—just barely—into a ribald rant of moral indignation, and this might be why many critics insist that this is more than satire. Here, it is important to remember that comedy has very little to do with mere humor. Humor, as Burke uses the term, includes satire and burlesque and various concepts of the grotesque. Or, as Celeste Condit notes, "comedic" is not synonymous with "the humorous" (355). Rather, Condit says, "humor asks us to laugh against something, whereas comedy asks us to laugh knowingly and sympathetically with something" (355). This is, at times, a difficult feat to achieve in literature that carries such a loud propagandistic message. In the case of post–9/11 war literature, it might be even more difficult and require even more overt stylistic choices like Fountain's, especially when one is obsessed with meeting the expectations of combat gnosticators.

War experience has little place in this novel, yet the satirical distance between experience and imagination is what this novel manipulates and that its various critics accept or discard at varying degrees. Of his concept of the comic corrective, Burke writes:

> A frame becomes deceptive when it provides too great plausibility for the writer who would *condemn symptoms* without being able to gauge the *causal pressure* behind the symptoms.... The progress of human enlightenment can go no further than in picturing people not as *vicious*, but as *mistaken* [*Attitudes* 41].

These are distinctions that Fountain doesn't bother attending to at times. With irony and exaggeration and mimicry, Fountain suggests that we have to laugh at the dealmakers of Hollywood, the massively wealthy, and the famous. As we saw above with March Hawey and his crew, these are the mistaken fools of America. However, Fountain's satire sometimes devolves into vicious ridicule instead of self-reflective dialectic comedy. This is what Burke means when he writes that "the intensity of a book's appeal is always based upon the reader's disposition to 'meet the author halfway'" ("Auscultation" 137). Fountain can only inspire a sympathetic laugh with his humor if the reader is able to see the characters as unaware clowns rather than vicious enemies. This also is the only way Billy and the other soldiers can serve as this novel's convenient motive-revealing scapegoats. If these fools are presented as fools, the novel, then, as Burke says, allows "people *to be observers of themselves, while acting*" (*Attitudes* 171; italics original). *Billy Lynn* is that study, though its comic frame does approach viciousness at times. That is, Fountain's style might ask too much of us as we try to meet him halfway. Of satire and comedy, Burke says, "Its ultimate would not be *passiveness*, but *maximum consciousness*. One would 'transcend' himself by noting his own foibles. He would provide a rationale for locating the irrational and the nonrational" (*Attitudes* 171; italics original). The argument can be made, however, that Fountain asks us to do very little noting of our own foibles. As Burke mentions in his essay "On Catharsis, On Resolution," Aristotle refers to excessive wit as "educated hubris" (349). Fountain's wit often is excessive as he asks "us" to laugh at "them" (the filthy rich, the numbly drunk, the overpaid athlete). Fountain's chosen mode of representation—irreverent comedy and unsubtle satire—results in a book with a gravitational pull toward a propagandistic message that simply cannot be missed or misunderstood.

As Burke posits in "Why Satire? And a Project for Writing One," satire like Fountain's, intended or not, operates as a "possibility of a compromise" (315). Satire, Burke says, is such a limited "offspring" of a historical situation, that it remains balanced between burlesque and successful rhetoric: "satire is universal, but burlesque is factional" (318). Satire, according to Burke, also "enables us to contemplate a situation to which we might otherwise close our minds, by self-deception, or by dissipation" (321). In order to understand the propaganda of *Billy Lynn*, it does matter the extent to which *Billy Lynn* succeeds in creating satirical spectacle as opposed to replicating a definite sense of the real. The narrator is a third-person omniscient voice, but it also is intended to be a witty and energetic stand-in for Billy Lynn's inner monologue, a limited but knowledgeable speaker whose voice comes across as a mix of Fountain's mature cynicism with a teenager's diction. For instance, in the very first paragraph Billy reflects about a hotel lobby full of "overcaffeinated tag teams of grateful citizens" who "trampolined right down the middle of his hangover" (1). This voice may play well in a movie since it can be eliminated without risking damage to the emotional core of the narrative, but in the novel, this language rings slightly out of tune.

For an example of *Billy Lynn*'s narrative blending of the real-seeming teenage language of its hero with the witty and mature observation of its author, one need not go any further than the opening scene when Billy settles in for a limousine ride to Texas stadium. Billy looks out the window, and his thoughts return to Bravo squad's departure from Iraq in an Air Force C-130 two weeks earlier; Fountain pounces on the opportunity to display his propagandistic message in fairly obvious—and far-fetched—terms. As Billy remembers it, "twenty or so civilians of various shades and accents … joined them for the ride" (4). These foreign men, it turns out, were gourmet chefs from all across Europe who had been shipped into Baghdad for some unknown function. "The coalition," Billy muses with a sigh, and then he remembers how these men began "partying hard" with "good whiskey, music blasting from a dozen boom boxes, a forest of Cuban cigars set ablaze" (4). One of these chefs, a "Swede," shows Billy a "calfskin attaché case" chock full of a "gold stash," a mass of "several pounds' worth of chains and ropes and coin, of such purity that they glowed more orange than gold" (5). As Billy remembers it, "the fuselage quickly filled with a witches' brew of smoke" (4), and Fountain—unsubtle to a fault—allows Billy a number of thoughts that belie a rather amazing astuteness for such a character. Of the chef's bag of gold, Billy reflects: "He was nineteen years old and had no idea that his war contained such things, and what a damn shame for him and the rest of Bravo that it has not been won in the two weeks since" (5). Of the throngs of eager hand-shakers Billy and Bravo squad have endured for days, Billy concludes,

> Desperation's just part of being human, so when relief comes in whatever form, as knights in shining armor, say, or digitized eagles swooping down on the flaming slopes of Mordor, or the U.S. cavalry charging out of yonder blue, that's a powerful trigger in the human psyche. Validation, redemption, life snatched from the jaws of death, all powerful stuff. Powerful [6].

This passage displays the novel's satirical voice, one that drives home Fountain's political message throughout the novel. It delivers a stream-of-consciousness, of sorts, one that blends adolescent slang with an adult's humorous commentary. One may argue that such a voice captures the way such a young soldier actually might talk and think, but such a choice is a costly indulgence, especially since it is how Fountain delivers much of his political message. His propaganda comes across brutally, like the punchline of a joke.

The speaker in these opening pages, and everywhere else in the novel, is this Billy-but-not-Billy persona. Fountain explains this technique:

> A lot of these pronouncements about America simply came from trying to put myself in his skin, and seeing as he sees things. And maybe Billy, as a poorly educated, relatively unsophisticated 19-year-old kid from a small town in Texas, isn't having these thoughts per se, not in so many words, but the narrative voice is conveying the substance of what Billy is thinking and feeling. If we could sit Billy down at any one moment and have him articulate precisely what he was experiencing—walking him through the experience, patiently, taking as much time as was needed—this, or something much like it, is what we'd end up with [Lepucki].

The issue here isn't whether or not a nineteen-year-old combat experienced soldier who recently began reading books actually thinks in the same language of the passages, nor is the issue whether or not Billy's cerebral experience of reality is a worthy instrument by which Fountain can access Billy's day. The issue, and its effect on Fountain's satire, is that many may find it difficult to slog through Billy's precise articulation of his experience.

Of Mark Twain's satire, Burke writes that "before setting pen to paper, [he] again and again transformed the bitterness that he *wanted* to utter into the humor that he *could* evoke" (*Counter-Statement* 53). The purpose of art and satire, as Burke sees it, is to evoke emotional responses in one's reader; it is not merely an opportunistic mouthpiece for a satirist's cynicism or frustration. As Burke writes, "the self-expression of the artist, *qua* artist, is not distinguished by the uttering of emotion, but by the evocation of emotion" (*Counter-Statement* 53). Thus, one can recognize Jim and Pudd'nhead Wilson and Huck Finn and Tom Sawyer even today. Fountain does not restrain his bitterness at all. He explains in an interview for National Public Radio:

> And when the initial impulse for the book came to me, it came to me with the notion of it needed to sound a certain way. There's got to be a certain kind of rhythm or speed to it. And it seemed, you know, from the very start, the correct rhythm, the correct sound for this book was going to be a headlong, you know, reckless, full-bore kind of rhythm to it. And I wanted to try to capture the intense experience that Billy and the other Bravos are having. I mean, this very vivid, almost overwhelming sensory experience—I wanted to try to capture that in the language—not just the images that the language is evoking but in the sound of the language itself. I didn't want to give the reader a rest [Sullivan].

Some readers need a rest though. "Vivid," "sensory," "reckless": these motives determine every word of the novel, and they drove Peter Molin, in his blog about war and art to describe them as the "hopped-up razzmatazz style of Tom Wolfe, with lots of over-the-top figures of speech and nonstandard ways of arranging text on the printed page to represent speech and sound" ("Thank You"). In the end, however, many of Fountain's choices highlight the novel's artifice rather than disguising it or displaying the "intense experience" of its characters. The result is what Burke identifies as an outdated tool of rhetoric, one that deploys invective and blame as artistic resources; such "stylistics of vituperation," Burke says, have limited effectiveness in modern "aesthetic satire" ("Dramatism" 328).

Perhaps Fountain's concern with "getting it right" refers to his preparation of a novel easily adaptable into a movie script; perhaps he has no worry that his language may cause his novel to wither as lasting satire. After all, he already has his own movie deal, something Billy Lynn and Bravo squad never get from their dealings with Norm Oglesby, who makes them a paltry, insulting offer toward the end of the novel. "Stylization is inevitable," Burke reminds us, and as Fountain ratchets-up the realism under the burden of seeming "real" and "authentic," he overcompensates to the point that his war novel can easily be read as accidental burlesque or dismissed as contextually-limited satire (*Philosophy* 128).

Fountain utilizes a number of mechanisms that can seem hyper-realistic, hyper-satirical, hyperbolic, or right on target, depending only on the resonance of the language and the transcendence of the novel's symbols for the individual reader. In Burke's estimation, "'pure' literature, as distinguished from 'propaganda' literature, would simply be literature 'weighted' as regards broader or less burning issues (preferring perhaps those issues which burn with the 'hard, gemlike flame')" ("Auscultation" 137). Beyoncé, a professional football game, Thanksgiving Day, Texas, sexy cheerleaders: all of these are effective symbols that *could* allow *Billy Lynn* a certain lessening of its propagandistic weight. Yet, war, 9/11, corruption, the decision to invade Iraq, ambiguities like freedom and patriotism: these burning issues add sufficient weight to *Billy Lynn* so that it falls closer to the extreme of utterance that is propaganda. Its ability to gravitationally pull us depends on the resonance of *Billy Lynn*'s voice and the ease by which a reader can draw any feeling of strategic ambiguity from its satire. After all, Burke says, "the satirist attacks *in others* the weaknesses and temptations that are really *within himself*" ("Why Satire?" 317).

Fountain rightly notices that there are fascinating rhythms and spoken accents in the language of a super-patriotic Texas, the tones of a hermetically sealed military, and the everyday speech patterns of a group of combat-hardened adolescents. In order to capture the "sound of the language itself" as it might be related by a teenager who barely graduated from high school, Fountain uses countless colloquialisms and slang expressions. For example, Hollywood is referred to as "Ho-wood" (7), and Billy describes being hung over and drunk at the same time as a "kind of sickly-sweet emo-funk" (11). One might argue that this is how young people talk and think today, that such terministic screens capture the language of a younger generation. For instance, the slang term "Dawg" appears sixteen different times throughout the novel, and it isn't always part of dialogue; Billy addresses an invisible "Dawg" in his thought processes too. The same is true for the word "Yo" (meaning something close to "hey"). "Yo" appears nineteen times in the novel, and, like "Dawg," five of them are not part of dialogue. Such "brutalization" and "over-bluntness"—as Burke describes "naturalism"—drives Fountain's narration (*Philosophy* 128).

In his drive to render such language as "full-bore" and as "headlong" as possible, Fountain also resorts to the copious use of italics, capital letters, bold face font, phonetic spellings, and an abundance of exclamation points. The officer in charge of this group of young adults is a hard-of-hearing, combat-wounded man named Major McLaurin. When one of the soldiers tries to get his attention in the opening scene, the text reads, "He turns to Major Mac and slows down his rate of speech to moron speed. 'MAY-JURH, MACK-LAAUUURIN, SIR! SAR-JINT, HOLLI-DAY, HERE, SAYS, YOU'RE, GAY" (3). Since the entire novel is set at the Cowboys' football game amid a cacophony of sounds, and Billy is increasingly intoxicated as the day progresses, Fountain tries to capture and express that noise in word clouds; important words haphazardly dot the page in a mocking rendering of a Texas accent and clichéd expressions. This display of the manner in which a drunk teenager might encounter such noise in a crowded stadium occurs six different times through the novel (2, 38, 45, 120, 148–149, 152). In one such smattering, a number of "Bush-isms" cascade down the page: "terrRr," "Eye-rack," "Sod'm," "nina leven," "dih-mock-cruh-see" (38). Fountain deploys a similar technique for the lyrics of the national anthem (203–207) and Destiny Child's halftime music (229–231). It engages the reader in some kind of phonetic game of sounding-it-out that is, for a fleeting moment, slightly enjoyable. Yet, in Fountain's effort to make the novel "sound" right, it rings false at times.

Such narration doesn't give the reader a rest, and it also doesn't require any sort of constructive imagination. "Moron speed" and the slur "gay" may be clever kitsch expressions that teenagers in the military use often, and the same may be true for "emo" and "scrooge" and "infilled." They also could, possibly, suggest that the young and unread do much of America's fighting. Indeed, these issues are directly discussed later in the novel when Billy and another soldier smoke marijuana with a dish washer in a hidden corner of Texas Stadium (69). The attempt to reduce language into phonemes also runs the risk of too much specificity. Without nuance, such examples of how soldiers really talk come across as dated replications of clichéd teenaged speech and little more.

David Lawrence suggests that the men of Bravo squad are "instantly recognizable to every person who's ever worn a uniform" (96). They barely are to me, and I don't think recognizing these "types" is dependent on insider knowledge about the military. The only way I understand the type these characters are drawn to represent is because they are the common characters of so much other war literature—there is a harsh but respected NCO, a clueless officer (or in this case, a literally deaf one), and a young hero involuntarily thrown into military service (Billy destroyed the car of his sister's boyfriend after a bad breakup, and the Texas judge offers either jail time or service in the Army). These men are caricatures that imply very little depth of character beyond the page. And thus, the members of Bravo join a long list of other perishable elements in the novel. Destiny's Child will be an obscure reference to a forgotten pop music group in another ten years, if it isn't already. There also is a sustained joke about Hillary Swank's tendency to play masculine roles in movies (she is rumored to be interested in playing the role of Billy Lynn if Bravo ever succeeds in selling the movie rights to their story). Many of these contextual mechanisms (or weightings) of *Billy Lynn* carry a definite shelf life, and we must take care to not read it "straight" or we would ascribe the untenable attitude of superiority, of being "holier than thou" to Fountain and his propaganda (*Counter-Statement* 183). As Burke says, "If a work of art were perfectly adapted to one situation, by this very fact its chances of subsequent perfection would be eliminated, as the identical situation will not recur" (*Counter-Statement* 181).

Ernest Hemingway finds similar problems in the dialogue of John Dos Passos' *Three Soldiers* (1921). He calls it the "'Twenty-three skidoo' and 'Ish ka bibble' school of American writing":

> There are certain words that are a permanent, but usually unpublishable part of the language. They are how men have talked actually, when under stress for hundreds of years. But to substitute slang expressions for these words, slang being a language which becomes a dead language at least every three years, makes a defect in writing which causes it to die as fast as the slang expressions die [Intro xvii].

Burke, like Hemingway, also singles out Dos Passos' style. Burke begins by calling him a "naturalist" (*Philosophy* 126). Dos Passos, Burke says, is a practitioner of the "'hard-boiled' style" that affects a kind of "academic school of naturalism" (126). All of this holds true for Fountain's mechanisms outlined above as well, and it is my argument that all of his stylistic decisions reflect his anxiety over meeting the aesthetic criteria for realism that today reigns as *the* critical approach to war literature: the ideology of combat gnosticism. What the language and the sometimes forced plot turns of *Billy Lynn* leave us with is a sort of palimpsest. Fountain has slightly effaced a moment cemented in time, an event fixed on YouTube and the archives of the National Football League. That makes it attractive and compelling, at least for the moment.

The Mortification of Billy Lynn

Despite its "over-caffeinated" style (as Mary Beard describes it), *Billy Lynn* bears examination according to Burke's scapegoating mechanism.

As Billy and his buddies move around the stadium, the scene in which they find themselves modifies all of their pronouncements, and pronounce is all they can do. The agents of *Billy Lynn* never really act unless we consider the soldiers' speech-acts as their only examples of agency. Their "utterances," as J.L. Austin would define them, are "performatives" only; or, as Austin writes, "to say something is to do something" (109). The members of Bravo squad (the agents, or act-ers) achieve articulacy according to the scenic conditions of the stadium and the shifting demands of each successive mini-scene. During war and their televised "Battle of Al-Ansakar Canal," they had agency, but inserted as they are into Texas Stadium, they mark time until they go back to Iraq by getting drunk, putting rowdy football fans in sleeper-hold headlocks, making out with cheerleaders, and getting in fights with stagehands from the halftime show. The reader is aware of this rounding out of their characterizations, but these physical "acts" all are hidden from the watchful and admiring eyes of the public. So, their agency is only located, as Austin would describe it, within their "locutionary acts" (109).

Failing to maintain the appropriate level of military bearing—or, failing to maintain their fittingness for their eventual scapegoating—through the appropriate speech-act is what Sergeant Dime, the group's leader, continuously calls "flaking." In the opening scene, as Billy ponders the strip clubs from the previous night and a "pale, spongy Twinkie of a human being crammed into starched blue jeans and fancy cowboy boots" who accosts him in the hotel lobby, he gets a little too introspective (1). As the narrator-Billy voice puts it, "Billy subsides into a gnarled, secret funk" (2). Sergeant Dime immediately notices Billy's "secret funk" and points it out to the group. "Billy," he says, "you're flaking on me" (3). So Billy's goal for the day becomes avoiding humiliation—via indirect speech-acts—in the face of adulation, or as he thinks of it silently, "no sir, thank you sir, I respectfully refuse to act like a moron, *sir*!" (10). This cheesy line might draw groans from any close reader, but it shows us how Billy and Bravo squad act in public by speaking, or better yet by not speaking, so they can remain the public's convenient scapegoats. Moreover, they all accept this role by modulating their diction and utterances according to the attendant social situation, all in the attempt to avoid flaking.

Fountain sets up the scene with the Jumbotron hailing the "HEROS OF AL-ANSAKAR CANAL!!!!!!!" (37). Scores of "well-adjusted citizens" descend upon the squad, mobbing them with handshakes and backslapping (37). Billy assumes what he calls, "the stance." Or, as the narrator-Billy voice describes it:

> Billy rises and assumes the stance for such occasions, back straight, weight balanced center-mass, a reserved yet courteous expression of his youthful face. He came to the style more or less by instinct, this tense, stoic vein of male Americanism defined by multiple generations of movie and TV actors, which conveniently furnishes him a way of being without having to think about it too much. You say a few words, you smile occasionally. You let your eyes seem a little tired. You are unfailingly modest and gentle with women, firm of handshake and eye contact with men [37].

Through this "stance" and a "few words," Billy passively accepts another load of public guilt, but he can only do so if he dons the proper mask. And this mask works wonders: "people totally eat it up.... They mash in close, push and shove, grab at his arms and talk too loud" (37). As these "affluent people" greet and accost Billy they "tremble" and they "quiver" with cathartic possibility (39). They "breathe in fitful, stinky huffs," for this "is the war made flesh.... His ordeal becomes theirs and vice versa" (39).

The entire novel follows this pattern as Bravo squad tours the stadium and mixes with the masses, and the soldiers are eager participants in the exchange as well. After all, their compliance affords them rare access to the inner sanctums of the stadium's society, and their potential failure as scapegoats lends the novel a much-needed sense of suspense. When they are treated to a Thanksgiving meal in the "Stadium Club" where "the carpet is coal-slurry gray, the furnishings a scuffed, faux-baronial mélange of burgundy vinyls and oxblood veneers reminiscent of a 1970s Holiday Inn," they are already drunk, but their speech-acts push the mask firmly back in place (51). As a number of "nearby millionaires" greet Bravo squad, Billy's mind again begins to wander, and Sergeant Dime "woofs" across the table, "Billy! You're flaking on me" (54). When a "ruddy fellow" sits down at the table and tells them all about his family's oil company, the "Bravos fold their hands and look down at their plates" (65). When the man is done speaking, Bravo squad responds together, literally. Sergeant Dime says something bland to the man in response, and then he asks, "Isn't that right, Bravo?" (65). They answer, "instantly, with gusto, **Yes, Sergeant!**" (65; italics and boldface original).

Fountain's decision to exaggerate how an adored and disciplined group of soldiers may actually behave in public is part and parcel of his propaganda and his capitulation to combat gnosticism. A certain audience may find such pandering to clichés of military behavior tiring, but that might be the whole point, though, as Fountain emphasizes the way that combat soldiers quite often become passive symbols of purgation within the Fantasy Industrial Complex. The public sees and hears what it wants to hear; the soldier sees what he wants; the reader sees something else. All consider their perspectives truth-providing. In public, Fountain's scapegoats stand at attention and say "sir" and "ma'am" and snap off sharp salutes during the national anthem. When the public's gaze is turned away, however, they belch (23); they "dip" chewing tobacco and spit the juice into "spit cups" (217). They sneak drinks, smoke weed, and talk about blowjobs at the strip club from the night before (69). When they meet Norm (né Jerry Jones) and his wife, Billy gets an erection—"her bitchiness makes him a little bit hard" (112). The civilians in *Billy Lynn* can thus reject any admission that these soldiers are just normal young men with flaws and questionable decision-making skills, but the reader is privy to these soldiers' normal acts, acts that more fairly and accurately paint them as immature adolescents having fun before they go back to war and the threat of death.

The hero's mask begins to slip, though, and we join Sergeant Dime in his worry that they all might fully "flake" and cheat the adoring public out of their cheap redemption. At one point, Billy talks to a businessman and asks marijuana-fueled questions full of childlike wonder: "I mean, okay," Billy asks the man, "like where do you start, where does the money come from for, well, the stadium?" (119). Billy keeps sneaking more drinks, with more frequency, and Sergeant Dime builds the suspense—really, the novel's only plotline—by continuing to accuse Billy of flaking and reminding him that they will be back "in the shit in two days" (121, 123). All of their scene-shifting passive action takes its toll on Bravo as a whole, and as they are repeatedly reminded of their sign-carrying significance, that "their fame is not their own" (28), they get increasingly close to breaking the unspoken contract that they are to be this society's purgative victims.

As we near the halftime show, the threat of Billy's flaking keeps the narrative moving. During a pregame press conference, Billy makes eye contact across a crowded room before the game with a born again Christian cheerleader named Faison. Billy is increasingly concerned with the status of his own virginity, and after a five-minute conversation, Billy and Faison grope each other behind the stage backdrop, and Faison achieves an orgasm. The plot here is somewhat anemic in its contrivance, but its coarseness highlights the importance of Billy's proportional response. The narrator-Billy even admits that the sexual encounter is rather unlikely: "It occurs to him to wonder was it even real. It's too perfect, just exactly the sort of delusion a desperate soldier would dream up" (159–60). It is a necessary distraction, though, and just enough of a release for the reader (and Billy) to get through the looming halftime show. Such an improbable plot twist may be horribly off-putting, but it deepens Billy's status as an object to be admired, desired, used, and then discarded.

Four: The Comic Corrective and Fountain's *Billy Lynn*

We follow Billy around Texas Stadium and observe his growing frustrations with his fellow Americans, or, as his refrain goes, "Oh my people" (23, 125, 212, and 298). But we need not worry that someone is going to discover the two lovers during their ridiculous sex scene any more that we need to worry that he will follow through with his daydream of running off to a Texas ranch with this cheerleader instead of returning to Iraq. Fountain may abuse his plot, but in such moments, when Billy is allowed to act like a preoccupied teenager, Fountain's satirical choices reinforce Billy's fitness as a scapegoat. Billy's single-minded obsession with sex and self keeps him from getting angry with his well-meaning sister (who wants him to go AWOL), and it allows us to accept his worry, brief though it is, about his mother in the event that he is killed in combat. He does so in a manner befitting any nineteen-year-old with a martyr complex: "All ego aside," he thinks, "it would be awful for her, possibly fatal, though not right away. He envisions a long slow process of interior numbing-out" (255). Billy may sound like a well-read, intellectually mature, and cleverly cynical cultural critic (even though he barely graduated high school and just started reading books), but he never fails in his role as our unsullied hero despite his teenager shenanigans. Instead, he survives two cheerleader make-out sessions with his virginity well intact, and he politely rejects his sister's offer to go AWOL. He won't flake on Sergeant Dime, and he won't flake on the grand narratives of war that make him feel most at home in Iraq. As the reader's convenient scapegoat, the sexual tension of his meetings with the cheerleader, the negotiations about Bravo's movie rights, and the other obnoxious things Billy does and says repeatedly serve to reassure us that Billy probably will think like a teenager in Iraq and ignore the moral implications of his agency in war. He worried Dime and the reader, but he will continue as our scapegoat. Who can blame a virgin-hero for doing what we asked him to do? That is what Fountain highlights with his novel's construction; the Fantasy Industrial Complex version of war allows us all to displace responsibility for the negative byproducts of the war.

Still, by the time the halftime show finally arrives, Bravo squad teeters on the balance between symbol and human, between flaking and maintaining their roles as scapegoats. "Short of blood sacrifice or actual sex on the field," the narrator-Billy voice muses as they take the stage, "you couldn't devise a better spectacle for turning up the heat" (235). One of the Bravos nicknamed Lodis is almost too drunk to stand. Another soldier, when he does mount the stage, is driven to tears by the "prime-time trigger for PTSD" of the halftime show (230). The narrator-Billy voice complains about being so manipulated: "It's not right. Nobody said anything about this. What might be merely embarrassing in real life is made obscene and hostile by TV" (239). The halftime show goes off without a hitch, though; the mask stays in place, and Beyoncé entertains the masses with Bravo squad right there at her side.

The climactic halftime show does end with an odd scuffle between stagehand roadies and the soldiers, and that fight carries over into the novel's final scene, but in its contrivance, this silly fistfight side story barely registers in the novel's scene-act-agent ratio. When they all get back to their seats after the halftime show, Sergeant Dime gives a flaking soldier named Sykes a "big fat Valium" (he just carries them around for just such an occasion), and they all settle in for the end of the game and the end of their Victory Tour (260). When they do speak again, they manage to speak again as one, with only one slang-driven term, to turn down Norm's pathetic offer. "Sorry, guy," Sergeant Dime tells Norm, "but fitty-five (the offer is for $5,500 each) don't cut it. And Bravo speaks as one on this" (283). In Burkeian terms, however, their "Victory Tour" is revealed as nothing more than public "advertising" for "courage and individual sacrifice for group advantage" that "enable[d] the humble man to share the worth of the hero by 'identification'" (*Attitudes* 35). And so, in the end, Billy redeems us all, for the hero's symbolic death (Billy's return to Iraq) allows him to "risk himself and die that others may be *vicariously* heroic" (*Attitudes* 36). Reunited and past any further threats of further "flaking," Bravo can return to Iraq, and we are ready to see them go, with our shame in tow.

In what I consider the cleanest passage in the entire book, one not cluttered with excessive slang or fouled with italics or phonetic translations of sound, Fountain's narrator—Billy—discusses the lasting conflict between war's experience and the problems that might prevent it from leading to a useful epistemology afterward:

> For the past two weeks he's been feeling so superior and smart because of all the things he knows from the war, but forget it, they are the ones in charge, these saps, these innocents, their homeland dream is the dominant force. His reality is their reality's bitch; what they don't know is more powerful than all the things he knows, and yet he's lived what he's lived and knows what he knows, which means what, something terrible and possibly fatal, he suspects. To learn what you have to learn at the war, to do what you have to do, does this make you an enemy of all that sent you to war? [306].

To repeat this chapter's epigraph from Burke, "The artist is like the man who cried 'Fire!' in a theater. The 'brilliancy' of the fellow arose out of the fact that he shouted the word best adapted to 'touching off' a stampede under these particular conditions" ("Auscultation" 137). The passage above is almost enough to light the fuse below a powder keg; it is almost enough to "touch off" a stampede that may rupture the "dominant force" of the "homeland dream" to which Billy finally surrenders. Whether or not one decides that Ben Fountain shouted elsewhere the appropriate words via the appropriate style in his novel depends on a reader's acceptance of his comic frame and the extent by which one recognizes Billy as a scapegoat. Only then, through the resulting perspective by incongruity, can we learn from *Billy Lynn*, as Condit puts it, that "laughing at our petty jealousies is the prerequisite to calming our war-like fervors" (278).

Five

The Convenient Scapegoat in David Abrams's FOBBIT

> We find our way through this everchanging universe by certain blunt schemes of generalization, conceptualization, or verbalization—but words have limited validity. Their very purpose being to effect practical simplifications of reality, we should consider them inadequate for description as it really is.—Kenneth Burke, *Permanence* 92

While the vast bulk of the American war literature that has received the most critical attention from our post 9/11 wars might indicate otherwise, comedy and satire have emerged as flexible vehicles by which an author can vigorously examine the way these wars have been fought and justified to a complicit public. Ben Fountain's *Billy Lynn's Long Halftime Walk* is a hyper-realistic attempt to present American citizens and their use of soldiers as pawns in a perverse moneymaking game. Fountain blends an overt political message with his version of a contextually specific historical moment in order to affect an extended attack on American pop culture. David Abrams's war novel *FOBBIT* (2012) takes a similarly colloquial and satirical tack, but it differs vastly as far as Kenneth Burke's concept of the comic corrective and his scapegoat mechanism is concerned. As such, *FOBBIT* merits analysis beyond the basic, reflexive laughter it pushes to the forefront of both its construction and its reception.

As Kenneth Burke says of comedy and the comic frame, it "is neither holy euphemistic, nor holy debunking—hence it provides the charitable attitude toward people that is required for purposes of persuasion and cooperation, but at the same time maintains our shrewdness concerning the simplicities of 'cashing in'" (*Attitudes* 166). Indeed, when the subject of literature is war and when the agents of that war are also the artists, there is an urgent ethical imperative to incorporate humor in contemporary American war literature, to bring laughter to otherwise

Five: The Convenient Scapegoat in David Abrams's FOBBIT

serious topics. Thus, humor and irony allow Abrams a frame by which he can shrewdly persuade his readers that today, when Americans go to war, a massive bureaucracy goes with them, and the resulting battle doesn't exactly look the way one might expect. In *FOBBIT*, the fighting does not happen in pitched battles in dusty Baghdad alleys; rather, war is fought by office workers, in cubicles. So Abrams is able to pay equal attention to buffoons and cowards in addition to the usual heroes and warriors. These less celebrated aspects of war often remain otherwise ignored or uncommented upon in traditional modes of war fiction. Of Civil War literature, Alice Fahs reminds,

> Instead of merely reaffirming the values of patriotism, discipline, obedience, and endurance, war humor acknowledged that sloth, laziness, cupidity, disobedience, and negligence were also among the values associated with the war. Most of all—and most transgressive of the heroic norms of patriotic literature—war humor made the simple but profoundly subversive point that war was ridiculous [224].

This transgressive place is where Abrams's novel thrives: it subverts the very concept of armed conflict by highlighting the more unappealing traits of warfighting as his text shifts the focus of war from the valorous to the absurd.

For this reason, *FOBBIT* is an important work of contemporary war literature. Abrams, like Fountain, highlights the disconnect that exists between the reality of war and the spin that it undergoes as soon as it passes into the various forms of reportage and art. Since Abrams seems to be primarily concerned with authenticity, he (again, like Fountain) relies on insider nomenclature and countless pop culture references to flavor his novel with authenticity-lending military kitsch. Such a style can be a liability, though. It is as if, the insider language of both novels suggest, war satire cannot be successful without first waving a recognizable flag of experience-based verisimilitude. In a recent review of Michael Pitre's Iraq War novel *Fives and Twenty-Fives* (2014), Helen Benedict suggests that Pitre's "technical descriptions" of an American platoon operating in Iraq ultimately damages the novel's literary worth since it causes the work to "veer away from honesty and towards glamorization" ("*Fives*"). Fountain avoids this by directing his lens away from the combat veteran, while *FOBBIT* suffers from an overreliance on the same stylistic crutch of rendering war into technical and colloquial jargon.

Benedict, a professor in Columbia University's school of journalism and the author of *Sand Queen*, argues that such "description reads like every other macho war novel, dwelling on the technology and jargon of military life rather than on the suffering the military inflicts, thus obscuring the horror of war while adding to the mystique" ("*Fives*"). In *FOBBIT*, rarely does a sentence pass that doesn't include military slang, an awkward military acronym, or a mundane detail that demands further explanation in parentheses or with another sentence. In one of the novel's opening scenes—which comes to be known as the Incident at Intersection Quillpen—a suicide bomber crashes a car full of explosives into an American tank in the middle of a busy Baghdad intersection. The bomb fails to explode, and the following is how Abrams's narrator describes the scene:

> A platoon from bravo Company (under the command of one Captain A. Shrinkle) had been escorting Alpha Company as it returned from mission in Khadhimiya, taking Route Franklin as briefed in last night's update. No issues; everything going swimmingly. Until they got to Intersection Quillpen where, at approximately oh-nine-thirty hours, the convoy of Humvees and tanks was forced to a halt by a herd of goats crossing the road.... Number Three Tank was the first to spot the suspected insurgent vehicle coming at a high rate of speed toward the formation. As the car accelerated up the frontage road, it quickly changed status from a *possible* Vehicle-Borne Improvised Explosive Device to a *probable* Vehicle-Borne Improvised Explosive Device. Gunners from Tanks Number Two and Three immediately applied Force Protection Measures 1 through 4 and would have implemented Force Protection Measure 5 except by that time the VBIED had already rammed into the left rear of Tank Number Three [23].

Unless the reader has driven a tank in Baghdad or is, for whatever reason, familiar with something called Force Protection Measures, it is difficult to wade through such language. To be fair, this is sort of the point Abrams seems to be making with such a style. He may be suggesting that powerful bureaucracies and excessive regulations hinder the effectiveness of the American soldier in war. Official language and contrived nomenclature slows down the readability of a passage like this one just as official procedures put in place by officers and leaders far from the battlefield have similar impacts on actual combat operations. Thus, one might argue, Abrams is merely criticizing such practices by exposing them as ludicrous.

Still, Abrams doesn't fully escape Benedict's criticism. He may question the effectiveness of officialese by displaying its obtrusiveness, but elsewhere in the novel he overtly glorifies American soldiers by celebrating their slang and their colloquialisms. But again this could be seen as another attempt to criticize something by exposing it. In *FOBBIT*, a character named Lieutenant Colonel Vic Duret is a prime example of a soldier we are supposed to admire as one of the few "real" warriors in the novel. However, throughout the narrative, this man becomes a veritable military slang machine as Abrams establishes Duret's personality and individual warrior ethos. Page sixteen alone—toward the beginning of the first chapter that focuses on Duret's warrior status—includes at least six of these awkward constructions: phrases like "*high pucker factor,*" "*manifest destination,*" "battering-ram headaches," "ballsy confidence," "kick the situation's ass," and "back-briefs" (16; italics original). However, just like the scene at the Incident at Intersection Quillpen, it is possible to see such language as a sort of veil, one that is designed to obfuscate and confuse rather than deepen Duret's characterization. At a minimum, it is safe to say that *FOBBIT*'s humor and style challenge us to question the way war and soldiers are managed, controlled, and packaged with language.

However obscure the novel's military jargon gets—indeed, *because* of it—the ethos of hero worship is what Abrams keeps at the center of his story. By illuminating the ludicrous and colloquial alongside the courageous and the official, *FOBBIT* invites a reading that exposes a system and order that is nothing but ridiculous. An army general clips his toenails during an important briefing. Everyone listening in on the conference call can hear the snipping sounds as he moves from toe to toe (182–83). For an entire deployment, one major does little else than play solitaire on his computer (155–56). Another soldier defecates in his commander's helmet and leaves a note that reads, "Have a Nice Day, Shithead" (148). While the novel's overall tone may obscure the destruction that the U.S. military inflicts, and while it may glorify the way people like Duret talk and think, Abrams's narrative style allows him to do something quite complex with his scapegoat mechanism. It affords him a way to critically assess *all* aspects of the society that makes war like the one in Iraq possible, criticism that includes the self-deceptions of American soldiers like Lieutenant Colonel Vic Duret. Abrams's language is annoying at times, but it allows us ample opportunity to note the massive foible that controls each character.

Benedict suggests that only two questions "matter" when one evaluates war literature of any style: "is it honest? And does it glamorize war?" ("*Fives*"). This test is an especially difficult one to apply to comedic treatments of war, but *FOBBIT* does manage to succeed in both regards through the extended scapegoat mechanism and the hierarchical psychosis he sets up in his novel. It also shows us how the typical American soldier likely experiences war, an experience that varies little between those who experience combat and those who don't. His text makes us admit that since buffoons and cowards people America, the cowardly and buffoonish should people Iraq too.

War is anything but glamorous in *FOBBIT* and neither are *any* of its agents. They fart; they curse; they complain; they lack compassion, self-awareness, honesty, and courage. As Abrams explains to David Lawrence, "everybody falls victim to satire at one point or another in the book. I'm an equal-opportunity offender" (169). Such a frank representation of the bureaucratic mess that attends modern warfare, then, stands as both refreshingly honest and painfully valid. In *Attitudes Toward History*, Burke writes that, "Like tragedy, comedy warns against the dangers of pride, but its emphasis shifts from *crime* to *stupidity*" (41; italics original). Stupidity and crime dominate *FOBBIT*, and every character suffers from an overweening sense of pride. Yet, when we analyze Abrams's text according to Kenneth Burke's concept of hierarchical psychosis and trace the scapegoat mechanism it engenders, it becomes clear that, with the proper critical approach, it is indeed possible to mock and criticize war, to treat its agents as stupid or misguided without risking an accusation of ethical insensitivity or unpatriotic propagandizing.

What Is a Fobbit?

Written by an Army public affairs sergeant whose wartime journal provided much of the novel's foundation, *FOBBIT* is set in Iraq in 2005 at a sprawling Forward Operating Base (or FOB) called FOB Triumph. The base is filled with two kinds of soldiers: combat grunts from the infantry (men like Vic Duret) and unfit office workers who never leave the safe confines of the base. The social order on this base follows a universally agreed upon narrative: while the combat grunts fight and die, the supporting force of staff and office workers (Fobbits) remain ensconced in the relative safety of Western-style cubicles spread throughout the passages and rooms of one of Sadaam Hussein's old palaces. There, these support troops count down the days left in their deployments; they craft press releases; and they build PowerPoint presentations. Thus, the hierarchy of FOB Triumph is based on—above all else—the social status that separates support troops and combat warriors, or "door-kickers" as they are called in the novel. Yet, this hierarchy of Fobbits and door-kickers is shaky at best and entirely untenable at worst. By examining the hierarchical psychosis at work within the novel, we can show how the line between a Fobbit and a door-kicker is a vague one indeed, how combat experience is a distinction that differs in very small ways from any other wartime experience.

As Burke sees it, hierarchy and order are principles that drive much of man's life, conflicts, and—most importantly—man's symbolic redemption via the vicarious victimage of a scapegoat.[1] War on FOB Triumph has very little to do with the ways American men and women fight against a tenacious or determined insurgency. The novel isn't a triumphant tale of individual sacrifice or heroic courage in the face of untold or untellable violence, nor is it an investigation into the human toll of war. It isn't about combat or battle or killing in the name of one's country; rather, it is a tale about a group of soldiers who are focused on one mission alone: maintaining the "pyramidal structure" (Burke, *Language* 19) that keeps combat troops and their presumed courage on the top while "supply clerks, motor pool mechanics, cooks, mail sorters, lawyers, trombone players, logisticians" remain relegated somewhat happily to the bottom (1).

As we will see, this order is not easily established. Hierarchies like the one that keeps the Fobbit in his or her place, Burke points out, are made possible by a sort of social mystery, a symbolic "magic" that leads to an overall "hierarchical psychosis" (*Rhetoric* 281–283), and this psychosis creates a "fog of social inequality" (*Rhetoric* 121). H.D. Duncan writes in *Communication and Social Order* (1966), "When the enactment of hierarchy becomes so dogmatic and the stages of development so rigid that doubt, question, or creation of new hierarchies are no longer possible and, indeed, are *punishable*, we enter into the realm of hierarchical psychosis" (122). Or as Burke explains, hypnotic-like linguistic constructions behind the "spirit of hierarchy" introduce "mystifications that cloak the state of division" (*Rhetoric* 141). The poseurs in *FOBBIT* definitely try to "cloak the state of division" between Fobbits and door-kickers with symbolic mystification, and each one tries to explain how the Fobbit deserves his or her lowest spot in the base's class system, but each one ends up looking very much the same: they are all poseurs.

When we pick up *FOBBIT*, it doesn't take long to see how pervasive this particular hierarchical psychosis is on FOB Triumph. Indeed, we are prepared for it before we even open the book, as "Fobbit" is defined on the cover: "Fobbit \'fä-bət\, noun. Definition: A U.S. Army employee stationed at a Forward Operating Base, esp. during Operation Iraqi Freedom (2003–2011). Pejorative." This definition is deliciously general. The nature of being "stationed" at a base in Iraq doesn't really clarify any meaning, nor does "Army employee." Strictly speaking, an "Army employee" could be anyone in any uniform, regardless his job description or his level of exposure to combat. Thus, we are left with one operative word, the final one: "Pejorative." Still, it tells us nothing about *Fobbit*'s negative connotations suggesting instead a vague multitude of reasons for the Fobbit hierarchy. Indeed, the rest of Abrams's novel invites us to do little else than examine the very concept of Fobbit-ness, to closely investigate the way this society manages to socially estrange a thing called a Fobbit.

What is a Fobbit and why is it pejorative? These are the questions Abrams poses, and he does so by giving us definitions and descriptions of the Fobbit from the perspective of five different primary characters, each one delivered in the voice of a common omniscient narrator. With every description, the subject (a less–Fobbity Fobbit) and the object (a more–Fobbity Fobbit) begin to dialectically blend into one. The first one comes from an American soldier named Chance Gooding:

> They were Fobbits because, at the core, they were nothing but marshmallows. Crack open their chests and in the space where their hearts should be beating with a warrior's courage and selfless regard, you'd find a pale gooey center. They cowered like rabbits in their cubicles, busied themselves with PowerPoint briefings to avoid the hazard of Baghdad's bombs, and steadfastly clung white-knuckled to their desks at Forward Operating Base Triumph [1].

So begins the long denigration of the Fobbit delivered here by a self-loathing public affairs office worker. He is the self-described "poster child for the stay-back-stay-safe soldier," the "Fobbitest" of them all (2). To be a "Fobbit" or a "Fobber" or a "Fob Dog," Gooding tells us, is no different than being "a dickless, lily-livered desk jockey back in the States" (3). All of this self-deprecating harshness comes across as hyperbole though, and so we are never quite convinced that things are as Gooding says. And that name—Chance Gooding—it announces the possibility that, despite what this man says in his opening salvo, a Fobbit like him may, eventually, have a "chance" to be "good." Or in other words, a Fobbit may always have a chance to shake the pejorative nature of the label.

The rest of Gooding's opening section continues with more imprecision. The first page announces that a Fobbit wears a uniform, works long hours, and lives near "Baghdad's bombs" (3). However, like the unfocused definition on the cover, all of this could be true of any soldier, combat exposed or not. The mark of a Fobbit, then, is branded somewhere in his character, in his personality. Apparently, that personality is one lacking a sense of selflessness or, more importantly, the opportunity to display it. In theory, this seems to be an easy thing to track, but as the rest of the novel's characters will prove, the eager exposure of oneself to danger is no easy metric. Each one will join Gooding in his disdain for the Fobbit, and each one will muddy the definition further, but no matter how severe Gooding is about himself or how hard he and the others work to mark the edges of a Fobbit, none one of their descriptions ever advances beyond the vague or the bombastic.

Since we get to know Gooding and become increasingly privy to his inner emotions and compassions, his Fobbit-ness ameliorates considerably. Thus, we continually fail to despise him as much as the combat/non-combat/door-kicker/Fobbit hierarchy suggests we should, especially as we begin to meet other Fobbits and other door-kickers. Since Gooding is the only likable character in the novel, we can somewhat forgive him for a sort of cerebral "piety" to a "trained incapacity" that attends his ideas about Fobbit-ness (Burke, *Permanence* 10, 7). The other characters are extremely shortsighted; thus, as we meet them, it is easy to dispute their versions of the same piety as we test each one out for scapegoat worthiness. In the multicolored picture they paint, it is easy to see that Fobbit-ness, like the human impulse to scapegoat, is a sad, unjust social construction. It is an untenable class system based on inequality and separation. Identifying the scapegoat and the hierarchical psychosis in this novel, however, makes it possible for us to bridge the gaps in the pyramidal magic that keep such divisions intact. Just as we find no triumph on FOB Triumph, we can't find any warriors either. This is the implication to be drawn from this novel: the war in Iraq may be driven by an internal American battle based on petty jealousies and grudges. Reducing war heroics into bureaucratic mundanity feels, ironically, somewhat more honest than the typical tale of heroic sacrifice. Dead Americans and dead Iraqis litter *FOBBIT*, but in the end, its scapegoats expose war for what it is, as Burke might say, as nothing but a "hierarchical embarrassment" (*Permanence* 279).

A Good Fobbit Is Hard to Find

When Gooding describes a Fobbit, he is not really describing a person. Rather, he is describing the "symbolic fog" that makes the hierarchy of Fobbit-ness possible. In *Permanence and Change*, Kenneth Burke explains:

> "Order" *as such* makes for a tangle of guilt, mystery, ambition ("adventure") and vindication that infuses even the most visible and tangible of material "things" with the spirit of the order through which they are perceived. In this sense, man as symbol-using animal must perceive even his most "animalistic" traits dimly through the symbolic fog arising from the social order of which he is part [288].

Only able to "dimly" recognize his own "animalistic" traits in that mix of "guilt, mystery, ambition, and vindication," Gooding is really describing the order that he and the other characters subscribe to, a social order that needs a Fobbit's symbolic existence for the order's very survival. A seductive and deceptive symbolic fog creates Fobbit-ness and holds him in that lowest place on FOB Triumph's hierarchy, but problems exist in that structure. It might foster unity, but it also creates scapegoats.

Gooding's hierarchical psychosis drives him to self-identify as a Fobbit so that he can join the rest of FOB Triumph in a collective effort to enact what Burke terms "congregation by segregation" (*Dramatism* 29). Congregation by segregation, as Burke describes it, is the habit of groups of people to "spontaneously identify ourselves with some groups or other, some trends or other" and then use that "identification" to establish a common enemy (29). Thus, after "segregation," the group can make use of the "tremendous pressures toward a *sacrificial* motive which the nature of human congregation builds up" (29). This human habit, to delineate society according to largely arbitrary categories (eg. Fobbits and door-kickers), is the basis of the hierarchy principle on FOB Triumph. Gooding calls himself a Fobbit, but he does so in order to congregate with the others; he does so to segregate himself from more loathsome Fobbits. Or, better yet, he does so in order to segregate himself from a scapegoat who doesn't fully subscribe to the unwritten but agreed upon concept of Fobbit-ness.

Gooding traces the legacy of the Fobbit and the tension that has long existed between support troops and combat troops: "In another war, REMF was the preferred term," Gooding reports, "but now, in this modern asymmetric theater of operations, there was no 'rear' echelon elite sitting in their motherfucking safe-from-harm shelter" (3).[2] There, in that self-loathing description, lies the need for a scapegoat. In such a "modern asymmetric theater of operations," what happens when it becomes increasingly difficult to distinguish the individual agents within the pyramidal structure of the order? We may both respect Gooding for his self-deprecations, but we also see that he has long ago lost his ability to recognize the extremely fluid nature of the established hierarchy on FOB Triumph. We wonder: where does the tension go when door-kickers and Fobbits start looking and acting very much alike? Instead of challenging the order that shuffles some soldiers to the bottom of the hierarchy, Gooding and his peers insist—repeatedly and confidently—that the hierarchy must be preserved at all costs, but for this to happen, some people must be pushed out. As we will see, the "Army employees" of FOB Triumph impulsively congregate by quarantining themselves from a soldier named Abe Lincoln Shrinkle who fails to wholly identify with Fobbits or with door-kickers, and this failure brings the framework of the hierarchy of Fobbit-ness into question. The challenge for the reader, then, is twofold: we must not only interrogate the ways FOB Triumph identifies a Fobbit and ejects scapegoats, but we also must question the inner workings of the hierarchy itself. Since the novel repeatedly insists that the hierarchy of Fobbit-ness is righteous, the reader can do little else but track the scapegoat mechanism and reveal the hierarchy as unjust.

As Gooding reports, Fobbits and non–Fobbits wear identical uniforms, but his uniform is "neat-pressed" (2) while the "infantry grunts" wear "wrinkled desert camouflage" (3). Gooding elaborates, saying that his "lavender-vanilla body wash" leaves him smelling "as if he bathed in gingerbread" whereas the door-kickers smell of "sweat, road dust, and, occasionally, blood" (3, 4). Other differences between Fobbits and door-kickers, Gooding claims, manifest themselves in the lines of the face. Infantry grunts are "the ones with worry and fear knotting the tight landscape of their foreheads" (3). Fobbits, however, apparently register nothing on their faces; they are merely nagged by the "irritation" and "annoyance" of "what felt like a yearlong camping trip" (3). This schema is a tenuous one, though. Fobbits and door-kickers can *all* own irons; they can *all* access the same washing machines; they can *all* buy the same lavender-vanilla body wash since they all have the same access to the same store. So, from Gooding, we can conclude two things about a door-kicker. He or she does something that makes him or her dirty, and he or she is also apparently held to a different standard of personal appearance than everyone else. After a trip to the shower and a change of clothes, all should be equal again, but a door-kicker is allowed a certain latitude in that regard. Deserving that leniency is not the issue here; the issue is whether or not one can appropriately and fairly apply the dictates of an entire social order with nothing to go on but dirty uniforms and sad faces.

Interestingly enough, all of Gooding's distinctions are based on each distinction's negative, and this explains why he insists on the clarity of a Fobbit's appearance. Just as evil has no meaning without an opposing concept of good, the smell of Gooding's body wash is unnoticeable without the sweaty smell of the door-kickers. A uniform isn't really wrinkly unless a pressed one is nearby for comparison. Without a clean Fobbit for comparison, a door-kicker is just a guy who needs a shower. Likewise, the presumptive heroics of the door-kickers have no meaning without the assumed self-preservations of the Fobbits. Without a public affairs officer sitting at a computer in a cubicle, a door-kicker on a patrol through Baghdad is just a guy or a gal driving around a city in a truck.

In fact, save one anecdote involving a relatively minor character,[3] the door-kickers in this novel never get any opportunity to display superior courage or to show how eagerly they embrace death and danger. Quite on the contrary, the center of FOB Triumph is, without a doubt, the most dangerous place to be for an American soldier. Four door-kickers do indeed die, but they are killed by a luckily-aimed mortar while eating hamburgers at the base's Burger King. Even then, these deaths occur before the events of the novel begin. The only American death that the reader directly witnesses happens on FOB Triumph when Captain Abe Shrinkle—the novel's eventual scapegoat—is killed while floating in a clandestine swimming pool in the very heart of Fobbit country (more on this later).

After Gooding, the second perspective of the Fobbit comes from Lieutenant Colonel Vic Duret. A champion door-kicker, Duret is our sorely mistaken enforcer of the Fobbit code. Initially, he is introduced negotiating the incident involving the suicide bomber and the American tank at Intersection Quillpen. The commanding officer on the scene, Abe Shrinkle, has failed to act decisively enough, so Duret must disarm the car bomb without killing the American troops inside the tank. This, we are supposed to conclude, is how one acts if one isn't a Fobbit, and Duret thinks this way, too:

> Lieutenant Colonel Vic Duret had come to the point where he hated Fobbits: self-preservationists who never admitted to the fear inside, and instead found ways to stay busy within the boundaries if the triple-rolled concertina wire and walls crenellated with shards of glass. Duret knew of an entire platoon's worth of officers who clung to the security of headquarters, their asses gradually molding into the shape of a chair. Their aftershave reeked of self-importance [95].

Duret's revulsion runs more deeply than Gooding's, but it doesn't take us long to see that what he despises in a Fobbit is really what he despises in himself. He thinks he behaves like a door-kicker during this crisis with the suicide bomber, but when we re-examine the scene, we can see that all he does is stand there, complain about Shrinkle and Fobbits, and make a radio call. He is the picture of self-importance. Instead of displaying competence, courage, or decisiveness, Duret does little else beyond whining. His ire for the Fobbit, delivered as it is in the rather obnoxious thought process of a proud, entitled officer, is just a different version of same hierarchical psychosis as Gooding's.

Duret intends to situate the door-kicker above the Fobbit, but he really manages to display their equality. Duret says he "hated Fobbits" because he has felt and experienced things he assumes the Fobbit never will, emotions that, according to him, justify his superiority complex (95). For Duret, these extreme emotions also disqualify him from any accusation of being a Fobbit. He tells us of "the nut-shriveling terror of careening through traffic" (he mentions his testicles a lot) (96). He congratulates himself for pretending to enjoy "having tea and sautéed camel entrails with the province's sheikh" (96). He recalls "the despair" he felt after his men helped to build a power substation that was bombed a week later (96). Duret also claims the privilege of being familiar with death, with never being "certain whether or not the car pulling up behind them was trunk-loaded with explosives" (96). *"No,"* he concludes, *"Fobbits would never know any of this"* (96). But, as we soon find out, the Fobbits have access to his experience-based epistemology too.

Clearly, a deep disharmony drives this entire hierarchy. Gooding, for one, experiences each one of Duret's special emotions. When the intelligence office reports that an attack on FOB Triumph is imminent, Gooding and his fellow Fobbits' "spines were chilled" by the very thought of "dark figures slipping over the concrete walls, slinking through the concertina wire, hundreds of them trying to overrun FOB Triumph en masse" (177). Yet, instead of congratulating himself as Duret does, he is more honest about his place in the army, and he remains understandably fatalistic about his lack of combat skills, concluding that, if the base is attacked, he is simply "screwed" (178). Gooding lacks a flair for door-kicker bravado when he ponders potential death in combat, but Duret's terror is just as present and just as imaginary. Based on their difference in training, Gooding's terror might even be more reasonable. Besides, we never actually see Duret "careening through traffic," and all we get are euphemisms for his door-kicker actions. For example, the narrator reports that "Duret and his men spent their days running from one molehill to the other, whacking anything that moved with their amusement-park mallets" (104). If the narrator is trying to convince us that a secret knowledge of a secret emotion is available only to door-kickers who have a secret experience, we never witness anything that would allow a resulting epistemology primacy over anything a Fobbit knows, feels, or experiences. Duret claims frustration as an emotion unique to door-kicker experience, but no one in the book experiences more of that particular emotion than the Fobbits. Duret also assumes that his closeness to death and the uncertainty of his own survival is what exempts him from carrying the Fobbit's stink. Yet again, not only does Gooding nearly bleed to death following a botched IV installation after drinking some bad water (291–307), he is closer to the death around him than anyone else. Since he works in public affairs, he is the first step in the onerous system of official notification of the next of kin. He was once a death "virgin," but now, he says, "death was just one of the commodities he traded on a daily basis" in the form of the notification processes he initiates (9). Death once was an unknown for Gooding; now, it is "a matter of course, one more task in a day already filled with a heavy workload" (12). Duret can't even remember the names of the men who are killed at the Burger King.

Gooding never holds a dying man's hand or fights off a horde of fanatic insurgents, but neither does Duret. In fact, the one person to describe Duret as an efficient, respected, and scarred commander of door-kickers is Duret. Thus, his repeated statement that he fears nothing more than becoming a Fobbit never convinces us. As the novel continues, we completely discount his perspective while we witness—again and again—a number of Fobbits experiencing the same emotions of despair, fear, and frustration. When two of the younger troops who work in Gooding's office—both self-proclaimed Fobbits—are sitting guard duty in a tower one evening, their covert lovemaking is interrupted by a mortar attack that barely leaves them alive (5). Do they deserve exemption from the disdain Duret levels a Fobbit's way? Not a chance, as far as the hierarchy of FOB Triumph is concerned. After all, Gooding had already prefaced this particular story with the announcement, "They were all Fobbits, everyone who worked in this palace" (4). But we know better.

After all, Duret lives and works in the palace too, though neither Duret nor Gooding ever note this detail. He even has his own office while the others work in cubicles. We are *tempted* to see Duret as the rest of the base does, and we are *tempted* to admire him as the hierarchy demands, but we can see through the hierarchical psychosis and recognize Duret's inconsistencies about door-kicker supremacy. We can see what he cannot, that what he considers knowledge is really nothing but banal experience reduced to cliché. We can see that his special experience is not all that special, and since nothing he does and nothing he says is courageous or selfless, we are invited to question the distinction between a Fobbit and a door-kicker. There may indeed be a special epistemology to be drawn from extreme suffering and trauma, but this is not the case for the self-described warriors in this novel. Duret tries to claim an epistemological supremacy in this world of war, but his knowledge comes from his Fobbit-hating and his fear of getting fat, of "his ass spreading" (97), of becoming "pale and farty" (125).

After Duret, the reader is given another door-kicker perspective of the Fobbit from Brock Lumley, the guy who actually saves the day during the incident at Intersection Quillpen. There, Lumley, Shrinkle, and Duret are waiting for a robot to defuse the bomb when the suicide bomber stirs to life and reaches for the detonator (38). On cue, Lumley quickly and

Five: The Convenient Scapegoat in David Abrams's FOBBIT

calmly kills the man with a miraculous 200-yard shot to the head, and the Americans all go home safe and sound. A lower ranking door-kicker than Duret, Lumley provides a crucial piece of the Fobbit's fuzzy image. This perspective, the hierarchy seems to say, is the one that we should accept as the least adulterated by bureaucracy and Fobbit self-preservation. After all, during the incident at Intersection Quillpen, Lumley played the role of the cool and collected warrior. However, Lumley's actions are not exactly heroic, and they certainly aren't self-sacrificing. He takes his shot from the safety of 200 yards of distance. Thus, it is difficult to accept his actions as adequate to grant him the highest place in the hierarchy. Yes, his marksmanship is admirable, but it has little to do with the way Gooding and Duret have taught us to conceive door-kicker supremacy.

This scene ultimately serves to establish Shrinkle as our scapegoat and place Duret and Lumley in their highly arbitrary but secure places on the scale of Fobbit-ness. Lumley—the enlisted door-kicker—makes the shot and kills the bad guy. He is on top. Duret—the deluded officer door-kicker—sees the suicide bomber wake up, but does nothing; he just freezes, "standing tall but paralyzed with indecision" (38). This, however, doesn't place him at the bottom because we have Shrinkle to serve as our convenient scapegoat, for he is the nervous and incompetent door-kicker who defecates in his pants, "giving himself completely to the dread and terror of close-order combat and releasing the clench on his bowels" (38). We are distracted by Shrinkle losing control of his bodily functions, but we also note, though the narrator calls this "close-order combat," that nothing resembling close-order or combat ever occurs.

It is from Lumley that we receive our requisite dose of combat gnosticism:

> Each time he came back from patrol, driving through the main gate of the FOB, his spleen rose between his teeth at the thought of all the coddled soldiers who never went beyond the wire. Fuck those high-ranking desk jockeys fat, dumb, and happy with their air-conditioning and the illusion they kept things under control in Iraq just by clicking a few icons on the computer screen, moving units around with a tidy drag-and-drop [41].

In *Permanence and Change*, Burke discusses the "magical" spell that makes people confuse the individual with the status that a hierarchy affords him or her (277). Lumley most certainly succumbs for this seduction. As we can see in his rant above, he only speaks in generalities and never has any real complaints about Fobbits other than the air conditioning they enjoy and the unwarranted job satisfaction he assumes they feel. The magical spell of hierarchical psychosis Lumley is under allows him to claim the qualities attached to the status he enjoys, and he can do so—like Duret—without actually displaying courage or seeing combat or without giving the reader any actual reason to join him in his hatred for "fat, dumb, and happy" non-door-kickers. But Lumley's place is less secure than he thinks. He may have claimed what he considers a rightful seat in his privileged position since he did make an impressive shot, and he did potentially save a number of lives in the process, but his self-pity doesn't quite allow him to advance to hero status. The ambiguity of Fobbit-ness illuminates such an irony: Lumley may be a great marksman, but as the novel progresses, he never becomes more than an unappreciated complainer. He was calm and collected and decisive in one moment, but the reader never witnesses an experience or an act that might in any way justify his self-described insight into war.

As Burke explains, "We take it for granted, that the pyramidal magic is inevitable in social relations, whereby *individuals* whether rightly or wrongly, become endowed with the attributes of their *office*" (279; italics original). Or, as Lumley lamely describes his fellow door-kickers, he and his buddies are all "kick-ass Warriors with a capital *W*" who are doing the "*real* work of Operation Iraqi Freedom" (140, 137; italics original). However, if the plot of *FOBBIT* is any indication, being a kick-ass warrior means driving around Baghdad in a Humvee. Beyond the magical linguistic constructions that keep the hierarchy in place, nothing else in the novel gives the reader any reason to follow Lumley's lead and endow door-kickers with the attributes of their office. Their unspecified efforts claim an epistemological privilege, but it is supported by insufficient information. Lumley's self-righteousness suggests that being a door-kicker might mean nothing more than indulging in extensive self-pity.

This brings us back to the line Gooding draws between door-kickers and Fobbits, the one that marks a soldier's comparable willingness to meet danger. "Let the door-kickers ride around Baghdad," Gooding exclaims, "in their armor-skinned Humvees getting pelted with rocks from pissed-off hajjis. Let *them* dodge the roadside bombs that ripped limbs from sockets and spread guts like fiery paste across the pavement" (4; italics original). To be sure, Gooding never goes "outside the wire," but no door-kickers in this novel ever get their limbs ripped from their sockets or their guts spread anywhere. Fobbits and door-kickers all meet the same hazards. Plus, a number of the "high-ranking desk jockeys" that Lumley despises actually do go outside the wire, but none of them are exempted from the strictly enforced and vaguely defined code of the Fobbit. When a convoy from another base has to stop alongside a dangerous section of Baghdad highway for a broken-down truck and wait for Lumley and Shrinkle to come to their aid, Lumley describes the officer in charge of the convoy as "another member of the Ass-Pucker Club" (142). This Lieutenant is outside the wire; he will probably smell like dust and death after his hazardous drive through Baghdad; worry and fear will probably mark his face. But, still, even he isn't granted full exemption from being a "softy," as Lumley describes him (137).

Gooding at least partially recognizes the definite ruptures in the Fobbit code; so he makes an exception that accounts for the "foolhardy officers gunning for promotion who grabbed every opportunity to ride on patrols" (4). These officers are *not* Fobbits, Gooding clarifies; rather, they are "ghosts" who are "gone outside the wire more often than not" (4). But "ghosts" still can't carry Lumley's proud label of "kick-ass Warrior" because of their concerns with self-promotion: as Gooding sees it, they made "damn sure everyone saw them depart, slurping loud from travel mugs of coffee, uniforms clinking and whickering" (4). But who's to say these men are slurping their coffee *too* loud? Who's to say these so-called "ghosts" seek promotion and recognition over doing the *real* work of Operation Iraqi Freedom alongside Lumley and his men? The cynicism associated with Fobbit-hate may be well founded in reality; it may indeed reflect self-promotion and self-preserving trends and behaviors that are common across the U.S. military, but in *FOBBIT* we are never convinced it is anything *but* cynicism.

Fobbits Who Don't Threaten the Hierarchy Need Not Be Purged

If it is difficult to distinguish Fobbits from non–Fobbits based on Gooding's, Duret's, and Lumley's examples, when we finally get to Lieutenant Colonel Eustace "Stacie" Harkleroad, we are given a perfect candidate for complete Fobbit-ness. No character has fully qualified for the disdain the label contains; so we almost exhale with relief at Harkleroad's cartoon presence. He fits all definitions. A less-dangerous "Gomer Pyle" from Gustav Hasford's 1979 novel, *The Short-Timers* (and the film *Full Metal Jacket*), his characterization nears farce:

> Harkleroad was a thick man. Thick in the way a bowl of risen dough is said to be thick. He filled his uniform amply; in truth, there was more flesh than fabric. When he leaned back in his chair, other soldiers flinched, afraid a button would pop off, come flying across the room, and put out an eye [60].

He is obese. He suffers chronic, spontaneous nosebleeds, and every other soldier he meets hates him. His superiors repeatedly call him a "doofus" (64), as do the troops he is supposed to lead. He is deaf in one ear from the time, years earlier, when he wandered too close to an artillery piece during training (62). In the public affairs office he runs, his second-in-command, a Major, calls him "Harklefuck" and often dreams of how Harkleroad might meet "his death in any number of abrupt, violent ways" (84).

However annoying Harkleroad is as an officer, what marks him as most deserving of the cruelty directed at him on FOB Triumph are the false claims he makes in his door-kicker-modeled emails that he sends home to his mother. These are, as the narrator describes them, "half-truths Stacie Harkleroad kneaded and pulled like Silly Putty" (62). When the four door-kickers are killed while eating at the Burger King, Harkleroad tells his mother that he ran into the carnage and saved lives, an act he compares to "Clara Barton on the battlefield" (119). Later, he completely fabricates a story about militants assaulting the FOB. According to this story, Harkleroad claims that he grabbed a weapon and ran to meet the assault with hand-to-hand combat, only to be pulled away by his superior: "So there you have it Mother—my bravery has once again been thwarted by my duty as a Public Affairs Officer.... Oh the damage I could have inflicted on those blasted Sunnis!" (236).

David Lawrence suggests that the immodest or false brandishing of one's combat bonafides is what Abrams seeks to expose with the novel's satire (163). Certainly, this is a safe analysis, and it is one with which Abrams doesn't disagree. As Lawrence puts it, "it's the soldiers committed to self-promotion over selflessness who find themselves in Abrams crosshairs" (163). Abrams agrees:

> For Fobbits—the ones who rarely go outside the wire—life can be comfortable, safe and mundane. The war is always "out there," far removed from their daily lives—a distant thing that both annoys and frightens them.... These are the guys who'll be spinning yarns down at the American Legion bar in years to come. The guys who were out there in the real shit, facing the real bullets and grenades, they won't talk about it much [163].

While I take considerable issue with Abrams's generality in that final sentence,[4] as far as Harkleroad is concerned, Abrams's point can be well taken. Clearly, the reader is supposed to encounter his fabrications with disgust and use them as adequate grounds to place him on the bottom rung of FOB Triumph's hierarchy. However, that's all they do; these made-up stories of bravado do not require any need for his removal from the hierarchy. Yes, embellishing past combat experience as one of the most despised things a military veteran can do.[5] However, just as Abrams's novel doesn't give us any examples of door-kickers who were "in the real shit," his narrative also never gives us any proof that any character in the novel is aware Harkleroad fabricates a single thing. These are harmless emails that he sends home to his mother. Abrams may personally subscribe to the popular notion that "real" veterans of combat mutely stare into their beers at the American Legion, and he may intend us to count Harkleroad as one who sits nearby "spinning yarns," but the novel doesn't support any suggestion that this reason is why the people FOB Triumph detest him so. He is never more than a cartoon buffoon.

So why, one may wonder, is Harkleroad not the convenient scapegoat of this hierarchy? The reason is because he, like the others, fits well within the Fobbit structure. He never does anything more than play the clown or fool's role, and thus he offers comic relief while he also reveals hidden truths about the structure itself. Since he doesn't threaten the hierarchy, his role can stand. Indeed, one of the reasons why the reader doesn't start rooting for or pitying Harkleroad is because we are privy to his lies. He most certainly doesn't contribute to or take part in the loathing that is inherent to the hierarchical structure of Fobbits and door-kickers. Also, unlike all the others, he never—not once—discusses Fobbits. While his manufactured stories show the reader that Harkleroad is well aware of the higher levels of respect paid to the combat experienced soldier, he never shows disdain for anyone who works in an office as he does. He covets the stories of door-kickers, but he never puts them on a pedestal where they can be admired.

From his position at the very bottom, Harkleroad holds up the entire hierarchy because he is its most oblivious patron. This is why the hierarchy must spare him. Door-kickers and Fobbits alike need him in order to measure and secure their own place on the Fobbit-ness scale. He is despised and ridiculed, but the disdain others feel for him never develops into a need for quarantine; there always remains insufficient incentive for his victimage. Throughout, he is nothing more than a type. As *FOBBIT*'s narrator tells us, "On every Army division staff there is always at least one officer who is the object of pity and/or ridicule" (64). His claiming of experiences and emotions that are reserved for the door-kicker deepens the reader's lack of empathy, but he is no threat to door-kickers or Fobbits. He would make a most inconvenient scapegoat.

Were Harkleroad to publish his tales in the *Murfreesboro Free Press* (as he keeps hinting to his mother that he might do some day), the entire hierarchy would be susceptible to exposure and collapse. But this never happens. The same goes for Gooding, who is able to fantasize about death during an attack on FOB Triumph and remain equally harmless to the FOB's social order. When Gooding walks through a bazaar and sees scraps of metal and scarves and fake silverware reportedly owned by Saddam Hussein, he says, "It is here that Fobbits can buy the false souvenirs that will later corroborate the equally false stories of their adventures 'outside the wire'" (53). But no Fobbits actually do this in the novel, and so this rule is one more item on a long list that does little to distinguish a Fobbit from a door-kicker. Besides, we are never convinced that the door-kickers in this novel refrain from doing the same thing. It definitely feels like something Lumley would do. At one point near the novel's end, Gooding nearly bleeds to death following a botched IV installation. Later, he looks down at the blood drops on his boots:

> When he returned to Georgia, maybe he could wear the uniform into the local American Legion and it would get him a few free beers from all the old battle-scarred veterans sitting at the bar. "Hey, look who's here," they'd say, "Rambo from Iraq" [307].

Again, this is nothing more than the conditional musings of a man with blood on his boots. After all, these imaginary "battle-scarred veterans" seem to be quite comfortable with whatever story accompanies the actual bloodstains. At a minimum, the sarcasm in that line—"Rambo from Iraq"—suggests that we probably shouldn't worry whether or not a Fobbit like Gooding would explain the marks on his uniform with the truth. That role, that danger, only exists in the form of Abe Shrinkle.

Abe Shrinkle and the Hierarchical Embarrassment of Fobbit-ness

From the other characters we can see that none of them deserve any exemption from the hierarchical psychosis that drives both Gooding's self-loathing and Lumley and Duret's self-congratulation. Duret and Lumley fall prey to the hierarchical psychosis because they mark themselves at the top of it. Gooding and Harkleroad acquiesce to it because they are at its bottom. All, however, share the assumption that the direct experience of combat discomfort and combat fear—however loosely defined these things are—is the only way to know "what is going on in Iraq," a knowledge that multiple characters claim (243). Regular, Fobbit-styled awareness of death, fear, and discomfort doesn't count as an epistemology to be respected, considered, or counted as part of this war at all. Still, as we have seen, the door-kickers who repeatedly proclaim that they know exactly what is going on in Iraq have nothing more to add to a collective understanding of this absurd war than do the Fobbits who never leave their air-conditioned offices. For this reason, a scapegoat is required to keep the hierarchy of Fobbit-ness in place, and that scapegoat is Captain Abraham Lincoln Shrinkle.

Hierarchies like the one on FOB Triumph are extremely resilient, for, as Burke writes in *A Rhetoric of Motives*, "the hierarchic principle is indigenous to all well-rounded human thinking" (141). But they also are extremely vulnerable; as Burke says, "hierarchy is inevitable," but "the crumbling of hierarchies is as true a fact about them as their formation" (141). All of the characters of *FOBBIT* display how the mystical nature of the criteria cloaks the divisions within the hierarchy of Fobbits and door-kickers, but Abe Shrinkle is the one who doesn't properly fit anywhere. He is both inside and outside the ordered world of Fobbits and door-kickers, and in order for the hierarchy to be reinforced—as it most certainly is in *FOBBIT*—there must be a release for the tension caused by the untenable class structure that keeps Fobbits and door-kickers separated. For the hierarchy to survive, there must be a purging, and it must be effected at the expense of a convenient scapegoat.

In *Dramatism and Development,* Burke discusses the term "identification" as it applies to his theory of "congregation by segregation" (28–29). "Identification," he says, "involves the working of antithesis, as when allies who would otherwise dispute among themselves join forces against a common enemy" (28). When the soldiers of FOB Triumph say, "we are at war," the pronoun "we" doesn't include the full population of the base, and "war" does not indicate a state-sponsored conflict against an armed insurgency. If the American soldier *par excellence* is the combat-experienced door-kicker (our god-term at the top of this particularly ordered world), and the Fobbit is the despised but necessary functionary at its bottom, the only available option for an enemy is Abe Shrinkle, since he manages to be consubstantial with both door-kickers *and* Fobbits. He also manages to be unwelcomed by both groups. The enemy in *FOBBIT* is not the Sunni militant or the faceless, identity-free hajji; it is anything that threatens to dismantle the system of Fobbits and door-kickers. And through Shrinkle's abject status, we can see that (after he fails as a door-kicker three different times) he is unfit for a place anywhere within the hierarchy's pyramidal structure. Again, it is for this that he must be purged, and when we demonstrate his construction as this drama's ultimate scapegoat we can lay bare the inherent problems in a world so ordered.

Shrinkle starts the novel as a door-kicker, but after some failures and crimes, he is relegated to life as a Fobbit. This backslide, from combat door-kicker status into a full-blown Fobbit and then, finally, into obliteration, is an interesting one to track. For one, Shrinkle's ejection from the hierarchy serves to remind the other soldiers that it is crucial that they continue subscribing to the order from which Shrinkle is cast out. Shrinkle's actions threaten to make Fobbits of every other door-kicker in the novel, so his unfitness as a door-kicker and as a Fobbit highlights how a door-kicker's status truly has nothing to do with door-kicker behavior, door-kicker bravery, or door-kicker knowledge. No, his expulsion exposes a ritualistic cycle of action-guilt-purgation-redemption that fulfills a collective American need to engage in hero worship in order to perpetuate and maintain our warfighting capabilities.

Shrinkle is never good at his job, but in the beginning of the novel he is safe from being called a Fobbit since, during the initial phases of his deployment, he fulfills all requirements to achieve door-kicker status. He is willing—even eager—to die for his country, but a series of decisions drive him back inside the wire and into Fobbit-dom. During this transition, we learn something important about Shrinkle and why he ultimately is unfit for membership in FOB Triumph's hierarchy. His suffers the worst from the door-kicker hierarchical psychosis; he *believes*, literally, that door-kickers are better Americans. As the narrator tells us, "Abe hoped he would never become so callous, so unpatriotic, so ... so *Fobbity*" (196; ellipses and italics original). As Burke says, "How can one better picture an issue in an appealing light than by showing that people were willing to be destroyed on behalf of it?" (*Permanence* 196). This is the threat Shrinkle poses for the hierarchy; he is the only character to link the vague concepts of patriotism and nationalism to such a flimsy hierarchy.

This following line comes during a crucial scene in the novel when Shrinkle meets Gooding for the first time, when his door-kicker status at FOB Triumph is in flux. Poolside at an American airbase in Qatar, the scene displays the extent of the hierarchical psychosis and its extensive effects on both Fobbits and door-kickers alike:

> "I'm in division public affairs" [Gooding says].
> "Oh, so you're one of those Fob—"Abe caught himself,"—uh, people who work at the palace."
> "You can go ahead and say it: yes, I'm a Fobbit."
> "You act like it's a bad thing."
> "To most people it is. But not to me."
> "Oh, why's that?"
> He leveled a flat gaze at Abe. "I'm still here, aren't I? Lot of door kickers can't say the same" [195].

Following that logic, being a Fobbit most certainly isn't a bad thing. But according to Shrinkle, Fobbit-ness violates the most sacrosanct ethic of American military service. That is, for Shrinkle, a Fobbit is a Fobbit not because he fails to meet danger in combat—as I pointed out above, *none* of *FOBBIT*'s characters ever see combat—a Fobbit is a Fobbit because he isn't a patriot. He doesn't love his country enough.

Though Shrinkle and Gooding situate themselves on opposite sides of the Fobbit divide, neither one can see that they are equals. For one, they are both sitting on the side of a pool. Gooding and Shrinkle are disinclined to interrogate the ordered world of Fobbits and door-kickers any further, but the reader is essentially dared to do so. Gooding is reading *Catch-22*, and when Shrinkle sees the book, he dismisses it, as a door-kicker should, as "classic antiwar rhetoric" (194). Shrinkle remembers how one of his old professors at West Point had "gone on a vein-throbbing rant against 'that ass-clown Yosarian,' who spent the entire book trying to weasel his way out of his patriotic duty" (194). Of course, Shrinkle has never read Heller's novel. We, however, know that in *Catch-22*, Yosarian wanted nothing more than to be a Fobbit, and so this concept of "patriotic duty"—what Shrinkle's equates with being pro-war, with being a door-kicker, with willingly sacrificing oneself in the line of duty—is the most salient aspect of this hierarchy's shaky foundation.[6]

Gooding plays along, saying that he "can't think of a better time to read" *Catch-22*, that it "helped to get [his] perspective skewed in the right direction," and that it is "sort of like an owner's manual for this war" (194). However, by this, Gooding merely means that the novel skewed his perspective so that he could cynically assess bureaucracy's place in war, not his place in the military. What Gooding and Shrinkle both miss is the fact that Yosarian would never fit within their hierarchy. They are both, as Burke would say, *"yearning to conform with"* what they consider the very *"sources of"* [their] *being"* (*Permanence* 69; italics original). By FOB Triumph's definition of a Fobbit, Yosarian would have been the least Fobbity of them all; he flies dozens upon dozens of combat missions and watches men die around him. Yet, by Shrinkle's view of Fobbit behavior, Yosarian is a disgrace because Yosarian does everything he can to avoid flying more combat missions. As far as Shrinkle is concerned, what makes him an "ass clown," then, is not the level of danger he actually meets while completing his "patriotic duty," it is the willingness he displays before and after doing so. Ironically, neither Shrinkle nor Lumley nor Duret ever come close to accumulating a level of combat experience anywhere close to Yosarian's.

After this conversation, both Gooding and Shrinkle return to FOB

Triumph, and after Shrinkle is pulled off his team of door-kickers, he is made to stand in the base gym and hand out towels while the rest of the novel proceeds until the scapegoat mechanism can be completed. We dislike Shrinkle along with all the other grunts and Fobbits, but we also want to empathize with him, far more than we do with Duret or Gooding or Harkleroad or Lumley. Thus, any questioning of Shrinkle's status simultaneously reflects the status of the subject. In other words, whatever makes the abject other different is really a reflection of the creating subject, not the quarantined object. Burke, in *A Grammar of Motives*, calls this the "dialectic of the scapegoat":

> For the scapegoat is "charismatic," a vicar. As such, it is profoundly consubstantial with those who, looking upon it as a chosen vessel, would ritualistically cleanse themselves by loading the burden of their own iniquities upon it. Thus the scapegoat represents the principle of division in that its persecutors would alienate from themselves to it their own cleanliness. For one must remember that a scapegoat cannot be "curative" except insofar as it represents the iniquities of those who would be cured by attacking it. In representing *their* iniquities, it performs the role of vicarious atonement (that is, unification, or merger, granted to those who have alienated their iniquities upon it, and so may be purified through its suffering) [406].

As we've seen, the wide possible range of Fobbit-ness means that anyone can carry a Fobbit's stink without deserving victimage. Shrinkle, however, can most certainly disturb the hierarchy or provide vicarious atonement because he is ready from the beginning for those who "seek to ritualistically cleanse themselves" by burdening him with their own "iniquities."

From the opening of the novel, the dialectic of the scapegoat makes Shrinkle the vessel of everyone's curse. We first meet him through Duret's eyes, and it is clear that Shrinkle is marked for removal from the clan of Duret's door-kickers; Duret sees him not as a peer but as "a pinch-faced captain named Shrinkle, known for his hems and haws" (20). Carter explains:

> At one moment the chosen victim is a part of the clan, being one of their number; a moment later it symbolizes something apart from them, being the curse they wish to lift from themselves. By the operation of dialectical change, they first identify with their victim; then they deny a connection altogether [18].

Even Shrinkle's name suits him for the role; it looks like a junk food cupcake but sounds like the nickname of a pet bunny. So Shrinkle is an easy target, and Duret's narration delivers all the early characterization of Shrinkle we need in order to load the balance in Duret's favor. Compared to Duret's self-described stoic leadership, we have Shrinkle, a young man who loses control of his bowels. We momentarily accept Duret as the perfect example for how a good door-kicker thinks because we are shown what he thinks. Thus, we initially ignore the fact that Duret, too, had a debilitating reaction to the Incident at Intersection Quillpen. The narration allows Duret many chances to hide his own incontinence (of action) with the imprecision of euphemisms and clichés while Shrinkle is never allowed a similar opportunity to brag and reflect. When Duret arrives at the Incident at Intersection Quillpen, he says, "solving this situation would be like trying to stuff eels into a can of grease. It could be done, but you had to know how to hold the eel" (21). Shrinkle is never afforded any similar assessment of his own reactions, nor is he allowed a chance to distract the reader with witticisms like Duret's. We are only allowed to look at him as Duret does, as an object to be despised and hated.

Duret calls him a "pale, visibly shaking captain" (21). He marches up to Shrinkle and tells him, "we don't have time for this wiffly-waffy bullshit" (21). Lumley overhears the haranguing, and the narrator allows him to jump on the Shrinkle-hating bandwagon. As Duret speaks, Lumley thinks to himself, "They (meaning, he, Lumley) could have handled this, if they were allowed" (22). As the scene at Intersection Quillpen develops, Shrinkle's abjectification continues, and no one else ever mentions him without disdain, even when he performs well. He calls in the bomb disposal team without being prompted, but the team arrives without his notice, and, predictably, Lumley jumps in and ingratiates himself with Duret by eagerly reporting the team's arrival (24). When Shrinkle dares to make a suggestion to a visibly angry Duret, Duret wishes that he could "tell his captain that he was a well-meaning but ultimately useless officer who couldn't find his asshole with a flashlight and a road map" (31). When Shrinkle breathes, his intake is "quivery" (23). When he swallows, Duret describes it as a "dry *click*" (26; italics original). When he talks, his voice has "a little seesaw in it" (30). As Duret confidently concludes, Shrinkle is "clearly a man out of his element" (21).

So, initially, we agree with the hierarchy, but once we dismantle it by peering through Duret's jargon-laden language and Lumley's eager self-concern, we can see that Shrinkle's mistake was *appearing* to hesitate; the rest of the complaints are unfortunate personality traits that have zero impact on the actual war. He was indecisive, but Shrinkle's hesitation actually resolves the situation and results in the death of only one man, the car-bomber. So, as a leader, he actually outperforms Duret. Does it really matter how someone swallows? Shrinkle doesn't fail as a door-kicker because civilians die or because a suicide bomber kills American soldiers or because a battle is lost; Shrinkle fails because he doesn't add to the prestige of door-kickers. He isn't a threat to American lives or to the American military mission in Iraq; he is a threat to the hierarchy because he shows how door-kickers stay on top, by doing nothing more that appearing as if they belong there.

After the incident at Intersection Quillpen, Shrinkle tries to fix his demeanor and appear as a door-kicker should, but he overcompensates. Instead of doing his job, he tries to act like a warrior. Shrinkle and Lumley and the rest of the door-kickers are called out to a local gas station one afternoon because a mysterious Iraqi man is walking around in circles and making odd noises, all while wearing a ski parka and a "jester's hat" (114). Or, as Lumley describes the situation, "Some hajji fool walking around a gas station making like he's going to do something" (109). Lumley and the other enlisted door-kickers try to leave Shrinkle at the FOB, but he insists on going along and yet again gets in the way of door-kickers acting like door-kickers. Actually, he acts like he thinks a door-kicker should when such imagined behavior is in no way necessary. As Shrinkle considers his options at the gas station, he worries about doing "his part in the war" and about how nice it would be to report to his future children that "he'd killed the enemy" (113). So he takes out his pistol and murders the man: "the heavy man crumpled to the ground, arms spread in a Y above his head, the jester's cap giving on last surge of bell music when it hit the ground" (113–14). But the dead man was no enemy; he was a mentally challenged adolescent who had wandered away from his Baghdad home.

This is Shrinkle's second failure, but this time, since a murder was involved, one would expect Lumley or Duret to respond by arresting him. But, as far as they are concerned, the murder is irrelevant. As Lumley sees it, this particular situation called for the opposite action of the incident at Intersection Quillpen. Then, Shrinkle chose to wait for help, which ended up being the right move. This time, however, Shrinkle acts too quickly, again against Lumley's advice. Lumley tells him politely that the appropriate action is to wait for "critical mass to arrive" (112). "We *wait*, sir," Lumley insists (112; italics original). But Shrinkle doesn't listen to Lumley, and this crime is the one that matters, not the murder of an Iraqi boy. So Shrinkle never is charged with a crime, but he most certainly is despised by Lumley and his men for challenging the dictates of the hierarchy.

Shrinkle's final failure comes when a U.S. convoy is forced to stop for a broken-down truck in a hazardous stretch of Baghdad highway. Shrinkle and Lumley are called out one more time with their team of door-kickers (Duret is in his office in the palace for both the murder at the gas station and for this scene, as well). This time, Lumley doesn't offer his advice or his rifle. He just sits back and lets Shrinkle fail for the third time. Actually, he helps him fail. A restless crowd forms at the scene; so Shrinkle decides to again act like a patriotic door-kicker and tries to destroy the truck with a thermite grenade so the convoy can keep moving. Lumley is the man who hands him the grenade after offering a meek protest: "Sir," he says, "I really don't think this is a good idea" (145). Lumley's self-pity is in full command of the scene, as the narrator sardonically announces, "Lumley and his squad had no choice but to follow" (147). When the Americans leave, the truck keeps burning, and when the local fire department puts it out, they find the body of another dead Iraqi man who had been hiding beneath the truck (134).

One might suggest that Lumley's protests in all three of Shrinkle's failures are extended commentary on the rank structure of the military. However, Shrinkle's crimes and failures don't resonate as complaints about rank; rather, they fuel grudges. They fuel Shrinkle's fittingness as a scapegoat. After all, during the incidents involving the burning truck and the murdered boy, Lumley is more concerned with his hierarchical reputation than he is with Shrinkle's negligence or the murder he committed. As he says, he and the other door-kickers enjoyed "a legacy stretching back to doughboys that needed to be preserved and upheld.... You couldn't just let bravery like that get tarnished by one indecisive officer who didn't know shit from Shinola" (140). Shrinkle misunderstands the door-kicker status as one based on mystical legacies, heroic stereotypes, and subjective reputations. These misconceptions make "it harder and harder" for Lumley "to mask his contempt for Shrinkle" (141). Shrinkle has our contempt too, but Lumley's scorn is not based on the concrete facts of Shrinkle's actions, which would have been entirely reasonable (remember, he killed two people and burned up a perfectly good truck). He hates Shrinkle and wants him quarantined because Shrinkle is a contagion that could potentially damage the door-kickers' collective reputation.

Luckily for us, the scapegoating of Shrinkle allow us to throw "light" (as Burke says) on Lumley's "practices of ostracism" ("On Carthasis" 352). As Lumley reflects long before Shrinkle is cast out from their midst, "Shrinkle was already a ghost, a nothing man on his way out" (140). If Shrinkle threatens Lumley and the legacy of the door-kicker with his ill-conceived door-kicker behavior and demeanor, his failures threaten Duret more. That is, he can turn Duret into more of a Fobbit than Duret already is, something Duret fears above all else. He goes so far as to vow "that he'd self-ventilate with a 9mm before he ever let" the Army chain of command turn him into a more obvious Fobbit (126). We taste his fear as Duret sits in his own office in the palace, just down the hall from Gooding and Harkleroad, a place he describes as his "refuge," a place that provides him a "little pool of silence" (125, 126). From this safest of perches, he learns of Shrinkle's escapades, and, like Lumley, he doesn't worry about the dead civilians or the burned truck at all. Instead, he begins to worry about how this "fuck-a-roo of all fuck-a-roos" will reflect back on him (151). By this point in the novel, however, the reader knows that Duret is oblivious to his own status as a Fobbit. Thus, we are not at all surprised when Duret fails to respond to Shrinkle's crimes with anything but self-concern. Shrinkle's behavior is not criminal to Duret. As far as he is concerned, he's an annoyance—"like a popcorn husk caught between" his molars (127). But Shrinkle still has the potential to unseat Duret from his place of superiority as the lead door-kicker, so, predictably, Duret doesn't ponder the effect that Shrinkle's actions have on the war or the local population; he just covers his own back by simply ordering Shrinkle's ostracism from the door-kicker clan. As Burke explains, "ostracism, we might say, attempt[s] to solve the problem of 'hubris' by amputating from the body politic whatever member seemed swollen to the point of becoming a threat" ("On Catharsis" 352).

Even then, Duret waffles in the execution of such a simple and justifiable move. When Shrinkle murders the "short-bus hajji"—as Lumley describes the boy Shrinkle murders (141)—Duret makes a grand, but empty, pronouncement to the other door-kickers. "Don't worry, gentlemen," he declares, "By this time tomorrow, Abe Shrinkle will be shitting out of two assholes" (135). When Shrinkle burns the truck and the Iraqi hiding underneath it, the narrator uses a Duret-styled euphemism to describe it: "This particular company commander was starting to feel like a hot poker rammed up Duret's pecker" (151). Such ridiculous language may work wonders with maintaining Duret's door-kicker status with his fellow Fobbits and door-kickers, but it falls flat with us. We know these are meaningless idioms that Duret and the narrator use to mask the problems in this hierarchy. Duret does begin "agonizing" over the "Shrinkle problem," but his agony has nothing to do with murders or the way Duret might judiciously, legally, administratively, or responsibly deal with a crime committed by one of his men (151). The "Shrinkle problem" only refers to the threat he poses to Duret's status.

Duret claims that he isn't "one of those grease-fingered Fobbits who let bad things fall slick out of their hands for someone else to catch before they hit the floor" (151), but in the end this is exactly what he does. Duret

Five: The Convenient Scapegoat in David Abrams's FOBBIT   149

doesn't charge Shrinkle with murder or negligent manslaughter or for destroying military property, nor does he reprimand him in any formal way (150). Paperwork or any other formal device of accountability would reflect too poorly on Duret, so, instead, he uses all the tools in the Fobbit self-preservation toolbox in order to avoid the "shitball" that he suspects is "already headed his way" (152). He "pulls a fast one" (as he puts it) by giving Shrinkle a Fobbit's job in order "to make it look like he, Vic Duret, was the first one to make a move" (152). He sends Shrinkle to Qatar for a week so he can "stifle the noise of this incident" (153), and then he fires Shrinkle from his door-kicking job as to "make a big show of cleaning house" (152). When Duret's scheme is complete, so, too, is Shrinkle's abjection. He has been safely quarantined away from the rest of the FOB; the hierarchy has been repaired, and Duret and Lumley's delusions regarding their place of superiority are restored, undamaged and unquestioned.

Shrinkle's Exile and Purging

Shrinkle is exiled, first to Qatar for a purgatorial rest and relaxation break, and then to what he considers the ultimate demeaning job: handing out towels at the fitness center in a polo shirt and khaki shorts. Stripped of rank and uniform, all outward signs of his place in the hierarchy are gone. The social order of FOB Triumph is intact, but Duret's plan has left the scapegoating mechanism unfinished, as is any self-reflection Shrinkle might undergo regarding his actions. As the narrator reports, "Abe still had not been able to completely exorcise the guilt of that night when, it was alleged, he'd barbecued an Iraqi to death" (174). Even Shrinkle imagines the various ways this might happen. As he wallows in worry and "the early onset of PTSD," he can't stop thinking about the "UCMJ, relief for cause, court-martial, execution by firing squad" (174, 175). These would be reasonable punishments for what he has done, but since Duret shirks his responsibility in favor of maintaining the hierarchy, none of these ever come to fruition. So when we find out that Shrinkle will be spared punishment beyond this simple demotion, we know a further purging is imminent.

Early on in his life, Shrinkle fell for the typical national myths of American identity, the same ones that led him to suggest that Fobbits lack a proper sense of patriotism. As a boy, Shrinkle thoughtlessly memorized the preamble to the constitution and the entire Declaration of Independence without really paying attention to the words or their meaning (77). As a teenager, he displayed his healthy American work ethic by mowing yards in order to prove his physical mettle and dependability (78). As a college student, he was convinced of "the absolute moral superiority of his Army, his country, and his role in both" (79). It seems this is all it takes to create an adult who subscribes literally to the metanarrative of American exceptionalism: "He loved America, he really did—purple mountains majesty and the whole nine yards. He believed there were no finer bedrock principles of government than the ones founded by those powder-wigged Philadelphia fathers all those centuries ago" (77). A true believer in "America at large," as the narrator puts it, what else is such an American (named Abe Lincoln) to do but join the Army like his grandfather and his uncles and eagerly do what he considers his "patriotic duty" (78)?

As Burke explains, a predictable tragic set up like this one acts in a more "homeopathic" fashion; it seeks to "provide a remedy for the pollution by aggravation of the symptoms under controlled conditions designed to forestall worse ravages of the disease" ("On Catharsis" 352). When Shrinkle is quarantined to the fitness center and removed from the hierarchy, the symptoms of his disease are most definitely aggravated:

> Abe Shrinkle couldn't help but think he was now straddling their worlds. Once an armore officer, he figured he'd soon be a Fobbit, the crème-center pussies his men constantly despised. Either that or he'd be dead within the month, courtesy of a reluctant but obedient firing squad [187].

Exiled as he is, forced to straddle the two worlds of the Fobbit and the door-kicker and then forced (momentarily) to question everything he thought was certain about war and service, Shrinkle's days are numbered. Not only is his uncertain status in the hierarchy untenable, but Shrinkle has also become, as Carter describes the scapegoat, "a fulcrum around which pivot self-justifying identifications and separations" for the rest of the FOB (18). When he was a door-kicker, he thought he knew what it meant to be a patriot and how to be part of his clan. But now, the men from his old company and squad avoid the gym where he works. In the chow hall, they avoid making eye contact (224). The boundaries have been redrawn to exclude him.

So Shrinkle, who "had never thought of himself a man of habitual sin" (though he has killed two men by this point) discards his identity as an American soldier and reinvents himself as a man named Richard Belmouth, a British contractor "who was there to advise the United States on historical preservation" (226). Complete with a backstory and an accent, Shrinkle "firmly" creates this new self at an off-limits pool run by a small group of Australian soldiers who humorously describe spending time at the pool as attending "Prayer Service":

Five: The Convenient Scapegoat in David Abrams's FOBBIT   151

> [Y]es, indeed, he *would* change his identity and leave the old Abe Shrinkle behind. It was as simple as entering an elevator and watching the doors close in front of him. At once, he was lifted up and away and, with the giddiness of a cold beer, bare breasts (the two eyes of nipples staring at him), and all these new eager friends, he felt that for at least the duration of a false prayer service, he could leave behind the death, stink, and shame of his failure at war [231; italics original].

But, despite this identity-shifting anagnorisis, this backsliding employee of the United States military cannot escape his role as the abject freak, a scapegoat that must be destroyed.

Call it poetic justice or blatant contrivance, Abrams's satire follows Captain Abe Lincoln Shrinkle all the way into his new identity and the amazing, erasing effects it has on his nagging guilty conscience. Before he makes up his new name and new identity, he does admit to a modicum of guilt along with a desire to exorcise it. But neither exorcism nor contrition ever comes, and Shrinkle buries his very real and very reasonable guilt underneath the same old hierarchies that got him to join the Army in the first place. Instead of voicing regret, Shrinkle aligns his own attitude with Duret's and Lumley's. That is, instead of accepting his culpability and the duties of his new job at the gym, he pushes it all away by blaming others. Before, he never said anything malicious about Fobbits, but after his banishment, Shrinkle adopts a door-kicker styled bitterness: "He was angry at the fat Fobbits who had nothing better to do in this war than waste a half-hour standing around waiting for a rinky-dink little fitness center to open" (267–68). There was a moment when Shrinkle thought Duret would court-martial him for his crimes, but when he becomes Richard Belmouth he comforts himself with Lumley-esque self-pity. "It's not fair, it's not fair, it's not fair," he repeats again and again whenever he thinks about his demotion (268). Instead of acknowledging and atoning for the momentary guilt he rightly feels for killing two men, Shrinkle now finds it possible to place blame for his liminal status on the victim: "that Iraqi—whoever he was—who'd crawled underneath that fuel truck and started this whole chain of events" (268). Whenever lingering feelings of shame bother him, he resorts to door-kicker name-calling; the "blubber-jiggling Fobbits" haunt his workdays, and the "Fucking hajji" he killed haunts his thoughts (269). He even manages, astonishingly, to never again spend another minute dwelling on the harmless boy he executed at the gas station.

In all this reinvention and redirection, Shrinkle begins to feel better because he has finally figured out how the hierarchy works. He starts thinking that the "barbecued Iraqi" was the "best thing to happen to him," and he rationalizes that "*maybe it was hajji's time to go and my time to realize*

I wasn't cut out for this Army life" (310; italics original). He still suffers pangs of guilt, but again, these pangs have nothing to do with his criminal actions as a door-kicker; they are linked with his new place outside the hierarchy: "Duret had removed him from the action, snatched him out of harm's way, and, though his men—his *former* men—still chewed at Abe's guilty conscience, he had to admit he was thankful" (312; italics original). Fully burdened with the guilt of the order he has finally figured out, there is little else to do with a character like Shrinkle than kill him.

The filthy purgation of the hierarchy of Fobbits and door-kickers is finally concluded when Shrinkle is literally disintegrated by a mortar while floating in a forbidden swimming pool in the center of FOB Triumph. As Burke explains,

> In his offense [the scapegoat] takes upon himself the guilt of all—and *his* punishment is *mankind's* chastening. We identify ourselves with his weakness (we feel "pity"), but we dissociate ourselves from his punishment (we feel "terror"). The *dis*sociation, however, coexists with the *as*sociation. We are onlookers but participants [*Attitudes* 144–45; italics original].

As news of Shrinkle's death spreads around FOB Triumph, each primary character goes through a ritualistic purging according to this cycle of association/dissociation and the resulting cure that follows it. Gooding drinks some bad water and spends a miserable day and night expelling fluid from every orifice in his body (292). Then, when he seeks medical attention and the rehydration of an IV bag of saline shortly before Shrinkle is killed, he notes that he is purified because he has finally "*shed blood for the first time … here in Iraq*" (293; italics original). Gooding's diarrhea and bloodletting is matched by Duret's vomiting when he is asked to identify Shrinkle's remains inside an "unzipped body bag—a solitary arm, rigor mortis fingers still clutching a can of beer" (351). The recognition of the arm and the man to whom it was once attached drives Duret to the toilet three times. Then, "with some small measure of relief…. He flushed the toilet" and "stood watching his sour yellow anger swirl down and disappear" (350).

As for Harkleroad, it turns out that Shrinkle is the two thousandth American to die in Iraq; so this buffoon tries to "spin" the news of the man's death so that Shrinkle's scandalous death will not occupy such an important place on the long list of the dead. He wants Shrinkle "obliterated" from the news, so he suggests to his boss that they merely pretend that Shrinkle never existed to begin with (337). He is unsuccessful, of course, but as he leaves his boss's office, with the brief annoyance Shrinkle caused in his life behind him, Harkleroad leaves purgative marks behind him on the marbled hallway: "He left a trail of nose blood that a Twee contractor named Majid would mop up later that night" (339).

Lumley and the other door-kickers are all in the shower when they find out about Shrinkle's death. Their new commander (Shrinkle's replacement) barges in and announces, "Men! He's dead!" (317). The door-kickers don't show sorrow; instead, they "blustered and bluffed their hidden grief with hard, impervious comments as they tiptoed through the murky water" that covered the floor of the shower (321). Some are even happy to hear of the scapegoat's death, but the narrator insists that most of the door-kickers are "genuinely shocked and saddened" by it, because "no one deserved to be 'obliterated.' Not even the worst officer in the United States Army" (322). The drains in this shower clog easily, though. So, as the narrator explains, the door-kickers use squeegees to push the "grayish mix of shampoos, soaps, and body washes—not to mention pubic hair, urine ... and snot oysters" to the center drain (318). Some of them are sullied by a momentary tinge of grief, but all of them are washed anew with the news of Shrinkle's death. The detritus of Shrinkle's short life as a misguided door-kicker follows their hair, their dirt, and their phlegm—their filth—down the drain.

As this analysis proves, tracing the scapegoating process in a book like *FOBBIT* levels each character's experience so that no one story or perspective is privileged over any other. In that leveling, we can see how war novels rarely convince that the complexities of combat experience can be generalized into one picture of combat trauma or that any picture that a door-kicker can paint is inaccessible to the uninitiated. Rather, *FOBBIT* demands that we interrogate the very nature of Fobbit-hating and the widely accepted reasons behind door-kicker-hero-worship as well. The hierarchy of Fobbits and door-kickers, as it is exposed in the novel, suggests that no matter what implicit line separates soldiers, war experiences are endlessly dissimilar but equally worthy of telling. Fobbits may work in air-conditioned cubicles and sleep in air-conditioned trailers, but even the door-kickers have to return to the FOB eventually, and in that moment each one becomes a "U.S. Army employee stationed at a Forward Operating Base."

This reveals the benefits of examining satire like Abrams's according to its scapegoats and hierarchies. The novel asks us to note again and again the disparities that exist between the hazards a Fobbit faces and those that a door-kicker faces. And—in a number of interviews—Abrams does suggest that he intended his novel to be read according to a rather stringent model of combat gnosticism. However, as Burke says, "One can mock death, but one cannot mock men in danger of death" (*Counter-Statement* 65). Of contemporary war, this analysis of *FOBBIT* teaches us that it is sensible to consider all men and women who experience war as sharing equal danger of death. Then, and perhaps only then, war may be treated—and avoided—as a way of life instead of as an aberration that can be reduced into easily digestible tales of heroic combat. Such an observation is an important one to make about war and war's representation, for, as Burke reminds us,

> The hierarchical psychosis (interweaving the social order with the motives of guilt, wonder, adventure, catharsis, and victimage) arises so spontaneously from the social order, it would seem that a free society should emphasize in its secular educational methods the kinds of observation that make the building of hierarchical magic most difficult [294].

War—according to *FOBBIT*—is not so easily reduced into a single firefight or the explosion of an improvised device. Rather, *FOBBIT* suggests that modern war shares much with the petty concerns of any number of American bureaucracies, combat-related or otherwise. That might be one of the most disturbing things about post–9/11 American war culture, but in its honesty, it rings true.

Six

Representing Hajji
This Generation's Enemy "Other"

> "We" are all here on this side; "the enemy" is over there. "We" are individuals with names and personal identities; "he" is a mere collective entity. We are visible; he is invisible. We are normal; he is grotesque. Our appearances are natural; his, bizarre. He is not as good as we are.—Paul Fussell, *The Great War* 82

A novel, a poem, a song, a movie, a phrase, a word: each one of these units of communication operates in American war culture as a symbolic act, an act that reveals a number of things about the author (the agent) and the sociocultural moment (the scene) in which they act (or write/create). Or, as Kenneth Burke would say, all of these linguistic creations are "the dancing of an attitude" (*Philosophy* 9). As the previous three chapters have shown, attitudes and hierarchies and guilt and catharsis and victimage dance all over contemporary war literature, a body of writing that is dominated by the ideology of combat gnosticism. This is what happens, symbolically, when the reality of war and experience is shaped, documented, restored, or altered when we seek to transfer experience into ritualistic, terministic systems. Yet, as James Carey writes in "A Cultural Approach to Communication," we all fall "under the sway of realism" when we try to present experience as if it is "there to discover in any significant detail" (20). So the question remains: can a study of the symbolic action that is the scapegoat mechanism in contemporary war literature extend into American war culture as a whole? Or, as I will examine in this chapter, is there a direct conceptual link between war literature's tendency to go scapegoat and the same in other forms of communication? I argue that, in the literature we write and in the language we use to communicate war's reality, writers and speakers and utterers of all stripes have a tendency to go scapegoat in story, in song, and in epithet. If we can identify and trace symbolic and ritualistic tendencies, then perhaps we can forestall and combat the tendency itself.

Similar to "charlie" and "gook" and "kraut" and "Jap" from United States' twentieth century wars, the word *hajji*[1] has become the latest epithet for the United States' enemy Other.[2] In some ways, *hajji* is just another iteration of the American habit to devise a slur and use it to describe an enemy, particularly an enemy that is seldom seen or that is rarely identifiable as a martial unit of a recognized nation-state. Much has been written about the large number and various names of the groups that oppose the United States' military action in both Iraq and Afghanistan, yet *hajji*'s appropriation and use by American military members to describe them all begs further analysis, especially as it appears in war literature and culture. On the one hand, as Ben Brody points out in his short "dictionary" of recent "U.S. Military Lingo" that he put together for National Public Radio, *hajji* is a "derogatory term for Iraqis, used widely during the Iraq War. A Hajii shop was an Iraqi-run shop on the base, often selling pirated DVDs, or Hajii Discs. Rarely used to describe Afghans." This is the type of definition that has been accompanying the word in news stories and memoirs and other works of nonfiction since 2003.[3] From such a simple accounting, any reader could gather a general understanding of the word, especially since it has become ubiquitous in contemporary representations of war. Indeed, a definition like this one, in post–9/11 America, is so reasonable—the word, a clever witticism even—as to defy further comment. On the other hand, it barely scratches the surface of *hajji*'s symbolic power. Geography, religion, ethnicity, skin color, culture: all of these determine *hajji*'s application today, yet none of them is an absolute requirement.

Again, Kenneth Burke's methodology/philosophy is quite useful and applicable in *hajji*'s case; the full symbolic power of *hajji* is much more complex than a simple definition might suggest. Joseph Gusfield describes the resilience of Burke's logology and his dramatistic method in his introduction to *Kenneth Burke: On Symbols and Society*:

> It is my contention that Burke's importance for the sociologist lies not so much in any particular content of any particular part of his writing but in the development of a method, a perspective about perspectives, which is a profound attempt to understand the implications for human behavior of the fact that humans are "symbol-using animals" [4].

I am no sociologist, nor is this a sociological analysis of *hajji*; regardless, Gusfield's point is a sound one. Burke was a student of language and meaning, so it is the "symbol" part of the "symbol-using animal" that I seek to

Six: Representing Hajji: This Generation's Enemy "Other" 157

examine in *hajji*. If *hajji* reflects a certain perspective on modern war, this chapter assumes a Burkeian perspective on that perspective.

In "'As Usual I Fell on the Bias': Kenneth Burke's Situated Dialectic," Elizabeth Weiser examines the title phrase as the defining characteristic of Burke's philosophy, one that exhibits his "propensity to situate his arguments *across* seeming dichotomies" that calls for "engaged intellectual activism of a particularly ambiguous sort, a celebration of multiple perspectives of a kind that often makes the most engaged among us uncomfortable" (134, 135). Thus, like Burke, this chapter also tries to "fall on the bias" and remain above the fray of moral outrage or distracting ethical arguments as I move from an analysis of literature to an analysis of other forms of communication. Since *hajji* is a real Arabic word, used by Muslims as a title of respect, some users of the word—usually veterans—dispute the word's pejorative connotations, citing this and a number of other reasons on open forums across the internet. Colby Buzzell, for instance, in his blog-turned-book, *My War* (2005), tells of grabbing a digital voice recorder and taking it out to ask "the first English-speaking Iraqi person [he] could find a couple of questions" (330). Toward the middle of this "interview" with his unit's interpreter, Buzzell asks, "Is the word *Hajji* offensive?" (335). The Iraqi interpreter responds:

> No. It is not offensive. People who go to Mecca and come back to Iraq, they call them Hajji, as you know the five duties in Islam, one of them is pilgrimage to Mecca. When the person come back from Mecca, that person is a Hajji [335].

Buzzell knows this already; so he digs deeper: "What about when Americans sometimes use the word *Hajji* to refer to an Iraqi, is that bad?" The man responds with a simple, "No" (335). While Buzzell does not address the rather suspect circumstances of this "interview" (how else would a cooperative Iraqi interpreter respond in such a situation?), the interpreter's response often is the one put forth by those who rebel against any suggestion that *hajji* is offensive or disturbing. They take a certain delight in pointing out socio-cultural inconsistencies regarding other American slurs, and they often rest their arguments on the inherent contradiction that exists when a society asks the military to kill a large number of human beings on its behalf but also expects that same military to maintain a lofty correctness in its language.

I dispute neither of these arguments, nor does my work directly enter any debate over the political or ethical implications of *hajji*'s existence as an epithet. Though I do—emphatically—argue that a word or symbol can be harmful, pejorative, and demeaning without actual injury or a speaker's awareness of its potential offensiveness, I make no demand regarding the way a soldier *should* speak or how he or she *should* view the people he or she chooses to describe as a *hajji*. As Kenneth Burke insists in *Permanence and Change*, "We are *not* saying that such *should* be the case. We are simply saying that ... such *is* the case" (284; italics original). After all, even if an Iraqi interpreter serving with the United States Army insists that he only receives the denotative or traditional sense of the word when an American uses it, the fact remains that the American speaker most certainly did not intend *hajji* in similar manner. However, because any close examination of a soldier's behavior—linguistic or otherwise—is often perceived as the enemy of patriotism or the military, any frank discussion can appear blasphemous or disrespectful.

Of this I am aware. As this chapter will show, however, whenever an American serviceman or servicewoman utters *hajji*, it is a sign-carrier of vast significance. My investigation of the epithet is intended, then, to discover what the sign carries and the ways a consideration of its appearance in contemporary war literature and war culture can help us understand the United States' expectations for the way its wars are fought. As Srinivas Aravamudan writes, "War can truly be prevented only when we mitigate its background conditions" (1512). *Hajji* grows out of the (linguistic) background conditions that Americans use to justify sending other Americans off to kill and die. Some readers may take this project as an affront to some supposed sanctity within the military-civilian contract, but if we conceive of the military as just another mouthpiece of the society it represents, even on the battlefield, we can mitigate the attitudes behind *hajji* and, by extension, the motivations behind war.

Thus, in line with the rest of this book, I will examine *hajji* as it appears in war literature and other forms of commination with Kenneth Burke's scapegoating mechanism in mind in order to extract a clearer understanding of *hajji*'s symbolic significance in the dramas of our post–9/11 wars in Iraq and Afghanistan. Burke writes,

> [I]f the great pyramidal structure of medieval Europe found its ultimate expression in a system of moral purgation based on the two "moments" of "original sin" and "redemption," it would seem to follow that the "guilt" intrinsic to hierarchal order (the only kind of "organizational" order we have ever known) call correspondingly for "redemption" through victimage [*Permanence* 284].

This is what I consider the most concise statement of Burke's scapegoat process as it exists in the drama that is human life, a cycle that I see at work in the mechanisms behind *hajji*. Therefore, I will apply Kenneth Burke's concept of "identification" and his ideas about the master trope "synecdoche" to *hajji*'s appearance in contemporary American war liter-

Six: Representing Hajji: This Generation's Enemy "Other"   159

ature to show how *hajji* is now part of a performance-based post–9/11 "rhetoric of insult" (to borrow Thomas Conley's phrase) that American soldiers employ to enact Burke's scapegoating process at a cultural level.

The Birth of *Hajji*

Hajji likely originated during the United States' invasion of Iraq in 2003. In two of the earliest, book-length, first-hand accounts that were published about the invasion (written by journalists embedded with U.S. troops), *hajji* appears as an epithet, and in both cases it is used to describe a dangerous enemy. In *Boots on the Ground* (2003), Karl Zinsmeister recalls bedding down for the night with the 82nd Airborne at what was once Iraq's Talil airbase: "If nature calls," he muses, "don't go out too far or you could be mistaken for a hajji" (80). In *The March Up* (2003), Bing West writes about a gunner named Chris Madia who, during the invasion, tells the complaining driver of his Humvee, "Some hadji will ding you sitting there behind the wheel, and I'll drop him, and after that I won't have to listen to you anymore" (54). Later, as the platoon digs in and prepares for sleep, West writes, "They scooped out their fighting holes and sat in the stinging dirt, whispering back and forth about how they would hit the hadjis in the balls or break their jaws or snap their necks" (60). Nothing similar exists in comparable book-length reportage from America's earlier invasion of Afghanistan, but as we can see in these two examples, *hajji* began as a reference to an unseen but present enemy.[4]

While neither West nor Zinmeister bother to explain the term further in their reports—context suffices in both cases—*hajji* did not escape the attention of the wider media beginning in late 2003. And, for a time, it primarily referred to an armed and organized enemy. The first person to report on the emergence of *hajji* as an epithet in Operation Iraqi Freedom was most likely Jay Price, a staff writer for *The News and Observer* in Raleigh, North Carolina, in September of 2003. "Every war spawns epithets," he writes, using a soldier in Iraq who had labeled his footlocker with the words "Hodgie Killer" as his prime example (A1). Price goes on to briefly examine *hajji*'s disturbing legacy by quoting John Balaban, a Vietnam-era war poet and writer in residence at North Carolina State University. "That sounds familiar," Balaban says, drawing a parallel to his own experiences in Vietnam:

> There were several words—"gook," "slope," "dink." Some of these were meaningless, but they were all working toward the same goal, of trivializing and depersonalizing the enemy. It makes it easier to kill these people and not feel bad about it [A1].

In May of 2004, Bob Herbert published a column in *The New York Times* about an Army staff sergeant named Camilo Mejia who was court-martialed for refusing to return to combat in Iraq after his mid-tour furlough at home. Mejia describes the way American servicemen and women began quickly using *hajji* following the invasion of Iraq: "You just sort of try to block out the fact that they're human beings and see them as enemies. You call them hajis, you know? You do all the things that make it easier to deal with killing them and mistreating them" (A23). That same month, Douglas Jehl and Andrea Elliot also explained how the term "haji" developed as a derogative in another story for *The New York Times* (A5). They quote a guard who worked in a detention center in Afghanistan, who speaks about the prisoners: "I think that giving them the distinction of soldier would have changed our attitudes toward them. A lot of it was based on racism, really. We called them hajis, and that psychology was really important" (A5). A year later, in May of 2005, Herbert followed with another column about an Army private and eventual conscientious objector who saw men in his unit shatter glass bottles over the heads of Iraqi civilians as their Humvees passed. When the private confronted one of these men, the man responded, "Look, I hate being in Iraq. I hate being stuck here. And I hate being surrounded by hajis" (A21).

Perhaps because there was, in the early months following the invasion of Iraq, a somewhat recognizable "front" in the Iraq war, many insist that *hajji* is unique to Iraq. To be sure, the bulk of American war literature and reportage has been focused on the combat there, and since March of 2003, there were more American troops on the ground in Iraq than there were in Afghanistan, a fact that applied until June of 2010 (McLean). Still, from the very beginning of the United States' military responses to 9/11, *hajji*'s reference system began to grow. The epithet may have begun on the battlefield, and it may have initially described an Iraqi enemy in dehumanizing terms, but as Price points out, as early as September of 2003 (the official bombing of Iraq began six months earlier, on 18 March 2003), *hajji* already described anyone from the Middle East or from anywhere in Southwest Asia (A1). Rick Atkinson noticed the same widening in *hajji*'s references during the invasion itself. In his chronicle of the two months he spent with the 101st Airborne Division—*In the Company of Men* (2004)—Atkinson explains, "Kuwaitis, Saudis, and all others with vaguely Semitic features were known collectively as hajjis" (33). Even if the individual American mil-

Six: Representing Hajji: This Generation's Enemy "Other" 161

itary member hasn't actually served within the borders of Iraq or Afghanistan, she or he probably has moved around southwest Asia with striking fluidity, and *hajji* made the trip too.

From 2005 through 2010, I served in Saudi Arabia, Bahrain, Qatar, Turkey, Kazakhstan, and the United Arab Emirates, and I flew all around the region in a KC-10 refueling tanker. Everywhere I went, on the ground and in the sky, I personally heard (and used) *hajji* to describe people from Saudi Arabia, Bahrain, Qatar, the United Arab Emirates, Kazakhstan, Afghanistan, Pakistan, Turkey, and even Bangladesh. A particularly quick-moving meme, *hajji* fulfills the American need to conceptualize the Other as homogeneous, different, and dangerous. Thus, *hajji* can readily describe any person in any country who may come into contact with any American in any deployed location after 9/11, regardless of that person's status as an enemy, a Muslim, a civilian, or even an ally. I once bought a cinnamon roll from a Cinnabon franchise in an upscale mall in Dubai while waiting to see the movie *Avatar* in a 3-D theater. A friend of mine, a captain in the Air Force, walked up to me and said, "Hajji makes a nice cinnamon roll, huh?" Clearly, *hajji* extends far beyond the battlefield.

Like I did, other support troops encounter the word in everyday parlance. In the nonfiction *Soldier Girls* (2014), Helen Thorpe writes about a woman soldier named Debbie whose unit was often tasked with guarding Afghan construction workers at an American Army base in late 2004. Debbie relates how many of the soldiers from her unit called this "hadji duty" or "hadji watch," even though these Afghan men were not enemies; they were employees of the United States (161). Debbie notes the racism behind *hajji*'s existence as a symbol (172), as does Kayla Williams in her memoir, *Love My Rifle More than You* (2005). Williams recounts her experiences as an intelligence specialist during the 2003 invasion of Iraq. She and her unit are working on a "relatively secure" base outside a town called Sinjar when another soldier gives her a "hajji-be-good stick" (256). She explains: "Some of the locals (who drove the buses) slept right behind the building where I slept. Matt didn't trust them. So he wanted to be sure I'd be safe. That's why he gave me the stick to keep under my pillow at night" (257). Earlier in the memoir, Williams admits, like Debbie does, that *hajji* is dehumanizing, and that it is designed to ensure that "we didn't see our enemy as people" (200). As Williams sees it, such a perspective is the "first thing any soldier [learned] in a combat situation" (200). Thus, *hajji* follows the usual path of logic: since 9/11, the threat of terrorism is everywhere, even if we can't see it. So, too, is the paranoia, and that paranoia might actually increase the further one gets from combat.

Note that while Williams is sufficiently retrospective about the epithet, she clearly considers herself to be in a "combat situation," and she intends that status to somewhat explain *hajji*. I certainly don't dispute the hazards she faced and the cautions she took in response to anything she did during her tour in Iraq. Yet, the fact remains that her "hajji-be-good stick" was not intended to be used against any enemy, and there certainly was no combat threat involved in its potential usage. Like Debbie's "hadji watch," the disdain conveyed in the slur is more general than that. Williams wasn't protecting herself from a wave of hardened Al Qaeda insurgents jumping the fence and firing AK-47s; she was protecting herself from friendly bus drivers.[5]

Sniping *Hajji*

These examples prove the pervasive nature of *hajji* in America's war discourse, but they do not explain the specific nature of *hajji*, a nature that allows it to travel so well, so that it simultaneously summons the specific and the general, the familiar and the foreign. *Hajji* is an extension of what Herman Melville calls, in the title of the penultimate chapter of *The Confidence-Man* (1857), the "Metaphysics of Indian Hating" in American culture.[6] Just as Richard Drinnon explains in his seminal work *Facing West: The Metaphysics of Indian Hating and Empire Building* (1980), *hajji* is an abiding expression of a "national animosity" that has driven the metanarrative of American war culture for centuries (xxii). *Hajji* is rooted in the Puritanical savage-civilian binary that drove western expansion, fueled the conquest of the American west, and justified the U.S. military's genocidal efforts to eliminate the native population of North American. While the hajjification of the post–9/11 enemy may not be explicitly directed toward native tribes in the United States, Indian hating at the sociohistorical level excuses, authorizes, and provides the model for its racist undertones. Symbols and mascots like the Washington Redskins and the North Dakota Fighting Sioux and Chief Wahoo culturally authorize *hajji*, "HAJIKLR" license plates, and the "Hajji Girl" song (more on these later).[7] Because Americans are so thoroughly inundated with widely accepted stereotypes of Native Americans, the American military member can easily accept and unquestioningly embrace words like *hajji* and deploy it in a manner similar to Puritanical nineteenth century savage Indian stereotypes. As Billy J. Stratton writes of the captivity narrative commonly attributed to Mary Rowlandson and Increase Mather's *A Brief History of the Warr with the Indians of New-England*,

> A primary function of writings such as them was to validate Puritan claims and justify the prosecution of the war through the graphic chronicling of "Indian depredations" and cruelties that functioned to demonize, marginalize, and effectively silence Native subjectivities [8].

Hajji can be conceived as a modern manifestation of the same function. Therefore, when we look at contemporary war culture through a similar lens, *hajji* becomes just as complex as the past examples of "native-hating" that Drinnon examines in his book, perhaps even more so (xxvi).

The most glaring example of the persistence of this Puritanical revenge metanarrative in contemporary war literature is Chris Kyle's "autobiography" (co-written with Scott McEwan and Jim DeFelice) entitled *American Sniper: the Autobiography of the Most Lethal Sniper in U.S. Military History* (2012). Chris Kyle never uses the term *hajji* in his "autobiography," but he explicitly invokes the Puritanical savage-civilian binary as he describes his mindset as a sniper:

> Savage, despicable evil. That's what we were fighting in Iraq. That's why a lot of people, myself included, called the enemy "savages." There really was no other way to describe what we encountered there [4].[8]

It is important for Kyle that he maintain this binary, and if the flood of responses to Clint Eastwood's cinematic adaptation of the book is any indication, many Americans are all too eager to accept his attitude as acceptable and representative.

Both the movie and the book present the story of an exceptionally effective and unapologetic Navy sniper with 160 confirmed kills. Perhaps expectedly, then, the movie adaptation takes considerable license with many other aspects of Kyle's life as it tries to shape individual scenes of the rather bland book into a narrative arc, and they speak to a larger project in the film, one that Michael Carson says is driven by "pure unadulterated kitsch" (*"American"*). This is where *hajji* comes into play as a symbol. Toward the beginning of the movie, the movie follows Kyle back to a mostly empty bunkhouse on his FOB in Iraq. The actor, Bradley Cooper, who plays Kyle, walks in and asks his friend Biggles, "Where is everybody?" Biggles responds, "Training those haji soldiers" (Hall 35).[9] Here, *hajji* describes the good guys—Iraqis willing to serve in the newly formed Iraqi military. Yet, this scene and this conversation never happen in the "autobiography." In the book, Kyle does express his unvarnished disdain for the newly formed Iraqi Army, but like many other departures from the book that the movie takes, *hajji* brings something more complex to the emotional core of the film that, presumably, Hall or Eastwood found lacking in Kyle's book.

Does *hajji* lessen or reinforce Kyle's repeated invocation of the savage-civilian binary or is it just one more insertion of military kitsch? While Hall says that he pieced together his dialogue and other authenticity-lending elements like *hajji* from sources other than Kyle's book, the scene above allows the movie Chris Kyle an opportunity to express his conviction that the enemy is guided by evil while a good God guides the Americans (a repeated refrain in the "autobiography").[10] Carson argues that the movie "manipulates substandard genre tropes to produce an innocuous and utterly uninteresting character study, turning a once breathing man into a figment, an avatar of our lazy imaginations" ("*American*"). That it does, and *hajji* is one of its tools.

Tone has a lot to do with its absence in Kyle's book. With some effort, one could read Kyle's "autobiography" as just that, a first-hand account of S.E.A.L. training and that training's culmination in one man's experience of war. Kyle's diction and narration would support such a reading. He deploys to Iraq four times, and the enemy changes, as it should, as time passes. During the invasion of Iraq and his first deployment, he largely sticks with "Iraqis" (76–78), and then soon thereafter he begins alternating between "insurgents" and "terrorists" and "Iraqis." But then his horribly limited savage/civilian worldview pushes itself onto the page. In one passage, Kyle adopts a professional tone as he teaches us about "terrorist forces," a force of fighters drawn from the "Ba'athist Party that Saddam headed" or the Fedayeen "paramilitary resistance group" or "Iraqi guerillas" or "al-Qaeda in Iraq" (119). He tells us about the "Iranians and their Republican Guard" and "what came to be known to the media as 'the insurgency'" (120). When his unit starts training Iraqi men to serve in the new Iraq Army, he says, "we called them all *jundis*, Arabic for soldiers" (251). Kyle retains this confident, almost condescending, tone throughout; however, despite all of his "officialese," Kyle cannot avoid the historic urge to conceive every one of these people comprehensively. And so Kyle reverts to his general label of "evil" to describe anyone who happens to end up in his gun sight. This is the message of both the book and the movie: if Kyle is shooting him, he is evil. The labels don't matter. And this is where *hajji* comes in; the incongruity of Kyle's perspective is obvious in the book despite—or even because of—his unwavering certainty, but the movie needed a little extra push to translate that to the screen.

Carson explains the movie's "kitsch" according to the Clement Greenberg definition of the term.[11] Carson writes, "our uniquely modern kitsch privileges authenticity to such a degree that it mistakes authenticity for art" ("*American*"). This partly explains why the *American Sniper* filmmakers used *hajji* as they did. In the movie, when Kyle is leading a group of Marines through a section of Ramadi, making sure all houses are empty as they move past, they discover a family. After a tense struggle, the father begs them all to come in from the alleyway: "please tell the others to come inside" (Hall 45). A Marine says, "This hajji wants us in here so he can blow us up." This line is from the movie only; nothing like it exists in the "autobiography," and the final draft of the script reads, "This sand nig' want us in here so he can blow us up" (Hall 45). Carson worries that cheap military kitsch like this instance of *hajji* can trick an audience into feeling "warm and fuzzy (or angry and titillated) without any guilt for the obviously contrived sappiness" ("*American*"). He is right. In this case, "Sand nig'" would have interrupted that flow. It would have introduced too big of a racist stumbling block into the flow of this scene designed to heighten the sentimental sappiness of the movie's plot. "Sand nig'" would have pulled our focus off the good-evil binary and onto the utterance. *Hajji*, on the other hand, allows us to pass right on by and ignore the fact that it operates in exactly the same way but avoids notice; its symbolic significance is nearly drowned out by everything else Kyle insists is true about himself and the enemy. These two *hajjis* contain every ounce of the loathing and superiority that Kyle conveys in his reference system. Or, more precisely, they quietly highlight that Kyle's logic is just as untenable and ridiculous as *hajji* itself whenever an American military member utters it.

Dismantling *Hajji*

In other American wars, there was little mistaking the demonizing function of "chinks" and "japs" and "gooks." In our more recent wars, however, as the heavy differences between the movie and book version of *American Sniper* reveal, *hajji* operates—at times—with both more ambiguity and more precision. For one, *hajji* is a byproduct of the American need to simulate the enemy in terms its symbol-using animals (both soldiers and civilians) are familiar with. It is used to assuage fear and vengeance and hatred and guilt. But its complexity comes from the fact that soldiers like Chris Kyle feel an obligation to force convenient metanarratives and historical myths of American exceptionalism onto their stories of war while they also attempt to leave their tales free of that order's attendant guilt.

As Umberto Eco writes in *Travels in Hyperreality* (1985), America has a taste for the "sign that aims to be the thing, to abolish the distinction of the reference" (7). The sign—in this case *hajji*—through repetition, takes the place of the thing (a mass of human beings that may or may not be considered American enemies) and becomes its double, its "plaster cast" (7). This impulse, Eco writes, "is the reason for this journey into hyper-reality, in search of instances where the American imagination demands the real thing, and to attain it, must fabricate the absolute fake" (8). *Hajji* is just as derogatory as "chink" and "gook," and like these other slurs, it is an "absolute fake" when it is uttered by an American in the context of war. It takes no large leap of logic to draw the conclusion that it is easier to kill an absolute fake, a double, or a plaster cast. However, *hajji* is still a sign-carrier of more nuanced, dialectic proportions because the "thing" or the "reference" itself covers such a wide range of possibilities. The object that *hajji* points to is both everywhere and nowhere.

As Drinnon suggests, "Societies are known by their victims" (xxii). Societies are also known by the way they describe their victims, and the ubiquity of *hajji* and its wide range of references reflect more about American fear and attitudes in this "Global War on Terror" than it does about the enemy itself. Such dialectic imagining is nothing new, though, in fiction, memoir, or autobiography. In 1938, Kenneth Burke outlined the steps that Hitler took in *Mein Kampf* to establish the international Jew as the perfect enemy of and scapegoat for the German people. "It may well be," Burke writes in "The Rhetoric of Hitler's *Battle*," that "people, in their human frailty, require an enemy as well as a goal" (20). Burke outlines the ways Hitler first essentialized the Jew as the perfect, deserving scapegoat, and then used that "international devil" as a "visible, point-to-able form of a people with a certain 'blood,' a burlesque of contemporary neo-positivism's ideal of meaning, which insists upon a material reference" (3–4). Hitler invented his concept of blood purity to isolate and mark Jewish people as worthy of victimage, but what happens when the "devil" or "evil" is more loosely defined?

As Robert Ivie and Oscar Giner write in their co-authored *Hunt the Devil* (2015), "Naming the demonic enemy constitutes the peculiar state of war that turns the nation against its democratic self" (13). The hajjification of the enemy in our enduring conflicts in Iraq and Afghanistan has left a mess of entangled meaningfulness that glossaries, non-fictive chronicles of war, and short journalistic explanations often fail to fully examine. As Englehardt points out (ironically) in *The American Way of War* (2010), it can be quite difficult to "spot a terrorist," or, for that matter, is just as challenging to find a material reference for something called "anti–Iraqi forces" or "Baathist remnants" or "insurgents" (96, 97). Englehardt's point is not that it is difficult to find an enemy and engage that enemy with military force; rather, he is arguing that language is nearing impotence in its ability to capture and describe the collective of human beings that can be called an enemy of the United States after 9/11. When movies like *American Sniper* deem it necessary to insert *hajji* into their tales, they prove that *hajji* is a colloquial answer for this conundrum.

There may be no Hitlerite voice naming the new devil and describing the new scapegoat for the American public, but as Ivie and Giner point out, Americans don't need such a director. We are well-trained in that respect. Like the Puritans, American military members grasp for slurs like *hajji* to create, as Stratton puts it, a "mythico-historical master narrative to order the world in a way familiar" to the narratives they grew up with (15). Out of the forces of fear, vengeance, historiography, and human frailty, our contemporary war literature and culture provides ample proof that we are quite skilled in our ability to name an enemy and pile upon that enemy a society's worth of animosity.

Of Hitler, Burke writes: "Let us try also to discover what kind of 'medicine' this medicine-man has concocted, that we may know, with greater accuracy, exactly what to guard against if we are to forestall the concocting of similar medicine in America" (1). *Hajji* has the potential to work similar Hitler-ian magic on American society, and that should frighten anyone into examining the word beyond glossing it in a special list of terms. As Edward Said writes in his preface to the twenty-fifth anniversary edition of *Orientalism* (1978),

> [I]t is incumbent upon us to complicate and/or dismantle the reductive formulae and the abstract but potent kind of thought that leads the mind away from concrete human history and experience and into the realms of ideological fiction, metaphysical confrontation, and collective passions [xxiii].

Part of *hajji*'s symbolic complexity as an enemy epithet comes from the fact that it is, at its etymological root, an Arabic word. Actually, it is an Arabic title. The *Oxford English Dictionary* agrees with Buzzell's interpreter as the term is used in Muslim cultures: it is "the title given to one who has made the greater pilgrimage … to Mecca." Since the pilgrimage itself is called the "hajj," adding the adjectival suffix thus makes *hajji* an honorific title of respect for countless men across the Muslim world (the feminine equivalent uses the feminine suffix, resulting in *hajjah*).

Since it can take years to save up enough money to pay for such a trip, the term usually refers to elderly men. So, oftentimes, *hajji* can simply be a term of respect, independent of any actual completion of the pilgrimage. In various cultures, *hajji* has been adopted into the surname itself and handed down to successive generations that may or may not remain tied to their Muslim heritage at all. Most often, however, the title comes to supplant the man's first name completely in common speech. For instance, Leo Tolstoy's eponymous hero of his historical novel *Hadji Murád* (1912) is never referred to or addressed with anything but the two-term "Hadji Murád." It is reasonable to suggest, then, that Tolstoy's warrior of shifting allegiances and shifting motivations made the pilgrimage to Mecca sometime before the events of the novel. Therefore, the convention as Tolstoy maintains it is both appropriate and culturally accurate. So, it stands to reason that an American soldier or an embedded reporter can indeed address an elder man in Iraq or Afghanistan with the title *hajji* and be taken in absolute earnestness. Yet, whereas Tolstoy only uses the word in its denotative sense, very few American soldiers do the same when they appropriate *hajji*.

Hajji has long enjoyed a troubled legacy in America, one that began with midcentury American pop culture when it brought an exotic, Oriental flavor to a cartoon character. In 1964, the *Johnny Quest* cartoon series introduced American children to Johnny Quest's sidekick, a twelve-year-old orphan from Calcutta named Hadji. This turban-wearing boy is the perfect companion (adopted brother even) for the series' hero; he is wise and gentle and possesses a skill set that makes him both indispensably useful and ultimately mysterious. In the series *I Dream of Jeannie*, Hadji is the name of the "master of all genies" who appears in four different episodes. Like the *Johnny Quest* character, this "Hadji" wears a turban and speaks with a Hindi accent.

Both of these examples are clear manifestations of Edward Said's concept of the patronizing Western attitude of "Orientalism." *Hajji*'s development, rooted as it is in these caricatured images of the "Orient," persists still today in western representations of the Middle East and South Asia. Indeed, Said could have been describing *hajji* in a 1980 essay that he wrote for *The Nation*:

> So far as the United States seems to be concerned, it is only a slight overstatement to say that Moslems and Arabs are essentially seen as either oil suppliers or potential terrorists. Very little of the detail, the human density, the passion of Arab-Moslem life has entered the awareness of even those people whose profession it is to report the Arab world. What we have, instead, is a series of crude, essentialized caricatures of the Islamic world presented in such a way as to make that world vulnerable to military aggression [490].

Today, *hajji* is an ethnic-religious-racial-antagonistic slur of massive symbolic implications that—sadly—reinforces the very attitude Said sought to critique and reshape.

In the language and discourse of American war culture, it is possible to accept *hajji* as just another specialized term in the confusing lexicon of the American military member and—in so accepting—perpetuate the stereotype that a wide swath of human beings are backward fanatics or war enthusiasts. Robert Ivie's admonition that "it is difficult to see something that is everywhere" is a worthy reminder in *hajji*'s case ("Savagery" 58). *Hajji*'s growing and unquestioned appearance in contemporary war art of all kinds, despite lexical attempts to explain it, suggests that its acceptance as a symbol is growing. As Northrop Frye posits, "typical recurring images" of a genre function as "communicable units" (*Anatomy* 99). *Hajji* appears so often and is accepted so easily that a reader or viewer can easily pass the term by as a convenient label for any anonymous, faceless enemy amid the baffling panoply of organizations and individuals who oppose the United States' global military actions since 9/11.

In the Academy Award winning movie *Hurt Locker* (2009), one American soldier observes, through binoculars, a would-be suicide bomber sitting in a car. The soldier knows nothing of this bearded man's background; so he simply calls him "hajji" in his report to his superiors. In an entirely different scene, another soldier pulls his pants down and "moons" a building where some enemy combatants are hiding: "We got you motherfuckers," he says, "You're fucking dead hajjis." In the Peter Berg's action film *Lone Survivor* (2013)—which was based on a co-written memoir of the same name by a Navy S.E.A.L. named Marcus Luttrell—three Afghan goat herders stumble upon a small group of American special operations troops who are spying on a compound. The Americans grab the goat herders and tie them up, but they are unsure about their next step. In the movie, one of the Americans says, "Look at them. They fucking hate us. We don't know how many hajji's they have down there. We can't let them go" (51).[12] They let the Afghani goat herders go, though, and the rest of the movie becomes a running battle between hundreds of brown men and four Americans. Interestingly enough, like *American Sniper*, neither the epithet nor the exchange above exists anywhere in Luttrell's original text. When the debate over the goat herders arrives in the memoir, one of Luttrell's fellow S.E.A.L.s named Danny Dietz says, "I don't give a shit what you decide. Just tell me what to do" (235).

Still, the word should not be dismissed as a Hollywood invention or an overused element of military kitsch or even as a natural expression of ingrained American attitudes about the Orient. Brody points out that "It is painful for U.S. soldiers to hear discussions and watch movies about modern wars when the dialogue is full of obsolete slang." It also is painful to hear military slang bandied about with linguistic abandon, but this does not mean filmmakers and authors are wrong to include *hajji* in their representations of war. Tobias Woolf pointed out in 2011 that in the "powerful tradition of writing about" war, conventions and a "jazzy vocabulary" that is "encrusted with cliché" incessantly grows up within war's art. Such clichés, he says, derive their power from the "ironic vocabulary" military members build up around "every corrupt thing" they do during war. Woolf is speaking of Vietnam, but *hajji* is no different, and Hollywood has not missed the authenticity-lending and guilt-driving resonance it can bring to contemporary war flicks. The trick is spotting the corruption through the crust, which is sometimes difficult to do when war literature must contend with those who merely accept the term at face value, shrug, and move on.

Robert Kaplan, in his neo-conservative celebration of American warfighting traditions entitled *Primal Grunts* (2005), places *hajji* right beside *chai* (the tea), suggesting they are equal terms U.S. soldiers must adapt for their own use in Afghanistan. Kaplan tells of a soldier nicknamed Big Country who shows Kaplan a village where he went to "inspect a minefield, and talk and drink *chai* (tea) with the *hajis*" (213). Kaplan pauses long enough to add an aside in a short appositive; he points out that *hajji* is "the nickname that American personnel had given the Afghans" (213). That is all he has to say about the term or Big Country's success or failure in communicating with the local population.

Clearly, a deep cultural pathology created and supports *hajji*, more so than its growing cliché-crust might suggest. As the pathological appearance of *hajji* continues to gain currency in war literature and war films, it becomes glaringly evident that it has less and less to do with an actual or imagined enemy or with the enactment of some sort of religious vituperation. It certainly does these things, but as it appears in American war literature, *hajji* is more a tool of American consensus building and a collective purging of war guilt. Moreover, fiction and other works of the imagination might be more appropriately poised for an honest presentation of *hajji*'s existence in war discourse. As my previous three chapters reveal, it is possible for artifice to provide more intense interrogations of war's complex hierarchies and vicarious purgings than history, more nuance than reportage, less parochial versions of wartime historiography than autobiography and memoir.

In the fall of 2014, I made similar observations in an article I wrote for *War, Literature, and the Arts*. In that essay, I wrote about my first exposure to *hajji* and its widespread use as a comprehensive pejorative to describe the Other. I identify the word's misappropriation by American servicemen and women (including myself), and I explain the growing unease I have since come to feel whenever I encounter *hajji* in the literature I read and the profession I live. Previously, I was primarily concerned with the ways various writers approach *hajji* in their representations of war. Some try to explain or mitigate the word's pejorative power with brief editorial notes, or they decide to include *hajji* in a special glossary of military lingo (like Brody). Sometimes—through footnotes or parenthetical asides—they insist the word is merely an innocuous nickname (like Kaplan). Others—usually professional journalists—simply excise the word completely from the dialogue of their work.

For example, Dexter Filkins (in *The Forever War*, a journalistic memoir about Iraq) and Sebastian Junger (in *War*, set in Afghanistan) only use the word denotatively, as an honorific (Buchanan 1, 8). I'm only speculating, but it seems reasonable to suggest that both writers heard the word being used in a derogatory manner in Iraq and Afghanistan. If true, they both chose to leave it out of their accounts of their experiences as journalists embedded with U.S. units. The marketing material that accompanies HBO's *Generation Kill* series (about the 2003 invasion of Iraq) takes a different approach, arguing—somewhat happily—that soldiers use *hajji* "not necessarily [as] a pejorative term." Instead, HBO claims, the word is more often used as an innocuous adjective to describe unfamiliar things (Buchanan 5).[13] Likewise, and even more difficult to accept, is memoirist Donavon Campbell's claim (in *Joker One*) that the term "wasn't meant to denigrate" when he and his fellow Marines used it in Iraq. Instead, he says, they used the term because the "two-syllable 'hajji'" was easier to say than the "three-syllable 'Iraqi'" (Buchanan 4). Admirable though (some of) these attempts are in their attempt to account for the term's potential significance, none of them fully acknowledge or capture the word's complexities. The mere fact that many authors and editors find it necessary to explain, obfuscate, or mislead the meaning of *hajji* indicates that, as I point out above, a "dancing of an attitude" attaches to the word whenever an American uses it in the context of war (Burke, *Philosophy* 9).

This is the problem with breezy glosses of military jargon and even some straightforward attempts to explain the word in a manner that keeps the explanation from intruding too far into the narrative. *Demon Camp* (2014) is Jennifer Percy's non-fictive story about her interactions with an Army sergeant named Caleb Daniels and the post-traumatic stress disorder that drove them both to seek out a formal, religious "exorcism" of the "demons" Daniels brought home from Afghanistan. Percy's is a unique style for war literature—Lea Carpenter describes it as "participatory journalism, in extremis" (BR11). Midway through her tale, Percy gives us an impressively inclusive list of wartime slurs that, like *hajji*, emerge from training that seeks to make it easier for "humans [to] pretend they're not killing humans" (120). As she summarizes, "Words used instead of person: Kraut, Jap, Reb, Yank, Dink, Slant, Slope, Skinny, Gook, Haji" (120). I have no problem with the list, per se, or Percy's decision to include it in her book. After all, I do the same thing in the first page of this chapter. I cite it here to point out the dismissive effects that such a simple categorizing can have.

Such a list picks up a certain analysis-denying momentum as it appears in various iterations in multiple publications. In his essay about Paul Fussell, John Wilson writes that "lists indicate how difficult it is to represent all aspects of reality, and how much distortion is required to subordinate reality to critical orthodoxy" (180). Percy likely doesn't include her list of epithets to illustrate this point, though; for one, it is nearly the exact same as another list in an essay by Stanley Hauerwas that appears in the *Journal of Religion, Conflict and Peace*—Percy adds "skinny" and moves the location of "gook" as if she cut, pasted, and slightly updated the exact list of terms. Hauerwas, a professor of "theological ethics" at Duke Divinity School, writes:

> Soldiers are often criticized for denying the humanity of the enemy by calling the enemy names such as *kraut, Jap, reb, gook, Yank, dink, slant, or slope, or haji*. Moreover, the enemy is not "killed" but knocked over, wasted, greased, taken out, mopped up, or lit up. But surely these attempts to depersonalize the enemy as well as rename the process of killing should be understood as a desperate attempt to preserve the humanity of those who must kill [italics added].

Lists like these do little to urge a reader to probe further into *hajji*'s place there, and they allow us to make casual assertions, as Hauerwas does, that human beings "must kill." It is entirely possible for one to read through it, momentarily pause, conclude that this is just what happens in war, and move on.

Elinor Levy, in "Upper Echelons and Boots on the Ground," does a close examination of *hajji* in her essay on military parlance, suggesting that such words grow out of the process of young men and women acquiring "cultural competency" as they "learn and internalize a wide array of new rules, procedures, and traditions" in their new lives within the military (99). When enlisted men and women have their "boots on the ground" in combat, she suggests, a special register of speech emerges, one that she describes with the neologism "enlistic" (100). She does admit that "hadji" is an expression of combat "soldiers' animus toward those who are different from themselves," but her primary concern is with creating this special glossary—she calls it a "disglossia"—for the uninitiated (108, 99). Levy's effort is admirable and probably necessary, but by so categorizing military slang and arguing why soldiers talk this way, she sort of celebrates its crudeness. Her essay may help to bridge the so-called civilian/military divide, but it also ignores larger, more troubling motivations. I doubt that anyone would make the same arguments about racial slurs and their persistent appearance in certain regions or subcultures of the United States.

To be sure, dictionaries and glossaries and lists clarify meaning, but they also limit it. As Mariana Birnbaum points out, "That slurs are the fastest vehicles by which national or regional antagonisms can be expressed is proven by the fact that often the very same motif takes widely different 'national tags'" (253–54). In the case of *hajji*, however, national tags are not even necessary; or, one could argue, they are not feasible. Without the space, the need, or the motivation, very few find the need distinguish between an Afghani or an Iraqi "Hajji shop" or to specify the allegiances of the person a "hodgie killer" is preparing to shoot. A "fucking hajji," as the word is often paired, is anything that stands as an element apart from the American military machine.

In his ambitious *Dictionary of International Slurs* (1944), A.A. Roback recognizes that describing a word as "slur" or "epithet" or "stereotype" or even as "slang" misses the full power of such a symbol; so Roback favors the word "ethnophaulisms" as a term to describe any "foreign disparaging allusion" (13). Regardless the term we use to denotatively categorize *hajji*, the strongest part of Roback's dictionary of slurs is the following point he makes in his introduction:

> [T]he moment a slang coinage is encountered ... we are immediately aware that we are no longer in the sphere of lexicography, but have skirted the realm of folklore and social psychology; for here we are studying attitudes of one people toward another [11].

In order to account for the attitudes that created *hajji*, a number of scholars have tried to examine it from a sociological point-of-view. Rightly so, Said's work and post-colonialism theory in general drives much of the extant scholarship about *hajji*.

One of the first was Daniel Egan in his postcolonial study, "Frantz Fanon and the Construction of the Colonial Subject: Defining 'The Enemy' in the Iraq War," which appeared in 2007. A sociologist, Egan looks at the "racialized nature" of the United States' "imperialism" as made apparent through our invasion and subsequent occupation of Iraq. Drawing from Fanon's theory of colonialism, Egan looks at the racist discourse of contemporary war that recasts the Iraqi people as "lazy," "unproductive," "savage," and "dangerous" (144). Soldiers do this, Egan argues, in order to ensure the colonized population remains appropriately subordinate to the "colonizer's" superiority (144). As he puts it,

> The racialized language of the Iraq war performs the important function of defining Iraqis as being "worthy" of subordination. In referring to Iraqis as "hajis," US forces make assumptions that all Iraqis are Muslims ... and that all Iraqis are the "enemy" or are potentially so, regardless of their political or religious affiliation [149].

Egan's work carefully outlines the sociological forces that have driven the agents of modern imperialism (soldiers) to recast every non–American as part of a massive, faceless, Muslim horde, one that must be controlled or eliminated.

Also in 2007, Keith Brown and Catherine Lutz examined seven war memoirs written by U.S. military personnel, not as literature or folklore, but as more documentary examples of Michel Foucault's concept of "subjugated knowledges" (322). Such "grunt lit," as they see it, forms a subaltern, yet important and "informed," source of "multiple, militarized transnational processes that help drive contemporary globalization" (322). They call it "warrior knowledge" (322). I don't necessarily consider "grunt lit"—which Brown and Lutz simply define as memoirs written by "junior officers and enlisted" (328)—as clear examples of "subjugated knowledges." None of the books they cite are, as Foucault describes his concept, "unqualified" or "disqualified," nor are they "buried" or "disguised in a functionalist coherence of formal systemization" (*Power/Knowledge* 81, 82). Indeed, one could easily argue that "grunt lit" really describes those products that are rooted in a clearly hegemonic social model. Despite these issues, Brown and Lutz, like Egan, rightly put *hajji* in a post-colonial context, and they accurately suggest that "grunt lit" authors "seek to master the environment through a language that lurches from technical to obscene but is always motivated by a taxonomic impulse" (325). On this point, Brown and Lutz make an important observation about *hajji*:

> Anyone is potentially a "Haji," a general-purpose epithet that appears as the direct descendant of Vietnam's "gooks" or "dinks" or Somalia's "skinnies." For many soldiers, as Williams wearily recounts, this category becomes synonymous with "enemy." But others, including most of these authors, seek greater precision.... These memoirs show the power—and danger—of analogical thinking in sense making [326].

I agree all the way up until the phrase "sense making." *Hajji* can definitely be conceived of as an imperialist's tool. It can, if one is often locked in the anguish of constant combat, also be counted as a response to the environment of war and a byproduct of hatred and fear and confusion. Yet, this conclusion about "sense making," one could argue, is a gentler way to say the same thing as Tobias Woolf, that soldiers develop an "ironic vocabulary for every corrupt thing" they do during war. Substitute "symbolic action" for "sense-making" and one can see how easily *hajji* begins to serve racist, scapegoating purposes.

Tyler Wall, in two separate essays about *hajji*, performs a closer examination of *hajji*. In his second essay, "Philanthropic Soldiers," he follows the same line of analysis as Egan, Brown, and Lutz, concluding that, after interviewing twenty-four soldiers regarding their deployments to Iraq, *hajji* is part and parcel of how soldiers "make sense of both themselves and Iraqi others" (481). While this yet again comes dangerously close to normalizing or rationalizing the use of a racial and religious slur in a crude attempt to achieve ontological clarity, some of these soldiers, Wall claims, are honestly ignorant to any suggestion that the word can be considered off-color, inappropriate, or even controversial. One soldier tells Wall about giving a presentation at a local high school on what the soldier titled "Hadji culture" and "Hadji geography" (496). The same willful ignorance, as Stacey Peebles points out, exists in John Crawford's memoir, *The Last True Story I'll Ever Tell* (2005). At one point, Crawford writes about a "hajji friend" but, as Peebles notes, Crawford is "perhaps unaware that his use of *hajji*, a pejorative American term for anyone Iraqi and/or Arab, as a modifier for 'friend' is rather oxymoronic" (113).

As far as the symbolic action that *hajji* represents as a scapegoating tool, Wall's other essay about *hajji*, "Imperial Laughs" is far more useful. In this essay, Wall examines *hajji* by "critically reading" a song written by a U.S. Marine named Joshua Belile and performed at Al Asad airfield in Iraq in September of 2005 in front of a large, laughing audience. A video of the performance was later posted on YouTube, in 2006.[14] The song, known as "Hadji Girl," reflects, Wall argues, "colonial sensibilities that help to mark difference as abject and disposable" ("Imperial" 81). That it does, and Wall's analysis of the performance thoroughly reduces the song to its value as a troubling artifact, or as a "cultural expression" of Derek Gregory's concept of the "colonial present" (74). It is, as Gerald Vizenor would likely describe it, a "colonial enactment" of dominance (*Manifest* 11). In "Hadji Girl," *hajji* is a simulation only, one that supersedes anything relating to a recognizable object. Furthermore, in the word's coarse misappropriation, an even deeper animosity is communicated, one that is actually intensified by the word's denotative sense. While I agree with Wall's analysis, I would add that Belile and his chuckling audience are reveling in their status as colonial superiors. This symbol abuse isn't sense making; it is scapegoat making, a performance of congregation by segregation.

The story of the song follows a Marine who encounters a "Hadji" girl while taking cover inside a Burger King during a battle "out in the sands of Iraq" ("Imperial" 74).[15] The Marine and the girl fall in love "at first sight" (74). So the Marine follows the "Hadji girl" to a "side shanty" where the girl's brother and father jump up, shouting and waving "their AKs" (75). The song concludes with the Marine using the "Hadji girl's" little sister as a human shield as he laughs "maniacally," and "[blows] those little fuckers to eternity" (75). Wall examines the reasons why an audience might find this song funny, concluding that "even if we grant that the intent of 'Hadji Girl' was to be inoffensive, 'dark humor,' a 'joke' in the eyes of its supporters, the song should not be dismissed as trivial or insignificant" (80). It is, he concludes, a distasteful example of how American soldiers make sense of combat and war. That should disturb us.

It is worth noting here, as Wall does, that the U.S. Marine Corps investigated Belile and the song, concluding that Belile did not violate any military regulations because he was not wearing a full uniform (he is visible from the waist up and wears a tan undershirt) and therefore did not represent the U.S. Marines at the time. And, for what it is worth, Belile did apologize later, though with major caveats, the most significant one (to me) being that the song was "nothing more than something supposed to be funny, based off a catchy line of a movie" (qtd. in Mazzolini).[16] The "catchy line," which forms the chorus of Belile's song, is undecipherable Arabic-sounding gibberish from the 2005 film *Team America: World Police*, a crude, but deeply satirical, comedy that was and is wildly popular across all corners of the U.S. military. Ironically, the popularity of the film among some soldiers and its presence in songs like Belile's displays how easy it is to misread or misunderstand satire; indeed, *Team America* criticizes the very attitude Belile celebrates in his song.

One might argue that Belile's use of both the phrase and the term *hajji* is a combat soldier's way of dealing with the trauma and threats of battle and expressing "what it's like to fight in Iraq." I know nothing of Belile's duty when he was deployed to Iraq; but as far as the performance of his song is concerned, he was on a stage on an extremely secure airbase being cheered on by more airmen and Marines when he quoted a movie made by the creators of *South Park*. Combat duty or sense making of war's violence had nothing to do with it.

The word *hajji* does not appear in *Team America*, but the phrase Belile says inspired his song is "Durka Durka Mohammed Jihad, sherpa

sherpa bak Allah," a punchline to an extended absurd joke delivered by one of the film's "heroes" named Gary. In the film, Gary tries to gain access to a terrorist hideout in Cairo; so he disguises himself with a turban and brown face paint and tries to pass for a "terrorist." As Gary approaches the hideout, two bearded guards holding assault rifles challenge him. "Durka Allah Muhammad jihad," one of the guards says. Gary hesitates. The tension builds. Agitated now, the guard says again, "Bakala! Muhammad jihad! Allah durka durka Muhammad Jihad!" As the tension builds, Gary breaks his silence and responds, meekly, with more gibberish: "durka durka mohammed jihad, sherpa sherpa bak Allah," he says. The guards allow him to pass.

In "Imperial Laughs," Wall discusses this phrase, and he describes the reasons why "Dirka Dirka Muhammad Jihad" might be so attractive to U.S. military members:

> [T]he perceived incoherence of the "other's" culture, especially the language of the colonized (is linked to) a logic of justification regarding the subjugation of the colonized.... Through the incoherence of the dark others' language, they are located in a field of racial and cultural hierarchy somewhere between civilization and savagery [77].

Wall doesn't explicitly make the link, but *hajji* operates in the same manner. It animalizes all speakers of Arabic and some who don't even speak Arabic. Whereas the classical Greek polis formulated the word "barbaros" to describe anyone who didn't speak Greek (because all non–Greek speakers sounded different, something like "bar bar"), the writers of *Team America* comically rendered Arabic speech into "durka durka" (Kitto 7–8). Indeed, elsewhere in the film, foreign terrorists are said to live in "Durkadurkastan."[17] This resonates with the typical American military member who often finds himself surrounded, not by flying bullets or improvised explosive devices, or death and blood, but by people he can't understand.

Still offensive in their ultimate effects of rendering all Arabic speakers as homogeneously subordinate to the speaker's culture and lumped into a religion that is popularly portrayed as one bent on creating terror around the world, *hajji* and "durka durka Muhammad Jihad" share a common etymological background: they are both nonsense. One could call such nonsense "sense making," but that sense making has less to do with the stress of combat or even religious vituperation than it does with symbol mongering, racism, and scapegoating. Indeed, Belile's "apology" may explain his intertextual borrowing of the phrase from *Team America* and his own sense of humor, but it does nothing to explain the phrase's sign-carrying significance. It does nothing to explain why a bunch of off-duty support troops cheered and hooted when they heard his song.

As Ivie writes, "The incomprehensible babble on the other side of the defensive walls surrounding democratic Athens was the threatening sound of the barbarian in ancient Greece" ("Savagery" 55). *Hajji* serves the same purpose. As nothing but sound, it resembles Arabic, because it *is* Arabic. But to American ears it is noise only; it carries no concrete denotative meaning at all. And this is what makes *hajji*'s misappropriation by American military members so dangerous and so meaningful. Even if we accept the dubious claim that no meaning is sent or received with its utterance, its pejorative meaning proliferates anyway. The soldier Wall interviewed—the one who taught a class in his old high school on "Hadji culture"—could have been happily unaware of the word's offensiveness, but his ignorance is almost irrelevant. If he did think "Hadji culture" was synonymous with "Iraqi culture," it is highly unlikely that is how that unfortunate classroom full of teenagers received such labeling.

In her article, "Harm's Way: Language and the Contemporary Arts of War," Mary Louise Pratt outlines the way language has been deployed by the U.S. military as a very real and very effective weapon in Afghanistan. After describing a unit of Marines who used loudspeakers and rock and roll music to draw the Taliban into a fight, Pratt writes, "The act of war here is the purposeful manipulation of the enemy's linguistic and symbolic codes in order to do the enemy harm, which is the purpose or currency of war making" (1518). *Hajji* is precisely this kind of manipulation of an enemy's symbolic code, but it is not *always* an overt attempt to verbally harm the described other. It is symbolic action. Pratt admits as much: "Do words," she asks, "when intended to wound, have an inalienable power to do so, or do addressees have the power simply to deflect them and refuse to be wounded?" (1522). In the case of *hajji*, addressees may have the power to deflect the insult or refuse to be wounded, but they may not be part of the dramatistic scene in which the utterance appears.

This is the case for both *hajji* and "durka durka," but they also differ in one important way. "Durka durka Muhammad Jihad" has no material reference whereas *hajji*'s reference is virtually unlimited. As a symbol, then, *hajji* carries far more contempt and loathing. This is why Colby Buzzell's interpreter was able to insist *hajji* is inoffensive; clearly, he was receiving a different meaning than the one intended. Or, at a minimum, he was being asked to define the word in an entirely different dramatic scene, a scene in which there was no symbolic clustering of alterity behind the word. He missed, as Emmanuel Levinas explains, that a word like *hajji* can operate much like a "third-person pronoun" which is "an impersonal, anonymous, but inextinguishable 'consummation' of being, which mur-

murs in the depths of nothingness itself" (52). Since it lacks an antecedent, the identity-starved subject can access a sense of substance and self via the absence implied in *hajji*. I'm guessing the interpreter's answer would have been quite different had Buzzell shown him the video of "Hadji Girl." Thus, *hajji* should be seen as—primarily—a performance of symbol mongering in the service of a scapegoating mechanism, as opposed to a useful part of wartime sense-making or an accumulation of cultural competence, unless, of course, that culture is to be defined as racist and hateful. Its original, denotative meaning left far behind without any object to perceive the intended or unintended insult, *hajji*'s utterance enacts a drama in and of itself.

Indeed, in the growing body of contemporary war literature penned by non–American authors, set in Iraq or Afghanistan and published in English, very few use the term *hajji* as an epithet or even discuss it as such, perhaps because they have no agency in the dramatistic scene of *hajji*'s typical appearance. Afghan author Nadeem Aslam doesn't use the term in either *The Blind Man's Garden* (2013) or *The Wasted Vigil* (2008), both of which are set in war-torn Afghanistan. Nowhere in *The Human Body* (2014) does the Italian Paolo Giordano's fictional squad of Italian soldiers on an isolated Afghan post use *hajji* or any other epithet for the enemy. The same is true about *The Corpse Exhibition* (2013), a collection of short war fiction written by the Iraqi author Hassan Blasim, and *The War Works Hard* (2005) a collection of poetry written by Dunya Mikhail, an exiled, Iraqi woman.

India-born novelist, Joydeep Roy-Bhattacharya, gently, uses *hajji* as an epithet in his novel, *The Watch* (2012), but he only does so once. In this one instance of *hajji*, Roy-Bhattacharya astutely uses the word to both lend authenticity to his dialogue (it is spoken by an American) and to complicate the labels of enemy and ally. After a small tribe of Taliban fighters die while attacking a remote American outpost in Afghanistan, a U.S. soldier prepares to escort the base's Afghan translator outside the walls of the small base. The officer in charge hopes the translator will recognize some of the dead so he can include the information in his report of the attack to his superiors. A lieutenant tells the interpreter: "He's going to take you to the hajjis" (102). The interpreter doesn't comment on the slur, but as he inspects the dead bodies, he begins "to feel a reluctant kinship with them—one that [he] cannot help but contrast with the way [he's] been made to feel inside the base" (103). I cite these examples of *hajji*, or more precisely the lack thereof, not to suggest that other cultures or countries avoid similar naming in war but to suggest that a performative unity exists in *hajji* as it appears in the stories and dramas of American war literature.

It does bear noting, though, that some American writers do attempt to simulate an Iraqi point-of-view pertaining to the epithet. In his second book of war poetry about the Iraq war—*Phantom Noise* (2010)—Brian Turner's poem "Stopping the American Infantry Patrol Near the Prophet Yunus Mosque in Mosul, Abu Ali Shows Them the Cloth in his Pocket" takes a view of *hajji* from an imagined Iraqi perspective (61). As the title indicates, the poem's speaker displays a sacred piece of cloth to some Americans he meets near the Iraq city of Mosul in the first three lines. The speaker tells the Americans that his father carried this "silk and cotton dyed black" all the way back to Iraq from Mecca (3). For this speaker, the cloth—like all other signifiers of his culture and religion—encompasses so much more than it may seem to an outsider. The poem concludes with the speaker explaining the pilgrimage, the "hajj," and the word *hajji*.

The delicate shifts in this discussion of *hajji* show how this scene is still a performative, one-sided though it may be. The title indicates an audience for the speaker's lesson, an audience to hear about the power of *hajji*'s misuse to disrespect, minimize, or dismiss its true meaning. However, the address is directed toward a collective of soldiers described vaguely as an "infantry patrol." Thus, it reads like a monologue, providing little reassurance, since in contains no named individuals and indicates no other agents, that anyone at all will hear and heed the speaker's message. We are left with the impression that this Iraqi man is speaking into a void.

It is a sad reality that, as Wall explains, combatant and support soldiers "have normalized the phrase 'Hadji' to where they fail to see the use of the term as morally and politically problematic; it is simply a descriptive term for the foreign Other" (495). It also is a natural expression of self-deception. If soldiers use the term to make sense of their war, might we not analyze the term to make sense of the soldiers? This brings me to my next question: if, as in much of contemporary American war literature, the speaker and the auditors are both American soldiers, does this change the nature of *hajji* as an epithet? Turner's poem and Pratt's essay would suggest that the answer is no. There may be no way to change *hajji*'s underlying offensiveness as Egan, Brown, Lutz, and Wall outline it, and we wouldn't want its imperial implications to be ignored either. But its role as a symbolic performance between two speakers of the same language/culture suggests that it also serves a wider, synedochic purpose.

In the novel *Book of Jonas* (2012), American author Stephen Dau crafts his narrative around a boy's wounding in an unnamed country (unnamed, yes, but the warzone is clearly somewhere in Iraq) and his subsequent emigration to the United States. The boy—named "Younis" in his homeland and renamed "Jonas" in Pittsburgh—survives a horribly misbegotten American operation due to the efforts of one American soldier named Christopher Henderson. Years pass as Jonas tries to assimilate to life in the United States; however, as he attends college and grows older, he is haunted by the fact that he retains very little memory of his homeland, his family, or the soldier (who was reported as missing in action and never heard from again). Fortunately, for his piecemeal memory and for Christopher's mother, Jonas still has the soldier's journal. He calls the man "his savior," and one of "his savior's" diary entries reads:

> What if you start calling all the locals hajjis? What if you start to see them less and less as human beings and more and more as things to be categorized as either very threatening or less threatening? What if your SAW gunner accidentally pops off a round or two in the general direction of a crowd of hajjis who have gathered for some purpose you don't fully understand, but don't like the look of? [140].

The musings of this exceptional, linguistically sensitive soldier highlights the symbolic implication—the synecdochic power—of *hajji*.

In an appendix to *A Grammar of Motives* (1941), Burke includes an essay he called "Four Master Tropes." In this short essay, Burke outlines the relative strengths he sees behind metaphor, metonymy, synecdoche, and irony. He begins by clarifying that his interest in these tropes is not only "with their purely figurative usage, but with their role in the discovery and description of the truth" (503). Truth is a slippery word as Burke uses it, as he intends it more as a description of the truth behind the link between figurative language and the reality it seeks to represent. In that pursuit, Burke places synecdoche[18] at the top of this list of master tropes. Richard Wess explains: "Synecdoches are representations that rhetorically qualify one another as they question and modify one another in a dramatistic dialectic" (118). As we can see in this short passage from *The Book of Jonas*, *hajji* qualifies everything else. It modifies the soldier, the local population, the vague concept of an unnamed and unseen enemy, and the soldier's ethical existence in war.

As Burke writes in *The Philosophy of Literary Form*, "synecdochic representation ... [is] a necessary ingredient of a truly realistic philosophy" (26). Burke uses the simple example of a "house" to demonstrate what he means. Just as "house" refers to more than just a building, it represents— as a proxy—all the other "things" that "cluster about it" (Burke's example is "the loved ones inside" the house) (27). Burke calls this linguistic phenomenon "house plus," which, he says, "suggests also the importance of the name as an important aspect of synecdoche (the name as fetishistic representative of the named, as a very revealing part of the same cluster)" (27). Thus, the name comes to offer a "fetishistic surrogate" for the cluster it stands for (30). Likewise, any impulse associated with or enacted via the name is therefore a symbolic or vicarious act directed at the represented object.

Remaining with the passage from Dau's novel, one might ask: What is "*hajji* plus"? What cluster surrounds *hajji* and its practically unlimited reference as far as the object's "polar otherness" is concerned (*Philosophy* 78)? As I have said, *hajji* has little to do with an enemy; the same is true for "*hajji* plus" in Dau's novel. In this soldier's diary entry, *hajji* is the only "name," and it is wedged in the middle of a long list of nouns, actions, and emotions that cause Christopher massive amounts of guilt. Jonas reads the passage; we read the passage; but, really, it is Christopher Henderson's solo performance that, as symbolic action, functions as a public admission of guilt—a confession—that enables this soldier to unburden himself at the reader's expense. But what does *hajji* synedochically represent for the reader, then? In short, it becomes a "fetishistic" naming of a soldier's paranoid imaginings of hate, of fear, of aggression that we vicariously share. But as Christopher castigates himself for *hajji*, he (and we) can see that inside *hajji* is unbridled loathing, not in the face of an enemy, but in the faces of a civilian population who need his help. Christopher stops short of completing the scapegoat mechanism, recognizing, as we do, that massive amounts of self-loathing reside inside *hajji*. Burke says that synecdoche is the figurative use of the "container for the thing contained" (*Philosophy* 25). When Christopher asks, "What if you start calling all the locals hajji?" he has landed on a name for the container of his guilt: *hajji* (140).

Of Coleridge's ancient mariner, Rueckert writes that "Confession itself is curative; simply verbalizing the pollution is the beginning of the purgative action" (*Kenneth Burke* 122). Christopher loads his guilt on the page of his diary and sends it off into the world via a frightened and injured Iraqi boy. In the private-public forum of Christopher Henderson's journal, Jonas, the reader, and then Christopher's mother (Jonas eventually gives her the diary) complete the scapegoat process away from *hajji*. The sin-guilt-penance-redemption cycle for the protagonist is clear: Younis' sister is killed and her village is destroyed (sin); Christopher (the scapegoat) saves the boy and suffers horribly in the process (penance); Jonas gives the journal to Christopher's mother (Jonas' and Christopher's tragic redemption). The audience's redemption never really comes.

Scapegoating *Hajji*

In *Permanence and Change*, Burke expands on much of the scapegoating process he first developed while discussing Hitler and *Mien Kampf*. He notes,

> But speech in its essence is not neutral. Far from aiming at suspended judgment, the spontaneous speech of a people is loaded with judgments. It is intensely moral—its names for objects contain the emotional overtones which give us the cues as to how we should act towards these objects [176–77].

Instead of letting language be a means of establishing binaries and a means of difference marking, however, Burke argues that the dialectic nature of language is the sole characteristic that unifies humans. Yet again, it is dangerous to rest on the conclusion that words like *hajji* naturally flow out of the babble and turmoil of war for combat soldiers or that they enact a colonizer/colonized hierarchy. These may be accurate analyses, but Burke would likely respond to them by saying, "Spontaneous speech is not naming at all, but a system of attitudes, of implicit exhortations. To call a man a friend or an enemy is *per se* to suggest a program of action with regard to him" (*Permanence* 177).

Note that Burke did not say, "to call a man a friend or an enemy is to suggest a program of action *upon* him." Rather, such spontaneous speech as *hajji* deserves examination at the uttered level or, in dramatistic terms, at the scene-act level. That is, attached to *hajji* (unlike "barbaros" or "durka durka") is a mass of "emotion or moral weightings" that "enforce the act itself, hence making the communicative and active aspects of speech identical" (*Permanence* 177). Furthermore, *hajji* falls well inside Burke's "inadequate" category of symbolic action, a category that includes occasions "when speech confuses the handling of non-racial issues by stimulating racial persecution" (*Permanence* 177).

The American combat soldier may be trying to make sense of the world of combat and death and killing (as Wall and Egan and Brown and Lutz conclude) when he responds to his environment with demonizing terms for an enemy that is trying to kill him, but what about the bulk of noncombat users of the term? In *The Other End of the Spear* (the "tip of the spear" being combat troops), John J. McGrath examines what he calls the "Tooth-to-Tail Ratio" in U.S. Army operations since World War I. That is, the balance of combat troops ("teeth") to support troops (the "tail"). The U.S. Congress actually mandates that the Army maintain a minimum acceptable level of combat troops between 29 percent and 34 percent of its total force.[19] With that in mind, McGrath reports that in January of 2005, the war in Iraq saw the lowest historical Tooth-to-Tail Ratio in the last century. At that point, shortly before the so-called "surge," 25% of Army troops serving inside Iraq did so in a "combat role," meaning they were categorized by job description in such a manner (86). Of course, this number still does not account for the percentage of those soldiers who actually saw combat, nor does it address any other branch of the military or any of the thousands of military servicemen and women who served outside the borders of Iraq.[20] In 2008, the RAND corporation published findings from a massive study of veterans who had returned from Iraq and Afghanistan and the "invisible wounds of war" that came home with them. Among other things, the study found that of 1,965 veterans who had deployed to either Iraq or Afghanistan, only 9.5 percent had engaged in "hand-to-hand combat" (Schell 97).

As we can see, combat and the rate of combat exposure among deployed military members, is a very difficult one to track down. Questions immediately arise: How does one define "hand-to-hand"? How trustworthy is self-reported information? What type of combat "counts"? Regardless, two things are clear; when we consider the full population of personnel who have deployed in support of the Global War on Terror, 9.5 percent is most likely a high number and it will continue to be difficult to define combat, combat zones, or what it means to be combat experienced. It is possible that combat exposure is immaterial or irrelevant to *hajji*'s appearance and symbolic resilience in the discourse of war.

Here, I should pause and say that I do not highlight this number in order to diminish the service of any individual who deployed in any capacity in Iraq, Afghanistan, and beyond in support of either conflict. Indeed, I argue for the exact opposite treatment of noncombat troops. In 2011, the Department of Defense reported that nearly 83 percent of military members who committed suicide that year had no history of direct combat (Luxton 30). All career fields in all branches of the military experience war guilt and the impacts of trauma. All also use *hajji*. One example may demonstrate my point. I flew a KC-10 refueling tanker over Iraq and Afghanistan for a total of roughly 1,200 "combat" hours between 2006 and 2010, and the whole time no hostile enemy ever threatened my airplane (though once my crew and I did think a rocket was headed our way, but it turned out to be an illumination flare 20,000 feet below us at an American Marine base). This is, admittedly, a relatively small amount of flight time compared to my pilot peers. At any rate, I landed after every one of those 120 missions at an airbase in the middle of the desert south of Abu Dhabi. There was plenty of paranoia and posturing about security there, but that sprawling base was as safe as my home base in New Jersey. I heard *hajji* everywhere though: at the chow hall, at the gym, in official presentations. A high-ranking officer on my base, in his welcome speech for my last deployment in late 2009, told me and the other support troops, "There are still a lot of *hajjis* who need killing out there."

So I ask: might the people (civilian or military) who never directly experience combat—which is a huge proportion of the people who deployed in support of the wars in Iraq and Afghanistan—(and those who *do* experience combat) use synecdochic symbols like *hajji*, not to pass on any information about their relationship with the described object, but, as Burke suggests, to "establish a moral identity with [their] group by using the same moral weightings they used" (*Permanence* 177–178)? Is this not what the song "Hadji Girl" actually enacts? Such a question can be extremely useful in our attempts to unearth the true attitudes behind a term like *hajji* in the war literature and war culture that has developed since 9/11.

We need to view *hajji* within Burke's understanding of language as symbolic action in order to unsettle its persistence as a tool of scapegoating in contemporary war culture. Thomas Ricks, in *Fiasco* (2006), his analysis of the invasion of Iraq, writes about an Army colonel named H.R. McMaster who taught his soldiers "from the outset that the key to counterinsurgency is focusing on the people, not the enemy" (420). In that spirit, McMaster issued a standing order that all soldiers would "treat detainees professionally" and, Ricks reports, he also "banned his soldiers from using the term '*haji*' as a slang to describe them because he saw it as inaccurate and disrespectful of their religion" (420). When McMaster took over this regiment, he was fighting a tradition of inaccurate symbol use among a group of noncombat soldiers. He was trying to improve the interactions of his troops and the local population. But what is it about the social order he was in charge of that so deeply ingrained such linguistic behavior?

Burke, in *A Rhetoric of Motives* (1969) suggests that "identification" is much more useful than "persuasion" as the key element of any rhetorical motive.[21] Whereas "persuasion" implies intention and specificity of purpose, identification is for Burke a process born out of a natural human need to overcome the isolation inherent in human order and hierarchy. As Levy points out in her discussion of a military "disglossia," the rhetoric of rank and submission, of class, and of regulations dominates military culture (99–101). But it also is dominated by countless collective acts that groups enact in order to overcome the difference that determines each level of the hierarchy. Levy says that one reason "military folks speak as they do" is to display a sense of "solidarity," and so she breaks her "disglossia" into two categories: *officialese* ("O") and *enlistic* ("E") (100). She goes to extensive lengths to point out how "both O and E are artificial constructs that serve to build cultural competence in a novel situation. And they do that by operating together" (112). She does not, however, recognize that *hajji* crosses all the categories she devises; it requires no "code-switching" or any other linguistic maneuver she praises the military member for mastering (111).

In *Ethics, Norms, and the Narratives of War* (2014), Pamela Creed "presents the stories of veterans of the Iraq War who expressed varying degrees of anger, shame and guilt over the public storylines" (100). She interviews a number of veterans who mention their unease with *hajji* as it appeared during their deployments in Iraq, but one subject, a man named "Gregg," explains in very clear terms how he heard *hajji* being used and abused in order to forge a cultural competency that crosses the lines between combat and noncombat troops and between enlisted soldiers and their officers. As he puts it, *hajji* helped established an entire "system that's put in place" (115).

The story, as Gregg tells it, begins with a Private First Class, a very young, low-ranking soldier, from Gregg's unit. One day this teenager is manning a checkpoint when he puts "more than 200 rounds" in a car that didn't slow soon enough, killing an unarmed family of four, including a four-year-old boy and a three-year-old girl (115). That night, a Colonel (a high-ranking officer, known as a "full-bird" because of the rank insignia he or she wears) has some choice words about the incident that Gregg remembered:

> [T]his full-bird colonel turns in his chair to this entire division of level staff and says, "If these fucking *hajjis* learned to drive, this shit wouldn't happen." And right then and there I looked around and nobody—everybody just went, "Mmmm, hmmm, fucking *hajjis*." And I was just like—you know, I expect it from the grunts, who to get through the day racially dehumanize (sic) but that's when I really started to look at the fact that it wasn't the lower ranking grunts on the ground that do this. It's a system that's put into place [115].

Gregg continues his rant against the way the phrase "fucking *hajjis*" was established as a major part of the wartime system he was part of, a system that manipulates language so that it serves a wider hegemonic function:

> I think back to the first night I was in Kuwait. It's your first briefing in the country and they say—they talk about going north and about how you can't trust any of these fucking *hajjis*. All these fucking *hajjis* are out to kill you. All these fucking *hajjis* are gonna stab you in the back. All these fucking *hajjis* are waiting to throw a grenade in your truck. Don't buy food off these fucking *hajjis*. These fucking *hajjis*

Six: Representing Hajji: This Generation's Enemy "Other" 187

> have no respect for life, blah, blah, blah. And it ends with this E-7 (a high-ranking enlisted man) who tells a story. He says—or gives us a scenario. He says, "So, your convoy's driving down the road. In the middle of the road is this little fucking *hajji* kid. What do you do?" And somebody yells, "Stop." And he says, "No, you just killed your whole fucking convoy. What do you do?" Someone else says, "Turn down another road." He says, "No time. What the fuck do you do?" And finally someone just says, "Run him over?" And he says, "You're damn right. You don't let any of these little fucking *hajjis* get in the way of getting you home, even if it's a little fucking *hajji* kid" [115].

The similarities of this speech and the one I heard when I was welcomed for one of my own deployments are startling. As Burke states, "often we must think of rhetoric not in terms of some one particular address but as a general body of identifications that owe their convincingness much more to trivial repetition and dull daily reinforcement than to exceptional rhetorical skill" (*Rhetoric* 26). Unlike Gregg, many military members blindly accept *hajji* as natural and miss the insidious strength of their need to symbolically identify with others. They also miss the guilt that comes with it.

Gregg would do well to read Burke's *A Rhetoric of Motives*. In Burkeian terms, we can conceive of American military members being "both joined and separate, at once a distinct substance and consubstantial with each other" according to levels of combat exposure, gender, rank, race, job type, and any number of other distinctions (*Rhetoric* 21). *Hajji*, however, serves mainly to effect consubstantiality among those who are merely imagining the hazards combat troops face. Yes, both the Colonel and the "E-7" from Gregg's story are doing their fair share of Chris Kyle-style dehumanization, but they also are institutionalizing the ways one achieves consubstantiation in this particular generation of war. However, Burke would remind us, this identification and consubstantiation is an exercise that "confront[s] the implications of *division*" (*Rhetoric* 22). Like the division between door-kickers and Fobbits in Abrams's novel, this division and the guilt it produces is the mechanism by which problems in a structure so ordered can be exposed, and by which competing narratives can be introduced. As Burke elaborates in *A Grammar of Motives*,

> To call a man a friend of brother is to proclaim him consubstantial with oneself, one's values or purposes. To call a man a bastard is to attack him by attacking his whole line, his "authorship," his "principle" or "motive" (as expressed in terms of the familial). An epithet assigns substance doubly, for in stating the character of the object it at the same time contains an implicit program of action with regard to the object, thus serving as motive [57].

Elizabeth Samet, in *Soldier's Heart* (2007), writes about teaching war literature at West Point. At one point, she discusses how a former student of hers, upon entering the active duty Army, became "frustrated" with the curriculum of a professional development and leadership course that he recently finished as a routine part of his progression as a career officer. Samet describes his ire:

> Even in the wake of Abu Ghraib and Guantanamo, the curriculum seemed to him to include insufficient instruction in just war theory and the laws of land warfare. He was also nonplussed by the fact that even a few of his instructors referred to the Iraqis as "hajjis" [164].

What the instructors at this stateside Army course were enacting had nothing to do with actual war; rather, they were demonstrating the ingrained ways military members rhetorically identify with each other. *Hajji* is a hegemonic manifestation of these people's attempt to be consubstantial with combat, with combat troops, and with the "real" experiences of war. Burke writes that "a speaker persuades an audience by the use of stylistic identifications; his act of persuasion may be for the purpose of causing the audience to identify itself with the speaker's interests" (*Rhetoric* 46). In the prologue to *A Rhetoric of Motives*, Burke explains his concept of identification further with the example of a politician who speaks to farmers at a rally and says, "I was a farm boy myself" (xiv). This is essentially what those instructors are doing with *hajji*; by using it in front of students, the instructor says, "I know about war. I am a warrior myself."

Yet, *hajji* also trades on congregation by segregation and what George Cheney calls "identification by antithesis," whereby the speaker seeks out "common ground" with others by drawing up the despised virtues of an "enemy" both share (148). Such antithesis can operate, as it often does in large collectives, via an "assumed we," meaning that a speaker acts linguistically in a way that goes unnoticed by most but still allows an almost unconscious grouping of anyone who is present (Cheney 148). Somewhat "magically" then, *hajji* becomes for those instructors a formal ritual that, Burke would say, "can awaken an attitude of collaborative expectancy" (*Rhetoric* 58). Once a member grasps the trend of *hajji*'s appropriation and use as a convenient tool of scapegoating, it begs participation. It is the division, the difference marking, the antithesis of *hajji* that Samet's former student and Creed's interview subject (Gregg) actively reject. Were either man to speak up and point out the symbol mongering to his higher-ranking superiors, no doubt he would draw the ire of members all along the hierarchy's structure.

Helen Benedict examines the roll of *hajji* as a tool of scapegoating via identification in her novel *Sand Queen* (2011). Early on in the novel, a number of Iraqis are crowding around the main gate of a compound where American soldiers are detaining a number of Iraqi men, most of whom are innocent of any wrongdoing. A man, a guard named DJ, says to the protagonist Kate, "We gotta get these hajjis to leave." Kate says nothing in response, but she thinks, "I wish he wouldn't use that word in front of Naema" (Naema is an Iraqi woman who quickly becomes a close friend of Kate's) (72). When Naema leaves, Kate talks to DJ about the incident: "Don't say 'hajji' in front of them like that ... it's not respectful" (72). DJ responds by recasting these individual Iraqi men and women as a monolith: "And I suppose it was respectful when those motherfuckers blew up Jones and Harman last week? Jesus Christ, Brady, whose fuckin' side are you on?" (73). Later, Kate reports another soldier for sexual assault, and her superior chastises her in similar manner: "Soldier, in case you forgot, we're at war. The cohesion of our unit is of paramount importance, and my job as a platoon sergeant is to preserve that cohesion. We have a common enemy, and that is the hajji" (148–149). Both of these characters are enacting, as Thomas Conley says in *The Rhetoric of Insult*, an "intimate sharing of both beliefs and values" with a racial/ethnic/religious slur (98). They are presuming that, to effect unification among their group, they must retain a position of moral superiority over the other side. However, in both of these scenes from *Sand Queen*, the incongruity of *hajji*'s reference confuses any chance for the construction of a concrete identity of friend *or* foe.

Benedict presents the paradox of *hajji*'s deployment in a warzone by contradicting the confidence of DJ and the self-serving certainty of the platoon sergeant with Kate's more open-minded perspective. The men apply a precision of reference that just isn't there, and Kate is castigated for not sharing such certainty. In other words, she fails to identify herself with the others via *hajji* and thereby display the appropriate perceptions, notions, imaginings, ideologies, and attitudes that would grant her consubstantiality with the others. DJ misses the ironic blurring of identity that exists within the word *hajji*. Does he mean *hajji* to refer to a group of women who are concerned for the future of their jailed family members? Does he use *hajji* to point to combatants who blew up his friends? Does *hajji* indicate the innocent men jailed inside the compound? Of course, DJ lacks the inclination and ability to care about the answers to these questions, but we do not. We can see that he abuses *hajji* to reinforce oppositions, to form "sides" quite literally. Kate's supervisor is equally mistaken. He even uses Kate's awareness of *hajji*'s symbolic power as fodder for his refusal to hold her attacker responsible for a sex crime. In this way, *hajji* is not only a tool of consensus building; it also provides the purgative cure for the guilt it engenders.

When an instructor in a classroom or a guard at a detention center or a drunken soldier in an isolated post in Iraq uses *hajji*, all are marking consubstantiality both within their culture and without. As Burke puts it, "And so, in the end, men are brought to that most tragically ironic of all divisions, or conflicts, wherein millions of cooperative acts go into the preparation for one single destructive act" (22). If order, Burke says, then guilt. Likewise, if identification, then separation. Since consubstantiality denotes a certain overlap between the two (for instance, all military members wear uniforms) and difference (no two uniforms are identical due to differing services, badges, medals, and other accouterment), we continually assuage the guilt we bear (and also acquire more guilt) by continually seeking association with new groups at the expense of others. Soldiers, airmen, marines, sailors, officers, enlisted troops, noncommissioned officers, combat troops, support troops: we all mark difference and separateness in countless ways. Both of the men from Benedict's novel insist that *hajji* refers to a "common enemy," but their argument is patently incorrect. They need *hajji* due to their anxiety about the order in which they exist. Both men abuse *hajji* to foster identification, and once that identification is established, the attendant division therein suggests that *hajji* must also act as the group's purgative cure, its symbolic scapegoat.

A symbol like *hajji* maintains its place in the scene since it combines two kinds of "form"—the "progressive form" and the "repetitive form"— according what Kenneth Burke calls the "Interrelation of Forms" (*Counter-Statement* 128). Burke breaks his "progressive form" into two categories: qualitative progression and syllogistic progression (*Counter-Statement* 124). In this scene from *Sand Queen*, qualitative progression describes the state of mind DJ and the platoon sergeant have been put in (that Kate rejects) and from which another, related mood of anger and revenge, can emerge (*Counter-Statement* 125). "Repetitive form" is the "restatement of the same thing but in different ways," with added details (*Counter-Statement* 125). Thus, DJ falls back on *hajji*'s vague references, repeatedly, right after he asks Kate which side she is on. When the two elements cross, the overlap creates a syllogistic fall, or a malign form of rhetoric, that creates the symbolic scapegoat, for the "scapegoat is dialectically appealing, since it combines in one figure contrary principles of identification and alienation" (*Rhetoric* 141). William Rueckert explains: "in every hierarchy, at every level of it, there are secret identifications that are in reality inducements to violence and victimization," and with *hajji* the inducement to violence and victimization is not limited to the military (*Encounters* 76). It most certainly isn't limited to those few American military members who directly engage a real enemy in real war. In the American war culture that has emerged since 9/11, *hajji* has become the latest victim of our tendency to go scapegoat.

Hajji in America

In "The Morality of Indian Hating," N. Scott Momaday writes about the way centuries of racism have created a space where the "Indian" lives within an imagined, purely symbolic place:

> The unique position of the Indian in this society is anomalously fixed and mutable, here and there, truth and fiction. The Indian has been for a long time generalized in the imagination of the white man. Denied the acknowledgment of individuality and change, he has been made to become in theory what he could not become in fact, a synthesis of himself [30].

He says that this "synthesis" reflects western (white) man's "inclination to impose the most convenient identities upon friends and acquaintances, strangers and enemies" (31). He calls this tendency the "rule of convenience" (31).

Hajji follows the same set of rules. It draws from a basis of symbolic stereotypes (or topoi) that began with our construction of the imagined "Indian," a symbolic simulation that has been reproduced again and again whenever we go to war in order to execute what has become a comforting and self-serving ideological purpose. Robert Ivie explains, "The topoi, metaphorically speaking, are a 'reservoir of ideas' or core images from which specific rhetorical statements can be generated" ("Images" 281). *Hajji* has emerged as this generation's rhetorical statement regarding the drama of our wars in Iraq and Afghanistan. *Hajji* is a Burkeian "god-term" of these wars because, as a tool of rhetoric, it is capable of "transcending brute objects" (*Rhetoric* 299, 276). In that transcendence, *hajji*, like the word "God," becomes a symbolic "summing-up" of the topoi-based motives and hierarchies that frame its very utterance (*Rhetoric* 300).

This also is what lends to *hajji*'s movement as symbolic action from rhetoric to reality and back again. In early 2011, the Virginia Department of Motor Vehicles revoked the tags of a veteran of the Iraq war—named Sean Bujno—who had been driving around with license plates that read "ICUHAJI" for four years. The revocation of the tags was based on the DMV's belated finding that the message of the plate encouraged violence

(Daugherty). Bujno appealed the decision (and won) on the grounds that, as his lawyer argued, "he got to know the culture in Iraq and was saying, 'I see you, brother'" (qtd. in Hawkes). Interestingly enough, Bujno's father had already attempted to obtain license plates that read "HAJIKLR" (Hawkes).

As far as I am concerned, the license plates show how pervasive symbol mongering, according to Momaday's "rule of convenience," has become in the United States. Some may argue, as Bujno's lawyer unconvincingly did, that *hajji*'s appropriation is a statement of solidarity, one that retains the Arabic word's denotative sense. Others yet may argue that *hajji* carries deeper, more performative implications that help soldiers survive a warzone that makes little sense. Regardless, *hajji* shows us that each generation of American war—and the agents who fight war and/or write about war—is skilled in absorbing the biases of a culture that has long confused defense with victimization. Sadly, *hajji* probably is already entrenched as a sign-carrier for another generation of victimizers, but we can still identify it for what it is: a perfected tool of scapegoating.

Nowhere else are the malign effects of the symbolic scapegoating significance of *hajji* more alarming than in Jim Frederick's nonfiction book *Black Hearts: One Platoon's Descent into Madness in Iraq's Triangle of Death* (2010). Frederick presents one of the most disturbing chronicles of hate and crime that took place during our war in Iraq. *Hajji* is a key operator throughout as Frederick outlines the actions and attitudes of one Army unit that, as his subtitle relates, slowly disintegrates into absolute moral depravity in Iraq in 2006. Early on in this unit's deployment, Frederick notes, one soldier, a man named Casica, stands out in his attempts to "retain his optimism" and "unflappable friendliness" about the Iraqis even though he had already been injured in a rocket-propelled grenade attack (69, 68). He is a well-liked member of the platoon even though the others call him a "Hadji Hugger" and a "Hadji Fucker" for trying to maintain his humanity in a unit that suffers from poor leadership and deep hate for the local population (69). Eventually, an insurgent's bullet kills Casica, and it is just the excuse these bored and frustrated soldiers need to commit horrible crimes against *hajji*. As a soldier named Payne reflected later, when Casica was killed, "That's when things started to turn" (143).

Emotions are running very high in the unit when a young soldier named Green has a heated conversation with his superiors, men named Lieutenant Colonel Kunk and Sergeant Major Edwards:

> "They all deserve to die" [Green says].
> "Goddamn it. That's not true," Kunk responded testily, "Ninety to ninety-five percent of the Iraqi people are good people and they want the same thing that we have

in the United States: democracy. Yes, there are five percent of them that might be bad, and those are the terrorists. Those are the bad guys that we're going after."
"Fuck the Hadjis," Green declared.
"Calling them that is like calling me a nigger," said Edwards. "This sounds like you hate a whole race of people."
"That's about it right there," Green said, "You just about summed it up" [144].

The hatred and animosity attached to this imaginary construct known as "hadji" continues to mount, though. At one point, the platoon's Lieutenant tries "to get the guys to focus more on the Iraqis as people, to consider that man over there as not just another fucking Hadji, but as Ali, who owns a falafel shop and loves his kids and has problems" (189). That effort fails though, and sadly, the brutal symbolic action of these soldiers' language stops being symbolic.

In *Collateral Damage: America's War Against Iraq Civilians* (2008), Chris Hedges and Laila Al-Arian discuss "haji" as a disturbing byproduct of the fear, stress, and hostility that troops face in Iraq, a place Hedges describes as an "atrocity-producing situation" (xiii). The soldiers of *Black Hearts* find themselves in this exact situation, one fueled by *hajji* just as much as it is fueled by Casica's death. The men begin beating up random Iraqis, and one group begins fantasizing about scenarios that would allow them to get vengeance on the faceless *hajji* for the deaths of their fallen brethren. At one point, a group of these soldiers are guarding a group of women and children. They are drunk on illicitly obtained booze, and they are drunk on power and fear. "All these Hadjis are motherfuckers!" one of the drunk soldiers yells, "we ought to just kill them all" (257).

Soon thereafter, four soldiers (named Steven Green, James Barker, Jesse Spielman, and Paul Cortez) planned their crime against *hajji*:

> Barker knew Green was always begging to kill Iraqis, if only someone would say the word.
> "You'll kill them, right?" Barker asked.
> "Absolutely," Green replied. "It don't make any difference to me," Green said. "A Hadji is a Hadji" [259].

Later that night, these four American soldiers burst into a quiet Iraq home and gang raped a fourteen-year-old girl. Then, they executed the family of four (including a six-year old brother) and burned the bodies.[22]

It is difficult to draw any cohesive lesson from this story, but one thing is certain: as this platoon descended deeper and deeper into their particular version of consubstantiation—a slovenly-conceived place of common ground and identification built on fear and hate—*hajji* was always there to describe this group's eventual victims, their scapegoats. It had nothing to do with sense making in a senseless warzone or with warrior knowledge.

Rather, as Burke writes in *The Philosophy of Literary Form*, these scapegoated victims were the final part of a mechanism that first assigned them a symbolic ambiguity and then used them like a "'suppurating' device," one that "brings the evil 'to a head'" (46).

We probably can't stop *hajji*, but we can indeed note its power and the way that war is perpetuated through extensive scapegoat mechanisms. We can note the true function of and need for scapegoats for a nation when it goes to war, and we can remain alert to what our need for a scapegoat reflects about us as a society. As Burke asks, "Would we not then be at least headed in the right direction?" ("Linguistic" 301).

Conclusion

When a country is at war for an extended amount of time (say, since 2001) a number of things start getting old. Death, destruction, war trauma, war politics: all of these things get very old, and everyone, it seems, falls prey to war exhaustion. Even in a post–9/11 world, a world in which war stays far away from a society protected by distance, technology, and an all-volunteer military, it is easy to simply forget that the United States is a nation at war. It is easy to compartmentalize the moral burdens that come with waging war as a politics-only or military-only concern. We get used to it. Or, better yet, we get tired of it. We willfully ignore it.

In this sense (as opposed to a military strategic sense) war exhaustion is dangerous. There is a certain level of normalization that accompanies one's limited attention span when it comes to hearing and talking about war, and this, of course, is one of the reasons why it is so important that we never stop telling and reading war stories. They need to be told, but more importantly, they need to be heard. So we should always try to find new and exciting ways to do both. There's a problem here, however, and that is the fact that war stories have a tendency to collect a definite baggage of familiarity and in so doing allow a complicit public the easy out of apathy. My wife is tired of hearing my own war stories. I am tired of hearing triumphant Navy S.E.A.L. tales of post–9/11 individual triumph over a mysterious and Islamic enemy. My wife says she can tell my stories in her sleep. I feel the same way about much of the contemporary war fiction I read.

I'm not the only one who feels this way. In a 2015 essay for *Harper's Magazine*, Sam Sacks discusses the status of contemporary war fiction. Something is missing, his subtitle announces, from contemporary war fiction. And he is at least partially right. Rarely does a novel or memoir appear that takes America's post–9/11 wars as its subject and shakes the impression that something has been left out. Be it the limiting effects of experience, the epistemological importance that most attach to war narratives rooted in combat, or the mere fact that the United States has been at war in Afghanistan for fifteen years and fighting in Iraq or its neighbor Syria for thirteen, contemporary war narratives often feel as if they are rehashing formulaic tales of redemption through trauma. As Roy Scranton puts it, the myth of the trauma hero surrounds a combat-experienced hero's struggle with "the need to bear witness to his shattering encounter with violence, and the compulsion to repress it." Scranton writes:

> Like all myths, this story frames and filters our perceptions of reality through a set of recognizable and comforting conventions. It works to convince us that war is a special kind of experience that offers a special kind of truth, a truth that gives those who have been there a special kind of authority ["Trauma Hero"].

It is the "bear witness" part, not necessarily the "trauma" part that seems to lurk behind Sacks's suggestion that something is missing from contemporary war fiction. The problem isn't that new fiction about war fails to engage the political (as Sacks suggests) or that it fails to present the suffering of the civilians whose country we have invaded (as Scranton suggests); it's that war's representation seems incapable of escaping its ultimate scapegoating function for an exhausted audience in need of continual vicarious purging and renewal. Our war heroes carry the audience's guilt away best when the author is a veteran and when the hero is wounded. Redemption is not always be available for the hero, but it almost always is for the audience.

To be fair, Scranton notes the scapegoat function of war heroes in contemporary film and literature in his article as well (his example is Chris Kyle and the *American Sniper* franchise), but what he doesn't note is that Kenneth Burke identified the same thing in war literature and other forms of war's representation almost ninety years ago. Americans like their war heroes wounded or about to be wounded, and in that common function, the wounded warrior becomes another military cliché, another example of military kitsch that carries massive amounts of authenticity capital. As Clement Greenberg defined it in 1939, kitsch is "mechanical and operates by formulas. Kitsch is vicarious experience and faked sensation … it is all that is spurious in the life of our times. Kitsch pretends to demand nothing of its customers except their money—not even their time" (35). War's setting and war's technologies may have changed, but contemporary American war fiction seems to have remained attentive to a rather unchanging reading public, one that is eager to identify with a traumatized and combat-experienced hero in order to achieve—through that hero's suffering—a purging catharsis and happily enjoy its associated redemption.

This function—tragedy—forms the common core of the American

war narrative. Indeed, the expectations that the reading public brings to authors of war fiction who happen to be combat experienced veterans may be the real reason why it feels as if there is something missing from the literature these veterans write, even though veteran writers (traumatized or otherwise) are all too happy to oblige. Philanteries (to borrow a term from Wyndham Lewis) or interpretive communities (to borrow a term from Stanley Fish) that recently have grown out of MFA workshops across the country have resulted in a commonality in perspective and self-involvement among this group of authentic and experienced writers. As Sacks writes, "nearly all recent war writing has been cultivated in the hothouse of creative-writing programs. No wonder so much of it looks alike.... The equivalence between American soldiers and helpless children runs throughout contemporary war fiction." As he sees it, this commonality has created a genre "that scrupulously avoids placing the Terror Wars within a larger political or ideological context. Redemption seems to rely on a shared incomprehension of what exactly these wars were about." There's a problem in his observation though. We fetishize war experience (as Sacks and Scranton and many other contemporary authors and critics do), but why should we expect that experience to bring any veteran a better, more clear, or more complex access to any political or ideological issues?

What we can expect, it seems, is cliché and kitsch. Or, better yet, we can expect well-worn symbols and expressions to appear in contemporary war fiction that operate like proverbs. As Kenneth Burke wrote in 1938, "Proverbs are designed for consolation or vengeance, for admonition or exhortation, for foretelling" ("Literature" 293). Writers have little recourse, Burke says, when they "find a certain social relationship recurring so frequently that they must 'have a word for it'" ("Literature" 293). Or, in the case of the clichéd trope of the wounded warrior, when veteran writers seek to inscribe the wartime experience and fulfill the audience's need for a vicarious purging, they return again and again to well-worn paths of narrative framing and plot shaping. As Burke asks: "Could the most complex and sophisticated works of art legitimately be considered somewhat as 'proverbs writ large'?" ("Literature" 296).

In *Authoring War*, from 2011, Kate McLoughlin suggests that each war tends to have its own poesis, or, as she writes,

> its "natural" way (or ways) of being represented.... [I]n ancient Rome, warfare was such an entrenched part of epic the *bella* ("wars") became a shorthand for the genre, while it now seems evident that the First World war's natural form was the lyric poem, that the Second World War's was the epic novel, that the Vietnam War's was the movie, that the Iraq Wars' may well turn out to be the blog [10].

Her speculation that the "blog" would prove to be the poesis of America's post–9/11 wars proved at least partially true (a number of soldier blogs were turned into commercially successful books), but it seems to me that the guiding poesis of our post–9/11 wars is observation-based, rather than medium-based. McLoughlin admits such a possibility as well. As she writes, "plunging a sword into the chest of someone a foot away involves very different notions of honour and bravery than does, for example, pressing a button on a computer that produces and explosion at a distance of hundreds of miles" (11). She goes on to ask, "But are the old war-joy and the old war-pain really recurring features of combat or are they ongoing constructions in war writing, in these instances imbibed from their classical representations?" (12).

In *Writing War in the Twentieth Century*, Margot Norris suggests that the main difference in twentieth century warfare was marked by a shift in the "locus of agency" among war's warriors (16). In the twenty-first century, the locus of agency hasn't necessarily returned to the warrior on the battlefield, but it has returned to the wounded warrior at home. Joseph Campbell's monomyth of the hero's journey may not always hold for every contemporary war story, but the trope of the wounded warrior doesn't alter it very much. Indeed, the *wounded* warrior carries home all the epistemological power as did the *wounding* warrior. This is a different sort of anxiety of influence, a generic seasoning that has travelled from one generation of wars to the next until all that remains today seems to be an overarching likeness in literature veterans produce about war. It runs the risk of losing steam. A public's apathy about war follows close behind, and the result is a limited communal healing for the wounded, returning veteran.

America's war fighting since 9/11 may look and feel different from its wars of the twentieth century, yet, despite vastly different political realities, an all-volunteer military force, precise weaponry, new communication mediums, and any number of different socio-strategic issues, when we read war literature, one is left feeling as if nothing much has changed. This is partially because, in a certain sense, it hasn't. Tim O'Brien's character Doc Peret, in his novel *Going After Cacciato* (1978) knew this. At one point in the novel, Peret holds court on war tropes as archetypal:

> War is war no matter how it's perceived. War has its own reality. War kills and maims and rips up land and makes orphans and widows. These are the things of war. Any war. So when I say that there's nothing new to tell about Nam, I'm saying it was just a war like every war.... I'm saying that the *feel* of war is the same in Nam or Okinawa—the emotions are the same, the same fundamental stuff is seen and remembered [190–1].

So, to say that something is missing from contemporary war fiction is the same as saying that something has sort of always been missing from narratives that take war for subjective representation. For every Tim O'Brien, there is a John Rambo. For every Phil Klay and every Kevin Powers, there is a Chris Kyle. The guiding poesis, in nearly every case, is the audience's need for redemption through the hero's suffering. It's an easy and cheap purging, and it seems to be available in just about any representation of war, traditional or otherwise.

This traditional Aristotelean catharsis is what seems to have soured Sam Sacks the most in his analysis of contemporary war fiction and, for the most part, I agree with his assessment. This group of war fiction is, as Sacks sees it, beautifully traditional yet tragically limited in perspective, a perspective that is handcuffed by experience. But he makes the same mistake so many others make. He still grants that experience the ultimate upper-hand in the truth-making game that is war writing. Sacks suggests that Powers and Klay and other writers are all stuck, as he puts it, in the "cul-de-sac of personal experience," but he is the one who put them in that cul-de-sac and asked for something in return. We need, Sacks says, "complex and imaginative approaches to the experience of war" in order to avoid "settling into the patterns of complacency that smoothed the path to the Terror Wars in the first place." And he is right. But he is rather silly to blame an entire subgenre of fiction for such a thing. What Sacks doesn't say is that maybe it is reasonable to expect war fiction writers who happen to be veterans to recycle the wounded warrior trope again and again. Perhaps we shouldn't expect them to provide any corrective after their experience. In a genre dominated by the forces of combat gnosticism, it may be quite some time for the next Stephen Crane or the next Joseph Heller to appear.

In *Writing War* (2000), Margot Norris points out that the discourse of war has not caught up with modernity. The way we write and observe war in language, she suggests, is still fixed within a Hegelian model in which "transcendence" is earned through the individual risking of one's life (19). The hierarchical psychosis on which combat gnosticism thrives draws from the same idea, but, with war literature, the reader needs a keen eye to identify the cure, the medicine, the vicarious redemption—the pleasure—that often accompanies such works of artifice. I am confident that literary criticism and the art it considers can overcome the problems Norris identifies. Honest assessments of war writing need not rely on accuracy or authorial resume or temporal immediacy or a popular hunger for realism to produce careful examinations of war, its agents, and its victims. When the reader accepts a proper quota of the moral burden that drives the scapegoat mechanism, she is thus denied easy and vicarious cathartic redemption. This book shows—even when redemption is undeserved—how criticism and fiction together can retain the ugly and the crude while also resisting the human habits of racist Othering when our nation goes to war. Cultural and literary criticism can thus invoke a healthy ambivalence, in all its frustrating and exasperating glory, instead of the easy pleasures associated with vicarious titillation.

Still, when we read war literature and war culture as I do, one observation remains salient. A painful paradox exists between the Hegelian model that Norris describes above and the changed ethical conditions of modern war. This nuance probably is the most important aspect to recognize in American war-fighting since 9/11. If writing and reading and discussing war literature (and other forms of art that represent war) can help us in the endeavor to foster peace instead of violence, cross-cultural understanding instead of difference making, and empathy instead of vicarious thrill seeking, it is paramount that we recognize how easy it is to slip into the same narratives and formulations of the past.

Yes, we must admit that writing about war is tricky. And we must also admit that it requires a deft hand and a unique perspective to make a war story appealing to the masses. But the reader has a role in war literature's meaning-making process, and it is an important one. The all-volunteer nature of the military may have left many Americans without personal connections to war, but we are all witnesses of war, and so we must all learn how to tell our war stories, but we also must learn how to read others' war stories. According to Elaine Scarry's formulation, in modern war "the *building-in of skill* thus becomes in its most triumphant form, the *building-out of consent*" (152; italics original). In other words, as war's technologies advance, out goes human agency and human risk, at least as far as the "firing" end of war is concerned. The scapegoats in *FOBBIT*, and *The Yellow Birds*, and *Billy Lynn's Long Halftime Walk*, and every American utterance *hajji* display this quality of war in one way or another. *FOBBIT*, for one, shows us that merely donning a military uniform carries with it a certain promise of risk. Door-kickers are at the firing end of the war in Iraq, but we should examine the stories they tell at the receiving end. This receiving end is, as *FOBBIT* reminds us, where door-kickers and Fobbits and Iraqis and *hajiis* all live and fight and die. As I put the final touches on this conclusion, I heard a story on the radio about suicide bombers denoting explosive devices in a Brussels airport, killing around thirty civilians and wounding over two hundred more. Combatants and noncombatants alike, it seems, live at war's receiving end. Fear and hate are difficult emotions to manage in such a world, but the implication regarding the way we observe war remains: it is probably improper to continue applying the old gladiatorial promise of transcendence to any contemporary war story.

Still, at the heart of the contemporary war novel is a message that we should not consider all deployments and all military members (or the enemy) as experiential equals. In his essay about *FOBBIT*, David Lawrence points out that "uniforms, tax-free wages, and hostile fire pay are just about the only things Fobbits have in common with the true warfighters" (162). At some basic level of unsupported gut instinct, I do not dispute that notion, nor do I dispute the notion that heroes serve a useful societal and military recruiting purpose. I also know firsthand that, as Tim O'Brien says in *The Things They Carried*, if we "Send guys to war, they come home talking dirty" (66). Authority is an awkward thing to negotiate in a democratic nation sullied by centuries of conquest and genocide and war and victimizing, and it becomes even more awkward when that nation seeks salvation at a national level by preventing these very things both at home and abroad.

I also do not suggest that true warfighters no longer exist in modern warfare. They are out there; I just think that there are more places to find them than I am usually given. I know a lot of soldiers and countless pilots. In fact, most of the ones I know would probably describe themselves as the truest of warfighters. But dealing in superlatives immediately fails Helen Benedict's test: it feels dishonest; it feels as if one runs the risk of glorifying the violence alone. Tales about the men and women we are to accept as the truest warfighters most certainly populate and dominate the vast body of war fiction, war memoirs, war films, news media, and journalistic accounts of the wars in Iraq and Afghanistan, but like a Fobbit, as soon I think I understand what a true warfighter is and does, as soon as one flashes into sight, it disappears just as quickly. That seems okay to me. I am certain of one thing, however; the epistemological worth of one man or one woman's wartime experience cannot be based on the number of bullets he or she dodged or unleashed.

Robert Ivie and Oscar Giner point out that "America's democracy is a myth" (135). That is, democracy is part of a story that gives our nation identity and meaning; it connects our better virtues with our better actions. Or as Ivie and Giner write, "It gives meaning to the national experience and infuses the story of American exceptionalism with promise" (135). America's war culture provides us powerful myths too, and we should never stop worrying about the ways America's war myths conflict with our democracy myths. We should never stop considering what it means to fight and kill (or ask others to fight and kill) in the name of a Constitution that charges us to respect and uphold the dignity and sacred rights of individual people. The calculus in that impossible calculation is even more difficult to compute when our stories pander to audiences that are prepared to breathlessly praise the combat narrative, unquestionably, as the sole arbiter of war truth. That metric isn't dangerous because the men and women who lose limbs in Baghdad streets or who die in the Hindu Kush have nothing to say about war. It also isn't dangerous because we love to hear those stories. After all, we couldn't ignore them if we tried. It is dangerous because, as Burke suggests, "vulgarizers," "epigons," and "steppers-down" all adapt experiential source material to their own purposes, and their purposes have a vast potential to "influence" mankind (*Counter-Statement* 70–71). Propaganda leaks out of every work of art, but when we focus only on stories of the combat gnosticators, we silence dissent and push civilian perspectives to the side. Our role as readers and critics, then, is to peer through experience and correct it by tracing the structure of the scapegoat mechanism within.

Ivie and Giner write that "the shadow of demagoguery darkens the democratic imaginary" (136). Combat gnosticism has the same effect on American war literature, culture, and language. In its elitism, it prevents the moral burdens of war from being publicly shared. With every *hajji* I hear, every recycled Indian War stereotype I encounter, every traumatic tale of hero-wounding I read, I fear that we slide deeper into the comforting shade that the scapegoat provides. It's nice in the shade, though, so the vicarious redemption that the heroics of war afford is probably here to stay. This deep dive into contemporary war literature, however, displays a third way, a way to transcend easy redemption via vicarious victimage so that we can continually probe and critique American ways of war from all angles.

Chapter Notes

Introduction

1. See Robert Ivie and Oscar Giner's recent book, *Hunt the Devil: A Demonology of U.S. War Culture* (2015), for an analysis of the repeated use of certain symbols in American culture that recycle stereotypes according to a militaristic "demonology" (their chapters: Evildoers, Witches, Indians, Dictators, Reds, and Tricksters).

2. See Chapter Five of this book for a close reading of the scapegoat mechanism in David Abrams's *FOBBIT* (2012).

3. For extended examinations of Native American and Indian War metaphors, proverbs, and stereotypes and their recycled use in modern discourse, see Slotkin (*Regeneration Through Violence* [1973]); Berkhofer (*The White Man's Indian* [1978]); Dower (*War Without Mercy* [1986]); Engelhardt (*The End of Victory Culture* [1995]); Bordewich (*Killing the White Man's Indian* [1996]); and Carrol (*Medicine Bags and Dog Tags* [2008]).

4. Kaplan also published a pair of books (*Warrior Politics: Why Leadership Demands a Pagan Ethos* [2002] and *Imperial Grunts: The American Military on the Ground* [2005]) that argue for a full return (strategically, morally, ethically) to the attitude with which America fought its genocidal war on native populations in the American West. Max Boot expresses similar sentiments his book *Savage Wars of Peace: Small Wars and the Rise of American Power* in 2002. For a different point of view, see Carroll's chapter, "The Same Forces That Went against Us as a People," that outlines the "parallels between U.S. domination of the Middle East and the Indian Wars" (198–206). For a comprehensive treatment of the resilience of Indian War stereotypes, see Michael Elliot's *Custerology: The Enduring Legacy of the Indian Wars and George Armstrong Custer* (2007).

5. In 1993, Ann S. Pancake published a similar study of metaphor exploitation and the invocation of the "wild west" in discourse about the first Gulf War (292).

6. For a book that illuminates the ways that Navajo conceptions of warfare, warriors, and the "legend" of Kit Carson differ from the metanarratives of mainstream American culture, see Tiana Bighorse's book *Bighorse the Warrior* (1990).

7. In *Language as Symbolic Action* (1966), Burke defines the "terministic screen" as a metaphor for the fact that "if any given terminology is a *reflection* of reality, by its very nature as a terminology it must be a *selection* of reality; and to this extent it must function also as a *deflection* of reality" (45).

8. See also Ted Remington's "Ceci N'est Pas Une Guerre: The Misuse of War as Metaphor in Iraq" for an analysis of the term "war" and the ways it "has become an uneasy and unstable metaphor, not offering perspective, but creating a deadly myopia."

Chapter One

1. Melville's *Battle Pieces and Aspects of the War* appeared in 1866, and Whitman published two collections, *Drum Taps* (1865) and *Sequel to Drum-Taps* (1866).

2. A few more war novels, written by civilians, did appear in the U.K. and the U.S. before 2011, but they were mainly considered Young Adult Fiction. Examples of these early Young Adult novels from the U.K. include *The Innocent's Story* (2007) by Nicky Singer, *Mixing It* (2007) by Rosemary Hayes, and *Guantanamo Boy* (2009) by Anna Perera; in the U.S., *Purple Heart* (2009) by Patricia McCormick, and *Sunrise Over Fallujah* (2008) by Walter Dean Myers.

3. For an early canon of books related to the wars in Iraq and Afghanistan, see Michiko Kakatuni's "A Reading List of Modern War Stories" that appeared on *The New York Times* website on 25 Dec. 2014. See also Peter Molin's

list in his essay, "The Iraq and Afghanistan Wars in Fiction, Poetry, Memoir, Film, and Photography: A Compendium."

4. A few of the more notable works of war fiction written by American civilians include Katey Schultz's *Flashes of War* (2013) and George Saunders' collection, *Tenth of December* (2013), which was shortlisted for the National Book Award (two of his stories deal with the Iraq war). A brief list of war novels written by American civilians includes *The Apartment* (2012) by Greg Baxter, *The Book of Jonas* (2012) by Stephen Dau, *Eleven Days* (2013) by Lea Carpenter, *Sparta* (2013) by Roxanna Robinson, *The Free* (2014) by Willy Vlautin, *Carthage* (2014) by Joyce Carol Oates, *The Kills* (2014) by Richard House, and *Wynne's War* (2014) by Aaron Gwyn.

5. The only direct reference to the Iraq or Afghanistan wars is in the final chapter, "The Cold War and the 'war on terror'" by David Pascoe. The "war on terror," in Pascoe's formulation, refers to American cultural fear and anger that followed 9/11. Iraq and Afghanistan are more of an afterthought than the essay's subject of study (239–249).

6. Gupta does not discuss what he calls "accounts of the invasion" of Iraq in his book, but he does admit, "It would, however, be simplistic to push such a distinction too emphatically. To begin with, the person and the profession do not necessarily coincide. There were undoubtedly U.S. and U.K. soldiers in Iraq who engaged the civil and civilian sphere sensitively in literary texts—the poetry of U.S. soldier Brian Turner in *Here, Bullet* (2005), for instance, often does so" (18).

7. *The Great War and Modern Memory* won the National Book Award and the National Book Critics Circle Award, and in 1991 Fussell edited the anthology *The Norton Book of Modern War* that is still widely used in classrooms across the country.

8. The five authors are Philip Caputo, Michael Herr, Larry Heinemann, Bobbie Ann Mason, and Tim O'Brien.

9. This passage from Lewis' book is borrowed from Philip Caputo's memoir, *A Rumor of War* (1977).

10. Eric Bennett satires this very legacy in his novel *A Big Enough Lie* (2015). According to Sacks, Bennett will soon publish a monograph that outlines the history of writing programs since World War II (*Workshops of Empire*).

11. The first story is "Tits-Up in a Ditch," by Annie Proulx, from 2008. The second is "Kattekoppen," written by Will Mackin, appearing in the 11 March 2013 issue. Luke Mogelson published a pair of war-themed short stories in *The New Yorker*: one is about a kleptomaniac National Guardsman in New York titled "Peacetime," and the other is "Total Solar," a short story about a journalist and a United Nations researcher.

Chapter Two

1. "Literature as Equipment for Living" was first published in *Direction* in April of 1938. It was also reprinted in *The Philosophy of Literary Form*. All citations refer to this later version.

2. This essay first appeared in *The Symposium* in October of 1933. It was later republished in unexpurgated form in *The Philosophy of Literary Form*, to which all citations refer.

3. Van Reet's essay briefly discusses Dillard Johnson's false claim in his non-fiction narrative—*Carnivore: A Memoir by One of the Deadliest American Soldiers of All Time (2013)*—that he killed more than 2,600 enemy combatants in Iraq. Were that true, as Dan Murphy points out in an essay for *The Christian Science Monitor*, Johnson would have accounted for 14 percent of all enemy deaths between 2003 and 2007, "an astonishing number for a single soldier who did not serve in the hottest battles of the post-invasion war."

4. Burke's "Dramatism" essay was first published in *Communication: Concepts and Perspectives* (1966), and then he revised it and republished it two years later for the *International Encyclopedia of the Social Sciences* (1968). In the version that appeared in the *Encyclopedia*, Burke added "congregation by segregation" to his parenthetical clarification of "perversions of the sacrificial principle" (451).

5. The essay was also republished in unexpurgated form in *The Philosophy of Literary Form*. All citations refer to the original *Southern Review* version.

Chapter Three

1. Alongside Ben Fountain's *Billy Lynn's Long Halftime Walk* (2012), Powers lost out to Louise Erdrich for her novel *The Round House* (2012). Some of the other notable awards that Powers and *The Yellow Birds* won include the French Prix littéraire du Monde, the 2013 PEN/Hemingway Award for first fiction, the Guardian First Book Award, co-recipient of the 78th Anisfield-Wolf Book Award for Fiction, and the Sue Kaufman Prize for first fiction from the American Academy of Arts and Letters.

2. Bowe Bergdahl, a soldier deployed to Afghanistan with the U.S. Army, walked away from his post and was subsequently captured by the Taliban. He was a prisoner of war from June 2009 until his highly publicized release in May 2014. For a comprehensive and penetrating examination of Bergdahl's service, capture, release, and subsequent court martial, see Season Two of Sarah Koenig's podcast *Serial*.

3. In every interview with Powers that I've found (NPR, *Time* magazine, *Style Weekly*, *Shelf Unbound*, and Virginia Commonwealth University's alumni newsletter, and others) each one includes the seemingly inevitable question about Powers's experience and its direct representation in the novel.

4. In *The Right Stuff*, Wolfe goes to extensive lengths to establish his use of the biblical "superstitious aura of the single-combat warrior" in the context of the space race in order to fit his tale within the formulae of combat gnosticism (231). The pilots who were chosen to be our first astronauts wore the "archaic mantles of the single-combat warriors of a long-since-forgotten time…. Thus beat the mighty drum of martial superstition in the mid-twentieth century" (97–98). These men were hardly warriors in any combative sense, so Wolfe invented the link to establish their martial hero status and fulfill the demands of combat gnosticism.

5. While I don't examine the metaphor in depth, the "yellow birds" also refers to Murph's story about his father bringing a dozen "caged canaries" home from the coal mine where he worked (139). According to Bartle, once the birds were let loose, they only "flitted and sang awhile before perching back atop their cages" (139). Like these birds, Murph and Bartle and Sterling voluntarily submit to the order that confines them.

6. According to Richard Burns, an African American soldier named Willie Duckworth "invented" the American military marching chant while he was running a marching drill in 1944 at a base in upstate New York (79). The army even called these songs "Duckworth chants" for a time before they eventually adopted the colloquial appellation of "Jodies."

7. Jody the Grinder is also a character in a Merle Haggard song, "The Old Man from the Mountain" (1974).

8. "The negative command," Burke writes, stands "as the moral center of man's linguistic genius" (*Counter-Statement* 216). Theological or otherwise, Burke says, "our character is built of our responses … to the thou-shalt-not's of morality" (*Language* 11). Even words, he points out, exist due to some "implied sense of negativity in the ability to use words at all. For to use them properly, we must know that they are *not* the things they stand for" (*Language* 12).

9. See Robert Ivie and Oscar Giner's *Hunt the Devil: a Demonology of U.S. War Culture* (2015) for an extensive analysis of how images of the Devil are manifested in American war rhetoric.

Chapter Four

1. This presentation took place on September 10, 2013, as part of the Seventh Annual David L. Jannetta Distinguished Lecture in War, Literature and the Arts at the U.S. Air Force Academy in Colorado Springs, CO. The speech appeared in *War, Literature, and the Arts* bearing the title "Soldiers on the Fault Line: War, Rhetoric, and Reality."

2. This interview originally appeared in *All Area*, and it was republished in *On Human Nature* (2003). All citations come from the later publication.

3. These five elements—agents, acts, agency, purpose, and scene—make up Burke's dramatistic pentad, first described in *A Grammar of Motives*.

4. Ang Lee specializes in adapting literature to film, such as *Life of Pi* (2012), *Sense and Sensibility* (1996), *Crouching Tiger, Hidden Dragon* (2001), and *Brokeback Mountain* (2006). Lee's movie is set to open on Veteran's Day in November 2016 (Gettell). Lee reportedly transformed the Georgia Dome in Atlanta into the Dallas Cowboy's AT&T Stadium for filming. Apparently, the movie updates the setting from the novel's 2004 timeframe when the Cowboys still played in Texas Stadium (Gettell).

5. Though, in the novel, the Cowboys lose 31–7. In the actual game on November 25, 2004, the Cowboys lost 21–7. Fountain must have wanted an even more lopsided defeat for "America's Team."

6. According to the NFL and Nielsen ratings, the average broadcast viewership of NFL games in 2004 was 9.8 million per game. For that specific game, the Fox network drew a rating of 29 for the game, a number that equates to 11.3 million "viewers" ("Final Nielsen").

7. See Lydia Wilkes's "'Now Here's What Really Happened': The Rhetoric of Authentic Experience in War Memoir" for an interesting analysis of the popularity of first-person shooter video games that trade on the public's desire for authenticity over empathy (179–80). Also see Sam Sacks' essay, "First-

Person Shooters: What's Missing from Contemporary War Fiction," for a quick review of a few veteran-penned novels that, as Sacks writes, "share a consistent perspective" that is focused on "the fighting itself."

8. As explained in Chapter One, James Campbell coined the phrase "combat gnosticism" to describe the dominant ideology in the war literature genre that emphasizes personal combat experience as a source of wartime epistemology, "a construction that gives us war experience as a kind of gnosis, a secret knowledge which only an initiated elite knows" (204).

Chapter Five

1. Hierarchy even earns a clause in Burke's definition of man: "Man is the symbol-using (symbol-making, symbol-misusing) animal, inventor of the negative (or moralized by the negative), separated from his natural condition by instruments of his own making, goaded by the spirit of hierarchy (or moved by the sense of order), and rotten with perfection" (*Language* 16).

2. In Vietnam, REMF stood for Rear Echelon Mother Fuckers.

3. In Chapter Seventeen, Gooding prepares a "door-kicker" named Kyle Pilley for a television interview about an episode—filmed by insurgents and posted online—in which Pilley is shot in the chest. His body armor stops the bullet and saves his life, so he pops up, shoots the guy who shot him, and then uses his own dressing kit to treat the insurgent's wounds (202–17).

4. Even Abrams seems to be under a bit of hierarchical psychosis regarding combat and noncombat experience. The historical record is full of combat veterans who were "in the real shit" and still couldn't avoid the "allure of mendacity," to borrow Lawrence's phrase (165).

5. In May of 2013, President Obama signed into law the "Stolen Valor Act," a law that levies fines and up to a year of imprisonment for making fraudulent claims about military service. Of course, it is designed for civilians who make such claims. Still, even when one rightfully accepts a war medal (as John Kerry once did), the slightest suggestion that a decoration is unearned can result in astounding public rage. In 1996, the highest-ranking officer in the U.S. Navy, Admiral Jeremy Boorda, stepped out his front door and shot himself in the chest after questions rose in the media regarding his eligibility to wear two "V" devices on his dress uniform (the V stands for Valor). The Navy later proved that he was rightfully wearing the devices (Shenon 1).

6. When asked about this reference to *Catch-22*, Abrams responded: "I'll admit that *Catch-22* was an influential book on *FOBBIT* ... [it] was both an inspiration and a burden. It was like the proverbial elephant in the room—I knew it was there, but I tried not to look at it. I gave Heller's novel a cameo in my novel as a sort of homage, a tip-of-the-hat to the master. That's the only reason I mentioned *Catch-22* in that swimming pool scene. Unfortunately, some critics thought I was using it as a semaphore to send a message that I was trying to compare myself with a classic. I have very few regrets about how the book turned out, but if I could go back and do it all over again, I would take out that reference to *Catch-22*" (Lawrence 167–68).

Chapter Six

1. Of all the phonetic approximations of the word in English ("hadji," "hodgie," "haji," etc.), *hajji* seems the most common and the closest Anglicized estimation of the word's Arabic pronunciation. Throughout this chapter, I italicize the word in order to distinguish it from the rest of the text and to highlight its value as a term or epithet (as opposed to an actual person), syntactically. When an alternative spelling is used in a quote, I retain the spelling and style of the original.

2. I use the capitalized "Other" in the sense established by Edward Said in his book *Orientalism* (1979) as an object within the concept of the Western-imagined "Orientalism," a way of seeing the "Orient" as "eternal, uniform, and incapable of defining itself ... the Orient is at bottom something either to be feared or to be controlled (by pacification, research and development, outright occupation whenever possible)" (301).

3. One of the first was in Colby Buzzell's *My War* (2005) that includes a section entitled "Hajji Shops" (150). A similar "definition" appears in Paul Dickson's updated tome, *War Slang* (2011) (395). I applaud the definition that appears in *War Slang*, for it admits *hajji* is a "blanket racist word for any person of color, usually non-American, in Iraq" (395).

4. It took a relatively long time for book-length reportage about the war in Afghanistan to emerge. For instance, the so-called Battle of Tora Bora occurred in December of 2001, but the first book about it—Sean Taylor's *Not a Good Day to Die*—did not appear until March of 2006. The United States' war in Afghanistan officially "began" and "ended" before and after the war in Iraq. Yet, all lit-

erature related to the conflict in Afghanistan has lagged far behind that of Iraq. This can be traced to any number of reasons. When the wars began, it likely had something to do with the smaller number of Americans who were actually fighting in Afghanistan or the fewer number of journalists embedded with troops there. Now, it remains a baffling trait of war literature's publication history.

5. Williams is unique in pointing out the following: "In Iraq we called them *hajjis* but we also called them *sadiqis*—which means 'my friends'—or *habibis*—'my darlings' (Soldiers seldom had any idea what these Arabic words meant)" (200). As far as I am aware, she is the only writer of a war memoir or of war fiction involving the Iraq war in any way who mentions *sadiqi* or *habibi* as interchangeable terms for *hajji*.

6. The full chapter title is "Containing the Metaphysics of Indian-Hating, According to the Views of One Evidently not so Prepossessed as Rousseau in Favour of Savages" (201).

7. Officially, the University of North Dakota dropped its Fighting Sioux nickname in 2012, but it persists in more than 2,200 logos around the multimillion-dollar arena that houses the popular UND hockey team. The arena is known as "The Ralph" after Ralph Engelstad, an alumnus who funded the arena's construction. Before his death in 2002, Englestad emblazoned the profile image of a stoic cartoon Indian all around the arena, creating a cost-prohibitive "safeguard" against the possibility that the mascot would ever be removed (Bowie).

8. All references to and citations from Chris Kyle's "autobiography" are from the 2012 first edition of the book. Since then, the publisher—HarperCollins—has issued two more editions, one to remove all references to a man Kyle calls "Scruff Face" and another to accompany the release of the movie. In drafts of the book and in an interview with Bill O'Reilly (and other interviewers), Kyle identifies "Scruff Face" as Jesse Ventura, a former S.E.A.L. and the former governor of Minnesota (O'Reilly). In his autobiography and elsewhere, Kyle made a number of claims about Ventura that have since been ruled to be fabrications and led to a defamation lawsuit the Kyle estate lost.

9. All citations and page references from the movie refer to Hall's "Final" script available at warnerbrothers.com. Some small discrepancies exist between the script and the words that appear in the movie.

10. The film ends with a note stating that the movie was based on the "autobiography."

In an interview with *Rolling Stone*, though, Hall reports that he collected much of the "nuances of war" from a trip he made to visit Kyle in Texas in 2010. As Hall says, "There was a lot of great material in [the book], but I knew there was more to this guy than was in those pages."

11. Greenberg writes, "Kitsch is mechanical and operates by formulas. Kitsch is vicarious experience and faked sensations. Kitsch changes according to style, but remains always the same. Kitsch is the epitome of all that is spurious in the life of our times. Kitsch pretends to demand nothing of its customers except their money—not even their time" (40).

12. All quotations come from Berg's screenplay available at screenplaydb.com.

13. The glossary is available both in the jacket that accompanies the DVD version of the series and online ("Glossary"). The definition seems to draw from Evan Wright's memoir of the same name that appeared in 2004. Wright mentions that he and his fellow Marines called flat bread "Hajji tortillas," as the HBO definition repeats, though Wright does not attempt a further accounting for the term in his memoir (226). I make it clear in my essay that I consider *hajji*'s part of speech irrelevant to its nature as a pejorative.

14. Currently, the performance can be viewed at www.youtube.com/watch?v=C_qz EY8R3rU.

15. Wall includes the full lyrics to "Hadji Girl" in his essay "Imperial Laughs" (74–75).

16. The video of the original performance has been posted and removed from YouTube a number of times, and a number of other "performers" have posted their own version of the song on the website as well. On 11 February 2008, a user with the name JDMEVO8 posted Belile's performance again, and as of 1 June 2015, this version had been viewed 225,773 times. See Chris Mazzolini's "Humor Attempt Falls Flat" for a news article about the song, the brief uproar it caused with the Council of American Islamic Relations, and for reactions from both Belile and the U.S. Marine Corps.

17. Matt Stone and Trey Parker, the writers of *Team America* and the creators of the animated television show *South Park*, first used "durka durka" to mimic spoken Arabic in episode 509 of the *South Park* series titled "Osama bin Laden Has Farty Pants" which first aired on 7 November 2001.

18. Burke defines synecdoche simply as "the figure of speech wherein the part is used for the whole, the whole for the part, the container for the thing contained, the cause for

the effect, the effect for the cause, etc. Simplest example: 'twenty noses' for 'twenty men'" (*Philosophy* 25–26).

19. The law that codified the "tooth-to-tail" ratio is the 1974 Nunn Amendment that sought to correct a perceived deficiency in the United States' force structure in Europe at that time (McGrath 32–35).

20. According to a recent Congressional Research Service report, in December of 2008, there were 15,111 military personnel deployed to locations outside of Iraq and Afghanistan, and there were 15,055 sailors aboard ships (Belasco 5).

21. See Lydia Wilkes' "'Now Here's What Really Happened': The Rhetoric of Authentic Experience in War Memoir" for an interesting analysis of Burke's concept of identification as an explanation for the popularity of first-person shooter video games that trade on the public's desire for authenticity over empathy (179–180). She writes, "identification also occurs between gamers and video game characters—but the emphasis is on identifying with a character rather than with a person" (179).

22. All four soldiers were eventually convicted for their crimes and all four are serving life sentences. Green is in the U.S. Penitentiary in Terre Haute, Indiana, since he had been discharged from military service before the crime was reported. The other three are serving life sentences in the U.S. Disciplinary Barracks at Fort Leavenworth, Kansas (Frederick 350–369). In 2007, a movie treatment—*Redacted*, directed by Brian de Palma—of these horrific events was released. See Martin Barker's *A Toxic Genre* for a short discussion of the film (37–42).

Bibliography

Abrams, David. *FOBBIT.* New York: Black Cat, 2012. Print.

Adams, Jon Roberts. *Male Armor: The Soldier-Hero in Contemporary American Culture*. Richmond: University of Virginia Press, 2008. Print.

Alexie, Sherman. "Relevant Contradictions." *The Stranger.* 27 Feb. 2003. Web. 16 Apr. 2015. www.thestranger.com/seattle/relevant-contradictions/Content?oid=13492.

American Sniper. Dir. Clint Eastwood. Screenplay Jason Hall. Warner Bros., 2015. Film.

Aravamudan, Srinivas. "Introduction: Perpetual War." *PMLA* 124.5 (2009): 1505–14. Print.

Aslam, Nadeem. *The Blind Man's Garden*. New York: Knopf, 2013. Print.

———. *The Wasted Vigil*. New York: Vintage, 2009. Print.

Atkinson, Rick. *In the Company of Soldiers: A Chronicle of Combat in Iraq*. New York: Henry Holt, 2004. Print.

Austin, J.L. *How to Do Things with Words*. 1963. 2d ed. Ed. J.O. Urmson and Marina Sbisa. Oxford: Oxford University Press, 1975. Print.

Barker, Christine R., and R.W. Last. *Erich Maria Remarque*. London: Oswald Wolff, 1979. Print.

Barker, Martin. *A "Toxic Genre": The Iraq War Films*. London: Pluto, 2011. Print.

Baudrillard, Jean. *The Gulf War Did Not Take Place*. Trans. Paul Patton. Bloomington: Indiana University Press, 1995. Print.

———. "War Porn." Trans. Paul A. Taylor. *International Journal of Baudrillard Studies* 2.1 (Jan. 2005). Web. 4 March 2015. ubishops.ca/baudrillardstudies/vol2_1/taylor.htm.

Beard, Mary, Harriet Gilbert, and Jeremy Paxman. "Good Reads." *British Broadcasting Corporation. BBC Radio4.* 7 Oct. 2014. Web. 8 Oct. 2014. bbc.co.uk/programmes.

Belasco, Amy. "Troop Levels in the Afghan and Iraq Wars, FY2001-FY2012: Cost and Other Potential Issues." 2 July 2009. R40682. *Congressional Research Service.* Web. 17 June 2015.

Bellesiles, Michael A. *A People's History of the U.S. Military: Ordinary Soldiers Reflect on Their Experience of War, from the American Revolution to Afghanistan*. New York: New, 2012. Print.

Benedict, Helen. "*Fives and Twenty-Fives* Review: Michael Pitre's Riveting Iraq War Novel." *The Guardian.* 2 Oct. 2014. Web. 4 Dec. 2014.

———. *Sand Queen*. New York: Soho, 2011. Print.

Bennett, Eric. *A Big Enough Lie*. Evanston: Triquarterly, 2015. Print

Berg, Peter. Adapt. *Lone Survivor*. Based on the book by Marcus Luttrell. *Screen playDb.Com.* 2014. Web. 1 April 2016. screenplaydb.com/film/scripts/lonesurvivor.pdf.

Bird, S. Elizabeth. "Savage Desires: The Gendered Construction of the American Indian in Popular Media." *Selling the Indian: Commercializing & Appropriating American Indian Cultures*. Ed. Carter Jones Meyer and Diana Royer. Tucson: University of Arizona Press, 2001. 62–98. Print.

Birnbaum, Mariana D. "On the Language of Prejudice." *Western Folklore* 30.4

(Oct. 1971): 247–268. Web. *JSTOR.* 9 Jan. 2015.

Blassim, Hassan. *The Corpse Exhibition and Other Stories of Iraq.* Trans. Jonathan Wright. New York: Penguin, 2014. Print.

Bowie, James I. "The University of North Dakota Dropped Its Offensive Nickname. How Does the School Replace It?" *Slate.* 13 Jan. 2015. Web. 15 May 2015. slate.com/blogs/the_eye/2015/01/13/university_of_north_dakota_is_in_search_of_a_nickname_and_logo_to_replace.

Brody, Ben. "U.S. Military Lingo: The (Almost) Definitive Guide." *NPR.* National Public Radio. 4 Dec. 2013. Web. 17 June 2015. npr.org/blogs/parallels/2013/12/04/248816232/u-s-military-lingo-the-almost-definitive-guide.

Brown, Keith, and Catherine Lutz. "Grunt Lit: Participant-Observers of Empire." *American Ethnologist* 34.2 (2007): 322–28. Print.

Brown, Randy. "'The Activity' Comes to a Close, While War Rages On." *Red Bull Rising.* 10 Feb. 2015. Web. 24 Feb. 2015. redbullrising.com/2015/02/activity-comes-to-close-while-war-rages.html.

Browne, Sir Thomas. *The Religio Medici & Other Writings of Sir Thomas Browne.* Ed. Ernest Rhys. London: J.M. Dent & Sons, 1920. Print.

Buchanan, David. "They Call It the Hajji Mall." *War, Literature, and the Arts* 26 (2014): 1–10. Web. 16 Dec. 2014. wlajournal.com/wlaarchive/26/Buchanan.pdf.

Burke, Kenneth. *Attitudes Toward History.* 1937. 3d ed. Berkeley: University of California Press, 1984. Print.

———. "Auscultation, Creation, and Revision." *Extensions of the Burkeian System.* Ed. James W. Chesebro. Tuscaloosa: University of Alabama Press, 1993. 42–172.

———. "Counter-Gridlock: An Interview with Kenneth Burke." *On Human Nature.* Ed. William H. Rueckert and Angelo Bonadonna. Berkeley: University of California Press, 2003. 336–89. Print.

———. *Counter-Statement.* 1931. Berkeley: University of California Press, 1968. Print.

———. "Dramatism." *Communication: Concepts and Perspectives.* Ed. Lee Thayer. Washington, D.C.: Spartan, 1967. 327–60. Print.

———. "Dramatism." *International Encyclopedia of the Social Sciences.* Ed. David L. Sills. Vol. 7. New York: Macmillan, 1968. 445–51. Print.

———. *Dramatism and Development.* Barre, MA: Clark University Press, 1972. Print.

———. *A Grammar of Motives.* New York: Prentice-Hall, 1945. Print.

———. *Language as Symbolic Action: Essays on Life, Literature, and Method.* Berkeley, University of California Press, 1966. Print.

———. "Linguistic Approaches to Problems of Education." *Modern Philosophies and Education: The Fifty-Fourth Yearbook of the National Society for the Study of Education.* Ed. Nelson B. Henry. Chicago: University of Chicago Press, 1955. 259–303. Print.

———. "Literature as Equipment for Living." *Philosophy of Literary Forms: Studies in Symbolic Action.* 1941. 3d ed. Berkeley, University of California Press, 1973. 292–304. Print.

———. "On Catharsis, on Resolution." *The Kenyon Review* 21 (Summer 1959): 337–75. Print.

———. "Othello: An Essay to Illustrate a Method." *The Hudson Review* 4.2 (Summer 1951): 165–203. Print.

———. *Permanence and Change: An Anatomy of a Purpose.* 1935. 2d ed. Indianapolis: Bobbs-Merrill, 1965. Print.

———. *Philosophy of Literary Forms: Studies in Symbolic Action.* 1941. 3d ed. Berkeley: University of California Press, 1973. Print.

———. "Realisms, Occidental Style." *Asian and Western Writers in Dialogue.* Ed. Guy Amirthanayagam. London: Macmillan, 1982. 26–47. Print.

———. "The Rhetoric of Hitler's 'Battle.'" *The Southern Review* 5 (1939): 1–21. Print.

———. *A Rhetoric of Motives.* New York: Prentice-Hall, 1950. Print.

———. *The Rhetoric of Religion: Studies in Logology.* 1961. Berkeley: University of California Press, 1970.

———. "The Rhetorical Situation." *Communication: Ethical and Moral Issues*. Ed. Lee Thayer. New York: Gordon and Breach Science, 1973. 263–75.

———. "Variations on 'Providence.'" *Notre Dame English Journal* 13.3 (Summer 1981): 155–83. Print.

———. "War and Cultural Life." *The American Journal of Sociology* 48 (Nov. 1942): 404–10. Print.

———. "War, Response, and Contradiction." *Philosophy of Literary Forms: Studies in Symbolic Action*. 1941. 3d ed. Berkeley, University of California Press, 1973. 234–57. Print.

———. "Why Satire, with a Plan for Writing One." *Michigan Quarterly Review* 13 (Winter 1974): 307–37. Print.

Burns, Richard Allen. "Where Is Jody Now: Reconsidering Military Marching Chants." *Warrior Ways: Explorations in Modern Military Folklore*. Ed. Eric A. Eliason and Tad Tuleja. Logan: Utah State University Press, 2012. 79–98. Print.

Buzzell, Colby. *My War: Killing Time in Iraq*. New York: Putnam, 2005. Print.

Campbell, James. "Combat Gnosticism: The Ideology of First World War Poetry Criticism." *New Literary History* 30.1 (1999): 203–15. Print.

Campbell, Joseph. *The Hero with a Thousand Faces*. New York: Bollingen, 1949. Print.

Carey, James W. "A Cultural Approach to Communication." *Communication as Culture: Essays on Media and Society*. 1989. Rev. ed. New York: Routledge, 2009. 11–28. Print.

Carpenter, Lea. "The Enemy Within." *The New York Times Book Review* (19 Jan. 2014): BR11. Web. *ProQuest Central*. 22 Jan. 2015.

Carroll, Al. *Medicine Bags and Dog Tags: American Indian Veterans from Colonial Times to the Second Iraq War*. Lincoln: University of Nebraska Press, 2008. Print.

Carson, Michael. "American's Sniper's Uniquely American Kitsch." *The Wrath Bearing Tree*. 23 Jan. 2015. Web. 1 April 2016. wrath-bearingtree.com/2015/01/american-snipers-uniquely-american-kitsch/.

———. "The Philosophy Hero: From Socrates to Scranton." *The Wrath Bearing Tree*. 27 Jan. 2015. Web. 1 April 2016. wrath-bearingtree.com/2015/01/20150127the-philosopher-hero-from-socrates-to-scranton/.

Carter, C. Allen. *Kenneth Burke and the Scapegoat Process*. Norman: University of Oklahoma Press, 1996. Print.

Cather, Willa. *The Selected Letters of Willa Cather*. Ed. Andrew Jewell and Janis Stout. New York: Knopf, 2013. Print.

Cheney, George. "The Rhetoric of Identification and the Study of Organizational Communication." *Quarterly Journal of Speech* 69 (1983): 143–58. Print.

Coker, Christopher. *Men at War: What Fiction Tells Us About Conflict from* The Iliad *to* Catch-22. Oxford: Oxford University Press, 2014. Print.

Colla, Elliott. "The Military-Literary Complex." *Jadaliyya*. 8 July 2014. Web. 12 June 2015. jadaliyya.com/pages/index/18384/the-military-literary-complex.

Collingwood, R.G. *The Idea of History*. 1946. Rev. ed. Ed. Jan Van Der Dussen. Oxford: Oxford University Press, 2005. Print.

Condit, Celeste Michelle. "Post-Burke: Transcending the Sub-Stance of Dramatism." *Quarterly Journal of Speech* 78.3 (1992): 349–55. Print.

Conley, Thomas. *Toward a Rhetoric of Insult*. Chicago: University of Chicago Press, 2010. Print.

Coupe, Lawrence. *Kenneth Burke on Myth: An Introduction*. New York: Routledge, 2005. Print.

Cowley, Malcolm. "Rev. of *The First World War*, by Laurence Stallings." *The New Republic* (20 Sept. 1933): 160–61. Print.

Creed, Pamela. *Ethics, Norms, and the Narratives of War: Creating and Encountering the Enemy Other*. New York: Routledge, 2013. E-book.

Daugherty, Scott. "For Second Time, DMV Denies Icuhaji License Plate." *The Virginian-Pilot*. 20 Feb. 2013. Hamptonroads.com. Web. 7 Mar. 2013.

Del Vecchio, John M. Afterword. "Code Word: Geronimo—Perspectives." *Code Word: Geronimo*. By Dale Dye and Julia Due. San Diego: IDW, 2011. Print.

Department of Defense News Release.

"DoD Announces Recertification of Imminent Danger Areas." Release No. NR-002-14. 3 Jan. 2014. Web. 3 Feb. 2015. defense.gov/releases/release.aspx?releaseid=16459.

Derrida, Jacques. *Of Grammatology*. Trans. Gayatri Chakrovorty Spivak. Baltimore: Johns Hopkins University Press, 1976.

Dickson, Paul. *War Slang: American Fighting Words and Phrases Since the Civil War*. 1994. 3d ed. New York: Dover, 2011. Print.

"DMV Says Iraq War Veteran's Personalized License Plate ICUHAJI Encourages Violence and Is Vulgar." Daily Mail.com. 20 Feb. 2013. Web. 10 Feb. 2015. dailymail.co.uk/news/article-2281804/DMV-says-Iraq-war-veterans-personalized-license-plate-ICUHAJI-encourages-violence-vulgar.html.

Dower, John W. *War Without Mercy: Race & Power in the Pacific War*. New York: Pantheon, 1986. Print.

Drinnon, Richard. *Facing West: The Metaphysics of Indian-Hating and Empire-Building*. New York: New American Library, 1980. Print.

Duncan, H. D. *Communication and Social Order*. London: Oxford University Press, 1966. Print.

Dyer, Geoff. "The Moral Art of War." *Otherwise Known as the Human Condition: Selected Essays and Reviews, 1989–2010*. Minneapolis: Graywolf, 2011. 215–27. Print.

Eco, Umberto. *Travels in Hyperreality: Essays*. Trans. William Weaver. San Diego: Harcourt Brace, 1986. Print.

Edwards, Paul, and Catherine Wallace. *Wyndham Lewis: Art and War*. Ann Arbor: Lund Humphries, 1992. Print.

Egan, Daniel. "Frantz Fanon and the Construction of the Colonial Subject: Defining 'The Enemy' in the Iraq War." *Socialism and Democracy* 21.3 (Nov. 2007): 142–54. Print.

Ehrhart, W.D. "Paul Fussell: A Remembrance." *War, Literature, and the Arts: An International Journal of the Humanities* 24 (2012). Web. 11 Feb. 2014. wlajournal.com/wlaarchive/24_1-2/Ehrhart.pdf.

Eliot, Thomas Stearns. "Reflections on Contemporary Poetry." *The Egoist* 6.3 (July 1919): 39–40. Web. *The Modernist Journals Project*. 23 Nov. 2013.

Engelhardt, Tom. *The American Way of War: How Bush's War Became Obama's*. Chicago: Haymarket, 2010. Print.

Fahs, Alice. *The Imagined Civil War: Popular Literature of the North and South, 1861–1865*. Chapel Hill: University of North Carolina Press, 2001. Print

Favret, Mary A. *War at a Distance: Romanticism and the Making of Modern Warfare*. Princeton: Princeton University Press, 2010. Print.

"Final Nielsen Ratings from Weekend Sports Events." *Street and Smith's Sports Business*. 3 Dec. 2004. Web. 31 May 2015. m.sportsbusinessdaily.com/Daily/Issues/2004/12/Issue-57/Sports-Media/Final-Nielsen-Ratings-From-Weekend-Sports-Events.aspx.

Fish, Stanley. *Is There a Text in This Class? The Authority of Interpretive Communities*. Cambridge: Harvard University Press, 1980. Print.

Foucault, Michel. *Power/Knowledge: Selected Interviews and Other Writing, 1972–1977*. Ed. Colin Gordon. Trans. Gordon, Leo Marshall, John Mepham, and Kate Soper. New York: Pantheon, 1980. Print.

———. "What Is an Author?" *Modern Criticism and Theory: A Reader*. Ed. David Lodge and Nigel Wood. 3d ed. Harlow, England: Pearson, 2008. 280–93. Print.

Fountain, Ben. "*Billy Lynn*: A Full-Bore Tale of a Day After Iraq." Interview by Laura Sullivan. *All Things Considered. NPR*. National. Public Radio. 30 June 2012. Web. 18 June 2015. npr.org/templates/transcript/transcript.php?storyId=155841872.

———. *Billy Lynn's Long Halftime Walk*. New York: Harper, 2012. Print.

———. Interview by Caroline North. "100 Dallas Creative: No. 8 Ben Fountain, Man of Letters." *Dallas Observer*. 20 Feb. 2015. Web. 21 Feb. 2015.

———. "Interview with Ben Fountain, Author of *Billy Lynn's Long Halftime Walk*." Interview by Teddy Wayne. *Huffington Post*. 30 April 2012. Web. 18 June 2015.

———. "Soldiers on the Fault Line: War,

Rhetoric, and Reality." *War, Literature, and the Arts* 25.1 (2013): 1–14. Web. 10 Oct. 2014. http://wlajournal.com/25_1/pdf/fountain.pdf.

Frederick, Jim. *Black Hearts: One Platoon's Descent into Madness in Iraq's Triangle of Death*. New York: Harmony, 2010.

Frye, Northrop. *Anatomy of Criticism: Four Essays*. Princeton: Princeton University Press, 1957. Print.

———. *Northrop Frye on Modern Culture*. Ed. Jan Gorak. Toronto: University of Toronto Press, 2003. Print.

Fussell, Paul. *The Boy Scout Handbook and Other Observations*. New York: Oxford University Press, 1982. Print.

———. *The Great War and Modern Memory*. 1975. Oxford: Oxford University Press, 1977. Print.

———. "My War: How I Got Irony in the Infantry." *Harper's Magazine* (Jan. 1982): 40–8. Print.

———. "The Real War: 1939–1945." *The Atlantic Monthly* 264.2 (Aug. 1989): 32–48. Print.

———. *Thank God for the Atom Bomb and Other Essays*. New York: Summit, 1988. Print.

———. *Wartime: Understanding and Behavior in the Second World War*. New York: Oxford University Press, 1989. Print.

Gallagher, Matt. "Anne Hathaway Plays Drone Pilot Fighting a New War in *Grounded*." *The Intercept*. 5 May 2015. Web. 19 May 2015 firstlook.org/theintercept/2015/05/06/grounded-vegas-anne-hathaway-plays-drone-pilot.

———. "*Billy Lynn's Long Halftime Walk* by Ben Fountain: The War Novel of Our Time." *The Daily Beast*. 27 May 2012. Web. 27 Oct. 2014.

George, Ann, and Jack Selzer. *Kenneth Burke in the 1930s*. Columbia: University of South Carolina Press, 2008. Print.

Geronimo, Harlyn. Cong. Senate. United States Senate Commission on Indian Affairs. "Stolen Identities: The Impact of Racist Stereotypes on Indigenous People." Oversight Hearing. 5 May 2011. Web. 16 Apr. 2015. indiancountrytodaymedianetwork.com/2011/05/06/geronimos-great-grandson-reacts-32639.

Gettell, Oliver. "Ang Lee Film *Billy Lynn's Long Halftime Walk* to Open in November 2016." *Los Angeles Times*. 17 Apr. 2015. Web. 13 May 2015. latimes.com/entertainment/movies/moviesnow/la-et-mn-ang-lee-billy-lynns-long-halftime-walk-release-date-20150417-story.html.

Giordano, Paolo. *The Human Body*. New York: Viking, 2014. Print.

Girard, Rene. *Violence and the Sacred*. Trans. Patrick Gregory. Baltimore: Johns Hopkins University Press, 1977. Print.

"Glossary." *HBO: Generation Kill: Inside*. Home Box Office. Web. 15 June. 2015. hbo.com/generation-kill/inside/glossary/detail/f-j.

Greenberg, Clement. "Avant-Garde and Kitsch." *The Partisan Review* 6.5 (1939): 34–49. Print.

Greenwood, Emily. "How to Write a War: Thucydides and the Literature of the First World War." *In the Company of Scholars Lecture Series*. Yale University. 20 Jan. 2015. Lecture. Web. 12 June 2015. youtube.com/watch?v=4KwilofMQg8.

Gupta, Suman. *Imagining Iraq: Literature in English and the Iraq Invasion*. New York: Palgrave Macmillan, 2011. Print.

Gusfield, Joseph R. Introduction. *On Symbols and Society*. Ed. Gusfield. Chicago: University of Chicago Press, 1989. 1–49. Print.

"Hajji." *Oxford English Dictionary*. Web. 1 June 2015.

Hall, Jason. Adapt. *American Sniper*. By Chris Kyle with Scott McEwen and Jim DeFelice. 17 July 2013. Web. 25 Dec. 2015. Screenplay. Pdl.Warnerbros.com/Wbmovies/Awards2014/Pdf/As.Pdf.

Hanley, Lynne. *Writing War: Fiction, Gender, and Memory*. Amherst: University of Massachusetts Press, 1991. Print.

Harjo, Susan Shown. Cong. Senate. United States Senate Commission on Indian Affairs. "Stolen Identities: The Impact of Racist Stereotypes on Indigenous People." Oversight Hearing. 5 May 2011. Web. 16 Apr. 2015. www.indian.senate.gov/hearing/oversight-hearing-stolen-identities-impact-racist-stereotypes-indigenous-people.

Harrison, Simon. *Dark Trophies: Hunting and the Enemy Body in Modern War.* New York: Berghahn, 2012. Print.

Hauerwas, Stanley. "Sacrificing the Sacrifices of War." *Journal of Religion, Conflict, and Peace* 1.1 (Fall 2007). Web. 22 Jan. 2015. www.religionconflictpeace.org/volume-1-issue-1-fall-2007/sacrificing-sacrifices-war.

Hawhee, Debra. "Burke and Nietzsche." *Quarterly Journal of Speech* 85 (1999): 129–45. Web. *Taylor & Francis Social Science and Humanities Library.* 6 March 2015.

Hawkes, Raymond, and Mark Holmberg. "Judge to DMV: Give Back Veteran's Vanity Plate or Find Better Reason to Keep Them." WTVR.com. 9 Nov. 2015. Web. 19 Feb. 2015. wtvr.com/2012/11/09/judge-to-dmv-give-back-veterans-vanity-plates-or-come-up-with-a-better-reason-to-keep-them.

Hawkins, Ty. *Reading Vietnam Amid the War on Terror.* New York: Palgrave Macmillan, 2012. Print.

Hedges, Chris, and Laila Al-Arian. *Collateral Damage: America's War Against Iraqi Civilians.* New York: Nation, 2008. Print.

Heller, Joseph. *Catch-22.* New York: Laurel, 1955. Print.

———. Interview. "On Translating *Catch-22* into a Movie." *A Catch-22 Casebook.* Eds. Frederick Kiley and Walter McDonald. New York: Thomas Y. Crowell, 1973. 346–62.

Hemingway, Ernest. *A Farewell to Arms.* 1929. New York: Scribner, 1995. Print.

———. Introduction. *Men at War: The Best War Stories of All Time.* Ed. Hemingway. New York: Crown, 1942. xi–xxi. Print.

———. "On Writing." *The Nick Adams Stories.* New York: Scribner, 1972. 233–41. Print.

Herbert, Bob. "From 'Gook' to 'Raghead.'" *New York Times* (2 May 2005): A21. Web. *ProQuest Historical Newspapers.* 31 Dec. 2014.

———. "'Gooks' to 'Hajis.'" *New York Times* (21 May 2004): A23. Web. *ProQuest Historical Newspapers.* 31 Dec. 2014.

Hosseini, Khaled. "Khaled Hosseini Discusses *Billy Lynn's Long Halftime Walk.*" Interview by Alexandra Alter. *The Wall Street Journal.* 4 Mar. 2014. Web. 27 Oct. 14.

Hynes, Samuel. *The Soldiers' Tale: Bearing Witness to Modern War.* Penguin: New York, 1997. Print.

Ivie, Robert, and Oscar Giner. *Hunt the Devil: A Demonology of U.S. War Culture.* Tuscaloosa: University of Alabama Press, 2015. Print.

———. "Images of Savagery in American Justifications for War." *Communication Monographs* 47 (Nov. 1980): 279–91. Print.

———. "Savagery in Democracy's Empire." *Third World Quarterly* 26.1 (2005): 55–65. Web. *JSTOR.* 27 Sep. 2013.

Jackson, Bruce. *Wake Up Dead Men: Hard Labor and Southern Blues.* Athens: University of Georgia Press, 1999. Print.

———. "What Happened to Jody." *Journal of American Folklore* 80.318 (Oct.–Dec. 1967): 387–96. Web. *JSTOR.* 1 Oct. 2014.

Jameson, Fredric. "War and Representation." *PMLA* 124.5 (Oct. 2009): 1532–47. Print.

Jehl, Douglas, and Andrea Elliot. "Cuba Base Sent Its Interrogators to Iraqi Prison." *New York Times* (29 May 2004): A5. Web. *LexisNexis Academic.* 31 Dec. 2014.

Johnson, Dillard, and James Tarr. *Carnivore: A Memoir by One of the Deadliest American Soldiers of All Time.* New York: William Morrow, 2013. Print.

Kakutani, Michiko. "Human Costs of the Forever Wars, Enough to Fill a Bookshelf." *The New York Times* 26 Dec. 2014: A1. Print.

———. "A Reading List of Modern War Stories." *The New York Times Online* 25 Dec. 2015. Web. 20 Apr. 2015. http://nyti.ms/1CJf3D0.

Kaplan, Robert. "Indian Country." *Wall Street Journal* 21 Sept. 2004: A22. Print.

———. *Primal Grunts: The American Military on the Ground.* New York: Random House, 2005. Print.

Kellogg, Carolyn. "Absurd Day for Soldier in *Billy Lynn's Long Halftime Walk.*" *Los Angeles Times* 1 July 2012. Web. 27 Oct. 2014.

Kieran, David. "'What Young Men and

Women Do When Their Country Is Attacked': Interventionist Discourse and the Rewriting of Violence in Adolescent Literature of the Iraq War." *Children's Literature Association Quarterly* 37.1 (Spring 2012): 4–26. *Project Muse*. Web. 10 Oct. 2012.

Kiley, Frederick, and Walter McDonald. Preface. *A Catch-22 Casebook*. Ed. Kiley and McDonald. New York: Thomas Crowell, 1973. v–vi. Print.

Kitto, H.D.F. *The Greeks*. London: Penguin, 1951. Print.

Klay, Phil. *Redeployment*. New York: Penguin, 2014. Print.

Komunyakaa, Yusef. Letter. *Poetry* 185.2 (Nov. 2004): 144–46. Print.

Koenig, Sarah. Host. "Season Two." *Serial*. Produced by WBEZ Chicago. Podcast. serialpodcast.org.

Kyle, Chris. *American Sniper: The Autobiography of the Most Lethal Sniper in U.S. Military History*. With Scott McEwan and Jim DeFelice. New York: HarperCollins, 2012. Print.

LaDuke, Winona. *The Militarization of Indian Country*. East Lansing: Makwa Enewed, 2013. Print.

Langness, David. "Them's Fightin' Words: A Tour of American War Fiction." *Paste* 18 (Oct.–Nov. 2005): 113–15. Print.

Lawrence, David. Interview. "Author Spotlight: Ben Fountain Interviewed by David Lawrence." *War, Literature, and the Arts* 24.1 (2012): 88–97. Print.

———. Interview. "David Abrams Interviewed by David Lawrence." *War, Literature, and the Arts: An International Journal of the Humanities* 25 (2013): 161–170. Print.

Lepucki, Edan. Interview. "Everything Is Political: An Interview with Ben Fountain." *The Millions*. 25 June 2012. Web. 11 Nov. 2014. themillions.com/2012/06/everything-is-political-an-interview-with-ben-fountain.html.

Levinas, Emmanuel. *Existence and Existents*. Trans. Alphonso Lingis. Pittsburgh: Duquesne University Press, 2001. Print.

Levy, Elinor. "Upper Echelons and Boots on the Ground." *Warrior Ways: Explorations in Modern Military Folklore*. Ed. Eric A. Eliason and Tad Tuleja.

Logan: Utah State University Press, 2012. 99–115. Print.

Lewis, Lloyd B. *The Tainted War: Culture and Identity in Vietnam War Narratives*. Westport, CT: Greenwood, 1985.

Lewis, Wyndham. *Blast: War Number* 1.2 (July 1915). Web. *The Modernist Journals Project*. 23 Nov. 2013. modjourn.org.

Liebrum, Jennifer. "Modern M*A*S*H*: Author Tackles Gritty Topic with Humor." *Idaho Mountain Express*. 15 May 2013. Web. 23 June. 2015. archives.mtexpress.com/index2.php?ID=2005147297#.VYmgb2C9o3Q.

Limerick, Patricia Nelson. "Live Free and Soar." Op-Ed. *The New York Times* 29 June 2005, late ed.: A23. *ProQuest Newsstand*. Web. 15 Nov. 2012.

Lone Survivor. Dir. Peter Berg. Screenplay Berg. Universal, 2013. DVD.

Loughery, John. *The Other Side of Silence: Men's Lives and Gay Identities: A Twentieth Century History*. New York: Henry Holt, 1998. Print.

Luckhurst, Roger. "Not Now, Not Yet: Polytemporality and Fictions of the Iraq War." *Trauma in Contemporary Literature: Narrative and Representation*. Ed. Marita Nadal and Monica Calvo. New York: Routledge, 2014. 51–72. Print.

Luttrell, Marcus. *Lone Survivor: The Eyewitness Account of Operation Redwing and the Lost Heroes of SEAL Team 10*. New York: Little, 2007. Print.

Luxton, David D., Janyce E. Osenbach, Mark A. Reger, Derek J. Smolenski, Nancy A. Skopp, Nigel E. Bush, and Gregory A. Gahm. *DoDsER: Department of Defense Suicide Event Report, Calendar Year 2011 Annual Report*. 15 Nov. 2012. Defense Centers of Excellence. 2012. National Center for Telehealth and Technology. Web. 17 June 2015.

MacLeish, Archibald. Rev. of *The First World War*, by Laurence Stallings. *The New Republic*. 20 Sept. 1933: 159–160. Print.

Mailer, Norman. "Introduction." *The Naked and the Dead*. 1948. 50th Anniv. Ed. New York: Holt, 1998. Print.

Marwilll, Honathan. "Paul Fussell's Wars." *Michigan Quarterly Review* 29.3 (1990): 431–52. Print.

Mazzolini, Chris. "Humor Attempt Falls Flat." *Daily News* (Jacksonville, NC). 14 June 2006. Web. *Business Insights: Global.* 5 Jan. 2015.

McGrath, John. J. *The Other End of the Spear: The Tooth-to-Tail Ratio (T3R) in Modern Military Operations.* Fort Leavenworth, KS: Combat Studies Institute, 2007. Print.

McLean, Alan, and Archie Tse. "American Forces in Afghanistan and Iraq." *International New York Times.* 22 June 2011. Web. 22 Jan. 2015. nytimes.com/interactive/2011/06/22/world/asia/american-forces-in-afghanistan-and-iraq.html.

McLoughlin, Kate. *Authoring War: The Literary Representation of War from the Iliad to Iraq.* Cambridge: Cambridge University Press, 2011. Print.

_____. Introduction. *The Cambridge Companion to War Writing.* Cambridge: Cambridge University Press, 2009. 1–3. Print.

_____. Introduction. *The Literature of War: Approaches.* Vol. 1. New York: St. James, 2012. xi–xiv. Print.

Melville, Herman. *The Confidence-Man: His Masquerade.* London: Longman, 1857. Print.

Mikhail, Dunya. *The War Works Hard.* Trans. Elizabeth Winslow. New York: New Directions, 2005. Print.

Miles, Donna. "Rumsfeld Thanks Troops, Likens Them to American Western Legend." *Defense.Gov.* 7 Oct. 2003. Web. *American Forces Press Service.* 18 March 2014. defense.gov/News/NewsArticle.aspx?ID=28364.

Molin, Peter. "Don't Kill the Messenger: Oren Moverman's Ode to Casualty Notification Officers." *Time Now: The Iraq and Afghanistan Wars in Art, Film, and Literature.* 16 Jan. 2015. Web. 24 Feb. 2015. acolytesofwar.com/2015/01/16/dont-kill-the-messenger-oren-moverermans-ode-to-casualty-notification-officers.

_____. "Grillin', Chillin', and Killin' with the Military 1%: Aaron Gwyn's *Wynne's War.*" *Time Now: The Iraq and Afghanistan Wars in Art, Film, and Literature.* 11 Jan. 2015. Web. 24 Feb. 2015. acolytesofwar.com/2015/01/11/grillin-chillin-and-killin-with-the-military-1-aaron-gwyns-wynnes-war.

_____. "The Iraq and Afghanistan Wars in Fiction, Poetry, Memoir, Film, and Photography: A Compendium." *Time Now: The Iraq and Afghanistan Wars in Art, Film, and Literature.* 5 Jan. 2015. Web. 20 Apr. 2015. acolytesofwar.com/2015/01/05/the-iraq-and-afghanistan-wars-in-fiction-poetry-memoir-film-and-photography-a-compendium.

_____. "Minnesota Turn-And-Burn: War Writing at AWP15." *Time Now: The Iraq and Afghanistan Wars in Art, Film, and Literature.* 18 Apr. 2015. Web. 1 June 2014. acolytesofwar.com/2015/04/18/minnesota-turn-and-burn-war-writing-at-awp15/.

_____. "'Thank You for Your Service': Ben Fountain's *Billy Lynn's Long Halftime Walk.*" *Time Now: The Iraq and Afghanistan Wars in Art, Film, and Literature.* 18 Aug. 2013. Web. 21 Oct. 2014. http://acolytesofwar.com/2013/08/18/thank-you-for-your-service-ben-fountains-billy-lynns-long-halftime-walk/.

Momaday, N. Scott. "The Morality of Indian Hating." *Ramparts* 3.1 (Summer 1964): 29–40. Print.

Murphy, Dan. "America's Deadliest Soldier or Stolen Valor?" *The Christian Science Monitor.* 26 June 2013. Web. 9 Dec. 2014. csmonitor.com/World/Security-Watch/Backchannels/2013/0626/America-s-deadliest-soldier-or-stolen-valor?nav=692833-csm_blog_post-promoLink.

Norris, Margot. *Writing War in the Twentieth Century.* Charlottesville: University Press of Virginia, 2000. Print.

O'Brien, Tim. *Going After Caccciato.* New York: Delacorte, 1978. Print.

_____. *If I Die in a Combat Zone Box Me Up and Ship Me Home.* New York: Delacorte, 1975. Print.

_____. *The Things They Carried.* Boston: Houghton, 1990. Print.

O'Reilly, Bill. Interview. "Most Lethal Sniper in U.S. Military History." *FOX News.* 5 Jan. 2012. Web. 29 Jan. 2015. foxnews.com/transcript/2012/01/06/

most-lethal-sniper-us-military-history.
Packer, George. "Home Fires." *The New Yorker* 7 April 2014: 69–73. Print.
Pancake, Ann S. "Taken by Storm: The Exploitation of Metaphor in the Persian Gulf War." *Metaphor and Symbolic Activity* 8.4 (1993): 281–95. Web. *Academic Search Complete.* 20 May 2015.
Pascoe, David. "The Cold War and the 'War on Terror.'" *The Cambridge Companion to War Writing.* Ed. Kate McLoughlin. Cambridge: Cambridge University Press, 2009. 239–249. Print.
Peebles, Stacey Lynn. *Welcome to the Suck: Narrating the American Soldier's Experience in Iraq.* Ithaca: Cornell University Press, 2011. Print.
Peterson, Nolan. "If You Want to Write About War Tell Us Something We Don't Know." *Blue Force Tracker.* 15 July 2015. Web. 4 Feb. 2015. blueforcetracker.com/article/if-you-want-to-write-about-war-tell-us-something-we-dont-know.
Percy, Jennifer. *Demon Camp: A Soldier's Exorcism.* New York: Scribner, 2014. Print.
Percy, Walker. "The Delta Factor." *The Message in the Bottle: How Queer Man Is, How Queer Language Is, and What One Has to Do with the Other.* 1954. New York: Picador, 2000. 3–45. Print.
Pipes, Candice. Interview. "*Flashes of War*: A Conversation with Katey Schultz." *War, Literature, and the Arts: An International Journal of the Humanities* 25.1 (2013): 139–147. Web. 18 June 2015.
Pitchford, Jenna. "From One Gulf to Another: Reading Masculinity in American Narratives of the Persian Gulf and Iraq Wars." *Literature Compass* 9.5 (May 2012): 357–70. Print.
Powers, Kevin. "Author's Note." *The Yellow Birds.* 2012. New York: Little, 2013. 156–57. Print.
———. Interview by Jeffrey Brown. *PBS Newshour.* PBS. 4 Oct. 2012. Web. pbs.org/newshour/art/conversation-kevin-powers-author-of-the-yellow-birds/.
———. Interview by Peter Slen. *Book Discussion.* C-SPAN. 5 June 2012. Web. www.c-span.org/video/?0306577-14/book-discussion-yellow-birds-novel.
———. *The Yellow Birds.* New York: Little, 2012. Print.
Pratt, Mary Louise. "Harm's Way: Language and the Contemporary Arts of War." *PMLA* 124.5 (2009): 1515–31. Print.
Price, Jay. "Epithet Shows Cultural Divide." *The News and Observer* (30 Sept. 2003): A1. Web. *NewsBank.* 31 Dec. 2014.
Remington, Ted. "Ceci N'est Pas Une Guerre: The Misuse of War as Metaphor in Iraq." *KB Journal* 7.2 (Spr. 2011). Web. 13 Sept. 2012.
"Reviews and Praise for *Letter Composed During a Lull in the Fighting and the Yellow Birds.*" Kevinpowers.com. Web. 1 June 2015. www.kevinpowers.com.
Ricks, Thomas J. *Fiasco: The American Military Adventure in Iraq.* New York: Penguin, 2006. Print.
Riggs, Thomas. Editor's Note. *The Literature of War.* Ed. Riggs. Vol. 1. Detroit: St. James, 2012. xv–xvi. *Gale Virtual Reference Library.* Web. 13 Feb. 2015.
Roback, A.A. *Dictionary of International Slurs.* Cambridge: Sci-Art, 1944. Print.
Robinson, Roxanna. "The Eight Annual David L. Jannetta Lecture in War, Literature and the Arts. U.S. Air Force Academy, 9 Sept. 14." Address. *War, Literature, and the Arts* 26 (2014): 3–10. Print.
———. "The Right to Write." *The New York Times* (29 May 2014): SR8. Print.
Rorty, Richard. *Consequences of Pragmatism.* Minneapolis: University of Minnesota Press, 1982. Print.
Roy-Bhattacharya, Joydeep. *The Watch.* London: Hogarth, 2012. Print.
Rueckert, William H. *Encounters with Kenneth Burke.* Champaign: University of Illinois Press, 1994. Print.
———. *Kenneth Burke and the Drama of Human Relations.* Berkeley: University of California Press, 1963. Print.
Ruppin, Jonathan. Interview. "A Conversation with Kevin Powers and Jonathan Ruppin of Foyles Bookshop, London." *The Yellow Birds.* New York: Little, 2013. 158–61. Print.
Ryan, Maureen. *The Other Side of Grief: The Home Front and the Aftermath in American Narratives of the Vietnam*

War. Amherst: University of Massachusetts Press, 2008. Print.

Sacks, Sam. "First-Person Shooters." *Harper's Magazine*. Aug. 2015. Web. 19 Feb. 2016.

Said, Edward W. "Islam Through Western Eyes." *The Nation* 230.16 (26 Apr. 1980): 488–92. Web. *Ebscohost*. 29 Dec. 2014.

———. *Orientalism*. 1979. 25th Anniv. Ed. New York: Vintage, 2004. Print.

Samet, Elizabeth D. *No Man's Land: Preparing for War and Peace in Post–9/11 America*. New York: Farrar, Straus and Giroux, 2014. Print.

———. *Soldier's Heart: Reading Literature Through Peace and War at West Point*. New York: Farrar, Straus and Giroux, 2007. Print.

———. "War Lies." *The Book: An Online Review at the New Republic*. 10 Sept. 2012. Web. 1 June 2015. newrepublic.com/book/review/war-lies.

Sanborn, Wallis R. *American Novel of War: A Critical Analysis and Classification System*. Jefferson, NC: McFarland, 2012. Print.

Scarry, Elaine. *The Body in Pain*. New York: Oxford University Press, 1985. Print.

Schell, Terry L., and Grant N. Marshall. "Survey of Individuals Previously Deployed for OEF/OIF." *Invisible Wounds of War: Psychological and Cognitive Injuries, Their Consequences, and Services to Assist Recovery*. Ed. Terri Tanielian and Lisa M. Jaycox. Santa Monica: RAND Corporation, 2008. 87–115. Web. 22 Jan. 2015. rand.org/content/dam/rand/pubs/monographs/2008/RAND_MG720.pdf.

Schroeder, Eric James. Interview. "Two Interviews: Talks with Tim O'Brien and Robert Stone." *Modern Fiction Studies* 30.1 (Spring 1984): 135–64. Print.

Scoggins, Michael. "Joseph Heller's Combat Experiences in *Catch-22*." *War, Literature, and the Arts* 15.1–2 (2003): 213–27. Print.

Scranton, Roy. "The Trauma Hero: From Wilfred Owen to *Redeployment* to *American Sniper*." *Los Angeles Review of Books*. 25 Jan. 2015. Web. 26 Jan. 2015. lareviewofbooks.org/essay/trauma-hero-wilfred-owen-redeployment-american-sniper.

———. Message to the author. 28 Jan. 2015. E-mail.

Scranton, Roy, and Matt Gallagher. Preface. *Fire and Forget: Short Stories from the Long War*. Boston: Da Capo, 2013. Print.

Searle, John. *Expression and Meaning: Studies in the Theory of Speech Acts*. Cambridge: Cambridge University Press, 1979. Print.

Shenon, Philip. "Admiral, in Suicide Note, Apologized to 'My Sailors': Top Officer Worried About Embarrassing Navy." *New York Times* (18 May 1996): A1. Web. *ProQuest Historical Newspapers*. 9 Dec. 2014.

Sherry, Vincent. "Guide to Further Reading." *The Cambridge Companion to the Literature of the First World War*. Ed. Sherry. Cambridge: Cambridge University Press, 2005. 302–10. Print.

Silko, Leslie Marmon. *Ceremony*. 1977. New York: Penguin, 1986. Print.

Silliman, Stephen W. "The 'Old West' in the Middle East: U. S. Military Metaphors in Real and Imagined Indian Country." *American Anthropologist* 110.2 (2008): 237–47. *JSTOR*. Web. 13 Sept. 2012.

Slotkin, Richard. "Our Myths of Choice." *The Chronicle of Higher Education* 48.5 (28 Sept. 2001): B11. *ProQuest Central*. Web. 15 Nov. 2012.

Spanos, Willaim. *American Exceptionalism in the Age of Globalization: The Specter of Vietnam*. Albany: State University of New York Press, 2008. Print.

Stahl, Roger. *Militainment, Inc.: War, Media, and Popular Culture*. New York: Routledge, 2010. Print.

Stanton, Doug. "*The Yellow Birds* by Kevin Powers: The Novel of the Iraq War." *The Daily Beast*. 11 Sept. 2012. Web. 18 June 2015.

Stout, Janis. *Coming Out of War: Poetry, Grieving, and the Culture of the World Wars*. Tuscaloosa: University of Alabama Press, 2005. Print.

Stratton, Billy J. *Buried in Shades of Night: Contested Voices, Indian Captivity, and the Legacy of King Phillip's War*. Tuc-

son: University of Arizona Press, 2013. Print.
Team America: World Police. Dir. Trey Parker. Paramount, 2004. DVD.
Thorp, Charles. "Jason Hall: Why I Wrote American Sniper." Rolling Stone Online. 28 Jan. 2015. Web. 19 Feb 2015. www.rollingstone.com/movies/features/jason-hall-why-i-wrote-american-sniper-20150128.
Thorpe, Helen. Soldier Girls: The Battles of Three Women at Home and at War. New York: Scribner, 2014. Print.
Tolstoy, Leo. Hadji Murad. 1912. New York: Barnes and Noble, 2005. Print.
Tredowe, Emily Gray. "Who Has the Right to Write About War?" The Daily Beast. 12 July 2014. Web. 12 June 15.
Trout, Steven. Memorial Fictions: Willa Cather and the First World War. Lincoln: University of Nebraska Press, 2008. Print.
Turner, Brian. "Stopping the American Infantry Patrol Near the Prophet Yunus Mosque in Mosul, Abu Ali Shows Them the Cloth in His Pocket." Phantom Noise. Farmington, ME: Alice James Books, 2010. 61. Print.
Van Buren, Peter. "America Loves Its War Porn: American Sniper and the Hollywood Propaganda Machine." Salon. 21 Feb. 2015. Web. 16 June 2015.
Van Reet, Brian. "A Problematic Genre, the 'Kill Memoir.'" New York Times Blogs. 16 July 2013. Web. Proquest. 14 May 2014.
Vernon, Alex. Introduction. "No Genre's Land: The Problem of Genre in War Memoirs and Military Autobiographies." Arms and the Self: War, the Military, and Autobiographical Writing. Ed. Vernon. Kent: Kent State University Press, 2005. 1–40. Print.
Vizenor, Gerald. Manifest Manners: Narratives on Postindian Survivance. Lincoln, NE: Bison, 1994. Print.
Vonnegut, Kurt. Slaughter-House Five: A Novel. 1969. New York: Dial, 2009. Print.
Wall, Tyler. "Imperial Laughs: A Soldier's Song and the Colonial Present." Social Justice 37.2/3 (2010–2011): 73–83. Print.
____. "Philanthropic Soldiers, Practical Orientalism, and the Occupation of Iraq." Identities: Global Studies in Culture and Power 18.5 (Sept. 2011): 481–501. Web. Taylor & Francis. 25 Sept. 2013.
Weber, Bruce. "Paul Fussell, Literary Scholar and Critic, Is Dead at 88." New York Times (24 May 2012): A29. Print.
Weiser, Elizabeth M. "'As Usual I Fell on the Bias': Kenneth Burke's Situated Dialectic." Philosophy and Rhetoric 42.2 (2009): 135–53. Web. JSTOR. 1 June 2015.
____. "Burke and War: Rhetoricizing the Theory of Dramatism." Rhetoric Review 26.3 (2007): 286–302. Print.
Wellesley, Dorothy. Letters on Poetry from W.B. Yeats to Dorothy Wellesley. London: Oxford University Press, 1940.
Wess, Robert. Kenneth Burke: Rhetoric, Subjectivity, Postmodernism. Cambridge: Cambridge University Press, 1996. Print.
West, Bing. The March Up: Taking Baghdad with the United States Marines. New York: Bantam, 2003. Print.
White, Hayden. "The Historical Text as Literary Artifact." Tropics of Discourse: Essays on Cultural Criticism. Baltimore: Johns Hopkins University Press, 1986. Print. 81–100.
Wilkes, Lydia. "'Now Here's What Really Happened': The Rhetoric of Experience in War Memoir." Literature, Rhetoric, and Values. Ed. Shelley Hulan, Murray McArthur, and Randy Allen Harris. Newcastle upon Tyne: Cambridge Scholars, 2012. 171–88. E-book.
Wilson, John Howard. "'Gross Dichotomizing' in the Work of Paul Fussell." The Midwest Quarterly 38.2 (Winter 1997): 172–84. Web. ProQuest. 5 Feb. 2015.
Wolfe, Tom. The Right Stuff. New York: Picador, 1979. Print.
Wolff, Tobias. Interview. "A Conversation with Tim O'Brien on Writing and War." Stanford University YouTube Channel. 24 Jan. 2011. Web. 20 Jan. 2015. youtube.com/watch?v=3vcmASDmEr8.
Wright, Evan. Generation Kill. New York: Penguin, 2005. Print.
Yeats, W.B. Introduction. The Oxford Book of Modern Verse. Ed. Yeats. New

York: Oxford University Press, 1936. v–xlii. Print.

Yellow Bird, Michael. "Cowboys and Indians: Toys of Genocide, Icons of Colonialism." *Wicazo Sa Review* 19.2 (2004): 33–48. *Project Muse.* Web. 13 Sept. 12.

Zinsmeister, Karl. *Boots on the Ground: A Month with the 82nd Airborne in the Battle for Iraq.* New York: St. Martin's, 2003. Print.

Index

Abrams, David 19, 38, 206*ch*5*n*4; *FOBBIT* 3, 9–10, 12–13, 122–154, 187, 206*ch*5*n*6
Afghanistan (conflict in) 4, 5, 11, 13–14, 30, 62, 184, 204*ch*1*n*5, 205*ch*3*n*2; and language 156, 158, 159, 160, 161, 166, 168, 170, 171, 178, 185, 191; *see also* war literature
Alexie, Sherman 3, 4
American Sniper (book) 39, 43, 163–165, 196
American Sniper (film) 43, 163–165, 167, 169, 196
Aristotle 76, 110, 199
Austin, J.L. 116

Baudrillard, Jean 97, 103, 104; *see also* war porn
Belile, Joshua 175–177, 207*ch*6*n*16
Benedict, Helen 17, 38, 123–125, 201; *Sand Queen* 17, 188–190
Bierce, Ambrose 16
bin Laden, Osama 5, 6, 57
Brown, Keith 10, 174, 175, 180, 183; *see also* Lutz, Catherine
Browne, Sir Thomas 74–75, 76, 77
Burke, Kenneth 7, 8, 9, 10, 11–12, 37–38, 45, 47–51, 53–60, 68, 71, 72, 76–77, 79, 85, 93, 95, 96–97, 98, 99, 100, 101, 102, 106, 107–108, 110, 112, 113, 115, 120, 127, 129, 130, 135, 136, 141, 142, 143, 148, 150, 153–154, 155, 156, 157, 158, 166, 167, 183, 185, 187, 188, 190, 191, 194, 197, 202, 203*n*7, 204*ch*2*n*4, 205*ch*3*n*8, 205*ch*4*n*3, 206*ch*5*n*1; comic corrective 12, 99, 101, 109, 122; cult of the kill 11, 86; heads I win, tails you lose 25, 40; hierarchical psychosis 11, 12, 13, 77, 125, 126, 127, 129, 130, 134, 135, 140, 142, 154, 199, 206*ch*5*n*4; psychology of form 70, 95; scapegoat mechanism 8, 9, 12–13, 47, 49, 50, 56, 57, 60, 84, 90, 99, 101, 115, 122, 126, 144, 158, 179, 194; super-agent 78–82; synecdochic representation 158, 181–182, 185, 207*ch*6*n*18; vicarious victimage 54, 98, 126
Bush, George W. 3, 4, 114

Buzzell, Colby 157, 167, 178–179, 206*ch*6*n*3

Campbell, James 10, 19–20, 21, 23, 26, 31, 34–35, 206*n*8; *see also* combat gnosticism
Caputo, Philip 67, 204*ch*1*n*8; *Indian Country* 2, 17; *A Rumor of War* 17, 66, 204*ch*1*n*9
Carroll, Al 3, 4, 6, 203*n*4
Carson, Kit 5, 203*n*6
Carson, Michael 28, 163, 164–165
Carter, C. Allen 60, 71, 85, 144, 150
Coker, Christopher 18, 22
Colla, Elliot 44
combat gnosticism 10, 11, 19–20, 21, 25–46, 47, 48, 50, 52, 53, 56, 58, 103, 107, 115, 117, 153, 155, 199, 202, 205*ch*3*n*4
Crane, Stephen 20, 199

Derrida, Jacques 76
Dos Passos, John 17, 115
Drinnon, Richard 3, 162, 163, 166
Dyer, Geoff 34

Eco, Umberto 165–166
Ehrhart, W.D. 31, 45
Eliot, T.S. 22–23
exceptionalism 10, 150, 165, 201

Fantasy Industrial Complex 96–98, 101, 103, 108, 117, 119
Foucault, Michel 48, 174; Author Function 48–49
Fountain, Ben 19, 37, 38, 96, 97, 103–104, 123; *Billy Lynn's Long Halftime Walk* 9–10, 12, 96, 97–121, 122, 204*ch*3*n*1, 205*ch*4*n*5; *see also* Fantasy Industrial Complex
Frye, Northrup 41, 169
Full Metal Jacket 17, 137
Fussell, Paul 19, 25, 26–27, 28, 29–32, 33, 34–35, 38, 44–45, 172; *The Great War and Modern Memory* 18, 23–24, 25, 39, 44; *see also* combat gnosticism

221

Index

Gallagher, Matt 36, 105
Garland, Hamlin 16
Geronimo (coding) 5, 6, 54
Girard, René 89–90, 94, 95
Gupta, Suman 13, 27–28, 44, 204*ch*1*n*6

hajji 13, 156–194, 200, 202, 206*ch*6*n*1, 206*ch*6*n*3, 207*ch*6*n*5, 207*ch*6*n*13; in *FOBBIT* 136, 141, 146, 148, 151; in *Sand Queen* 189; in *Yellow Birds* 81, 83, 84, 89
Hasford, Gustav: *The Short-Timers* 17, 137
Hawkins, Ty 33
Heller, Joseph 31, 105, 199; *Catch 22*, 31–32, 83, 143, 206*ch*5*n*6
Hemingway, Ernest 17, 20, 45, 66, 68, 78, 115
heroism 5, 8, 9, 11, 27, 33, 41, 50, 52, 54, 57, 62, 63, 64, 80, 85, 154, 168, 177, 196, 198, 199, 201, 202; in *Billy Lynn* 12, 97, 98, 104, 107, 108, 116, 118, 119, 120; in *FOBBIT* 13, 123, 127, 129, 135, 136, 147; hero worship 8, 13, 29, 60, 70, 125, 142, 153; in *Yellow Birds* 83
Hitler, Adolf 56–57, 84, 166, 167
Hurt Locker 169
Hynes, Samuel 18, 32–33, 45

Indian as stereotype 2, 5, 6, 7, 162–163, 191, 203*n*3, 207*ch*6*n*7
"Indian Country" 2, 5
"Indian Hating" 3, 13, 162
Indian War 2, 4, 7, 10, 202, 203*n*3, 203*n*4
Iraq (conflict in) 3, 4, 5, 13–14, 30, 43, 160–161, 184; in film 163; and language 2, 156, 157, 158, 159, 166, 168, 171, 174, 175, 190, 191, 207*n*5; *see also* war literature

Jameson, Fredric 25, 45–46, 58–59
Jody (military cadence) 73–76, 77, 84, 86, 87, 93, 205*ch*3*n*6, 205*ch*3*n*7
Johnny Quest 168

Kakutani, Michiko 41, 43, 48
Kaplan, Robert 5, 7, 170, 203*n*4
Klay, Phil 19, 32, 37, 199
Komunyakaa, Yusef 17, 42, 44
Kyle, Chris 43, 163–165, 187, 196, 199, 207*ch*6*n*8, 207*ch*6*n*10

LaDuke, Winona 3, 4
language: appropriation 3, 5, 6, 7, 54, 156, 171, 175, 178, 188, 192; and demonization 13, 73, 163, 165, 183
Lawrence, David 15, 19, 36, 105, 107, 114, 138, 201, 206*ch*5*n*4
Levinas, Emmanuel 178–179
Lewis, Wyndham 22, 23, 41, 42, 197
Limerick, Patricia 4
Lone Survivor 169

Luckhurst, Roger 15, 20
Lutz, Catherine 10, 174, 175, 180, 183; *see also* Brown, Keith

Mailer, Norman 17, 67–68
Marwill, Jonathan 26–27, 29, 39, 41
McLoughlin, Kate 8–9, 10, 18, 20, 21, 23, 26, 28, 39–41, 60, 197–198
Melville, Herman 16, 162, 203*ch*1*n*1
Molin, Peter 36, 37, 112, 203*ch*1*n*3
Momaday, N. Scott 191
Norris, Margot 19, 21, 22, 23, 35, 37, 46, 60, 198, 199–200

O'Brien, Tim 17, 66, 67, 68, 88, 91, 204*ch*2*n*8; *Going After Cacciato* 64, 198; "How to Tell a True War Story" 69; *If I Die in a Combat Zone* 45; *The Things They Carried* 42, 68, 201
operation (military) 5, 6, 13–14, 183
Operation Homecoming 42, 44
Othering 9, 11, 161, 171, 175, 177, 180, 182, 206*ch*6*n*2; *see also* Said, Edward
Owen, Wilfred 22

Packer, George 34, 35, 39
Powers, Kevin 19, 32, 67, 68, 69, 199, 204*ch*3*n*1, 205*ch*3*n*3; *The Yellow Birds* 9–10, 12, 61–95

Robinson, Roxanna 15, 16, 17, 35, 37, 204*ch*2*n*4
Rueckert, William 49–50, 76, 182, 190
Rumsfeld, Donald 4–5, 7

Sacks, Sam 41, 42, 52, 195, 196, 197, 199, 204*ch*1*n*10
Said, Edward 167–168, 173, 206*ch*6*n*2
savage (as stereotype) 6, 7; as binary identity 4, 6, 162–164; *see also* scapegoat
scapegoat 4, 5, 7, 8, 9, 10, 13, 30, 56, 57, 58, 60, 155, 167, 175–176, 177, 179, 182, 188, 190, 191, 192, 194, 196, 200, 202; in *Billy Lynn* 97, 98, 99, 104, 106, 108, 109, 116–119, 121; in *FOBBIT* 125, 129, 130–131, 132, 135, 139, 141, 144, 147, 149, 150, 151, 153; in *Yellow Birds* 71, 74, 75, 77, 80, 81, 83, 85, 87, 88, 89, 92–95; *see also* Burke, Kenneth; Girard, René
Scarry, Elaine 200
Scranton, Roy 51–52, 196, 197
Silko, Leslie Marmon 64
Slotkin, Richard 4
specter of Vietnam 10–11
Stallings, Laurence 54–55
Stout, Janis 18, 21, 27
Stratton, Billy J. 4, 6, 162–163, 167

Team America: World Police 176, 177, 207*ch*6*n*17

trauma 28, 47, 52, 65, 74, 75, 88, 171, 176, 184, 196
Twain, Mark 16, 112

Van Reet, Brian 51–53, 55, 204*ch*2*n*3
Veblen, Thorstein 99
Vernon, Alex 28–29, 32, 33–34, 48, 49, 51, 67
Vietnam War 2, 11, 159–160, 174, 206*ch*5*n*2; *see also* war literature
Vizenor, Gerald 4, 175
Vonnegut, Kurt 17, 69

war literature: Afghanistan in 15, 17, 19, 23, 34, 42, 43, 44, 62, 159, 171, 179, 201, 203*ch*1*n*3, 206*ch*6*n*4; authenticity in 10, 17, 20, 21, 37, 46, 47, 73, 74, 107, 123, 164, 179, 196; Civil War in 16, 123; and genre 8, 10, 11, 17, 18, 19, 20, 21, 23, 26, 28, 31, 32, 35, 38, 44–45, 47, 48, 50, 52, 53, 58, 70, 75, 95, 197, 199, 206*ch*4*n*8; and "Grunt Lit" 10, 174; Iraq in 7, 9, 12, 15, 18, 19, 23, 27, 34, 37, 42, 44, 52, 61, 62, 64, 65, 66, 77, 78, 80, 81, 86, 87, 88, 95, 96–99, 103, 110, 113, 119, 123, 126, 127, 129, 135, 136, 146, 152, 164, 179, 180, 185, 186, 189, 192, 193, 200, 201, 204*ch*1*n*4, 204*ch*1*n*5, 204*ch*1*n*6, 204*ch*2*n*3; and kill memoir 51–53, 54, 56; kitsch in 123, 164, 196, 197, 207*n*11; and postgenre 21, 35; Vietnam in 17, 33–34, 40, 67; World War I in 17, 18, 21, 41, 70; World War II in 17, 27, 31, 64
war porn 103, 104
White, Hayden 83
Whitman, Walt 16, 203*ch*1*n*1

Yeats, W.B. 22–23

www.ingramcontent.com/pod-product-compliance
Lightning Source LLC
Chambersburg PA
CBHW032052300426
44116CB00007B/698